HowExpert Guide to Live Streaming

The Ultimate Handbook for Building Your Live Streaming Channel, Growing Your Audience, and Monetizing Your Live Streams

HowExpert

For more tips related to this topic, visit
HowExpert.com/livestreaming

Recommended Resources

- HowExpert.com – How To Guides on All Topics from A to Z.
- HowExpert.com/free – Free HowExpert Email Newsletter.
- HowExpert.com/books – HowExpert Books
- HowExpert.com/courses – HowExpert Courses
- HowExpert.com/clothing – HowExpert Clothing
- HowExpert.com/membership – HowExpert Membership Site
- HowExpert.com/affiliates – HowExpert Affiliate Program
- HowExpert.com/jobs – HowExpert Jobs
- HowExpert.com/writers – Write About Your #1 Passion/Knowledge/Expertise & Become a HowExpert Author.
- HowExpert.com/resources – Additional HowExpert Recommended Resources
- YouTube.com/HowExpert – Subscribe to HowExpert YouTube.
- Instagram.com/HowExpert – Follow HowExpert on Instagram.
- Facebook.com/HowExpert – Follow HowExpert on Facebook.
- TikTok.com/@HowExpert – Follow HowExpert on TikTok.

Publisher's Foreword

Dear HowExpert Reader,

HowExpert publishes quick 'how to' guides on all topics from A to Z.

Our mission is to make a positive impact in the world for all topics from A to Z…one HowExpert book at a time!

We are dedicated to creating quick, easy-to-read 'how to' guides that are structured, comprehensive, and approachable, empowering our readers to effortlessly explore and learn about their passions and interests in a meaningful and enjoyable way.

We hope our HowExpert books bring you immense value and make a positive impact on your life. Every reader, including you, plays a vital role in helping us fulfill our mission of making a positive difference in the world across all areas of interest from A to Z.

If you enjoyed one of our HowExpert guides, we would greatly appreciate it if you could take a moment to share your feedback on the platform where you discovered this book.

Thank you, and I wish you success and happiness in all aspects of your life.

To your success,

BJ Min
Founder & Publisher of HowExpert
HowExpert.com
John 14:6

Table of Contents

Book Overview

HowExpert Guide to Live Streaming: The Ultimate Handbook for Building Your Live Streaming Channel, Growing Your Audience, and Monetizing Your Live Streams

If you want to build a successful live streaming channel, grow a loyal audience, and monetize your streams, then *HowExpert Guide to Live Streaming* is the ultimate handbook for success. Whether you're a gamer, creator, educator, entrepreneur, or influencer, this guide equips you with everything needed to thrive in live streaming's fast-paced world.

What You'll Learn Inside This Guide:

- **Introduction** – Unlock how this guide will transform your live streaming journey and help you stand out.

- **Chapter 1: Live Streaming Basics** – Master the fundamentals, evolution, and benefits of live streaming to create impact and grow your audience.

- **Chapter 2: Choosing the Right Platform** – Discover platforms like Twitch, YouTube Live, and other emerging options to find your perfect streaming home.

- **Chapter 3: Essential Equipment** – Get cameras, microphones, and tools to create pro-quality streams—even on a budget.

- **Chapter 4: Streaming Software and Tools** – Take control with OBS Studio, Streamlabs, overlays, alerts, and automation for seamless performance.

- **Chapter 5: Content Planning** – Build a content calendar, generate viral ideas, and leverage trends to grow faster.

- **Chapter 6: Brand Identity** – Create logos, banners, and storytelling techniques to stand out and earn viewer trust.

- **Chapter 7: Stream Setup and Optimization** – Fine-tune your setup and troubleshoot issues to keep broadcasts smooth and professional.

- **Chapter 8: Engaging Your Audience** – Maximize interaction, moderate chats effectively, and create community-driven experiences.

- **Chapter 9: Growing Your Audience** – Use social media, collaborations, and events to attract and retain loyal viewers.

- **Chapter 10: Analytics and Retention** – Track performance, identify growth strategies, and keep viewers coming back.

- **Chapter 11: Monetizing Your Streams** – Unlock revenue streams like ads, sponsors, subscriptions, and merchandise.

- **Chapter 12: Advanced Revenue Streams** – Scale income further with courses, consulting, memberships, and evergreen content.

- **Chapter 13: Leveraging AI Tools** – Use AI-powered tools for automation, analytics, and content creation to future-proof your channel.

- **Chapter 14: Accessibility and Inclusivity** – Make your streams inclusive with subtitles, translations, and accessibility features.

- **Chapter 15: Staying Ahead with Technology** – Explore trends like VR and AR to keep your content innovative.

- **Chapter 16: Success Stories** – Get insights and strategies from top-performing streamers to fuel your growth.

- **Chapter 17: Legal and Ethical Essentials** – Protect your channel with copyright rules, privacy practices, and platform compliance.

- **Conclusion and Appendices** – Finish strong with glossaries, FAQs, reflection prompts, and tools to simplify your success.

Why *HowExpert Guide to Live Streaming* Is Essential:

- **Complete Coverage** – Covers everything from live streaming basics to advanced monetization strategies and AI tools.

- **Practical Strategies** – Step-by-step tips to build, optimize, and monetize your channel fast.

- **Future-Ready Insights** – Keeps you ahead with AI, VR, AR, and accessibility features for modern audiences.

- **Proven Success Tips** – Insights and strategies from successful streamers to inspire and accelerate your growth.

HowExpert Guide to Live Streaming gives you the tools and confidence to grow your audience, build your brand, and succeed in live streaming. **Go live with**

confidence, captivate your audience, and turn your streams into success — get your copy now and start live streaming like a pro!

HowExpert publishes quick "how to" guides on all topics from A to Z. Visit HowExpert.com to learn more.

Introduction

Welcome to *HowExpert Guide to Live Streaming: The Ultimate Handbook for Building Your Live Streaming Channel, Growing Your Audience, and Monetizing Your Live Streams*! If you're ready to turn your passion into a thriving live streaming channel, attract an audience, and build a sustainable income, then this guide is for you. Whether you're stepping into the world of live streaming for the first time or looking to take your channel to the next level, this book provides the tools, techniques, and strategies you need to succeed. Let's dive in and explore how live streaming is revolutionizing content creation, who this book is for, and how to use it as your roadmap to success.

I. The Rise of Live Streaming: Why It's Revolutionizing Content Creation

Live streaming has rapidly evolved into one of the most powerful forms of content creation, transforming how people connect, learn, and entertain. Unlike pre-recorded videos, live streaming provides real-time interaction, allowing creators to build authentic relationships with audiences while delivering fresh and engaging content. From gaming marathons and educational workshops to product launches and personal vlogs, live streaming opens endless opportunities for creativity and growth.

The growth of platforms like Twitch, YouTube Live, and Facebook Live has democratized content creation, enabling anyone with a camera and internet connection to share their passion with the world. This rise is fueled by advances in technology, faster internet speeds, and a shift in viewer preferences toward interactive, unscripted content. Today, live streaming is not just entertainment—it's a career path, a business model, and a platform for influence.

Whether you're an aspiring gamer showcasing your skills, an entrepreneur promoting your brand, or an educator reaching global audiences, live streaming offers a unique way to amplify your voice, monetize your expertise, and connect with others on a deeper level. This guide will show you exactly how to leverage this growing medium to achieve your goals.

II. Who This Guide Is For: Gamers, Creators, Educators, Entrepreneurs, and More

HowExpert Guide to Live Streaming is tailored for a diverse range of readers, each with unique goals and aspirations. This book is for:

- **Gamers** looking to share their skills, build fan bases, and create entertaining gaming content that attracts loyal viewers.

- **Content Creators** interested in showcasing their talents, passions, and ideas while building personal brands and generating income.

- **Educators and Coaches** aiming to teach, train, and inspire audiences with live tutorials, webinars, and interactive classes.

- **Entrepreneurs and Business Owners** seeking to market products, host live events, and engage with customers in real time.

- **Influencers and Social Media Enthusiasts** wanting to expand their reach, enhance engagement, and collaborate with brands.

- **Hobbyists and Enthusiasts** eager to share personal interests, hobbies, or causes with like-minded communities.

No matter your background or experience level, this book provides actionable strategies and step-by-step instructions to help you master live streaming, connect with your audience, and monetize your efforts effectively.

III. How to Use This Book: A Roadmap to Live Streaming Success

This guide is divided into five parts, each covering essential aspects of live streaming success:

- **Part 1: Foundations of Live Streaming** – Learn the basics, including the history and evolution of live streaming, platform options, essential equipment, and software tools. This section sets the stage for building a strong foundation.
- **Part 2: Content Creation and Engagement** – Explore strategies for planning content, building your personal brand, optimizing your stream

setup, and engaging with viewers in real time. This part is all about creating content that captivates and retains your audience.

- **Part 3: Growth and Monetization Strategies** – Unlock growth techniques and revenue models, from social media promotion and collaborations to subscriptions, sponsorships, and merchandise. Discover how to grow your channel and turn your passion into profit.
- **Part 4: Future-Proofing Your Streaming Career** – Stay ahead of the curve with insights into emerging technologies like AI, VR, and AR. Learn how to make your streams inclusive, adapt to platform changes, and prepare for future trends.
- **Part 5: Expert Insights and Real-World Success Stories** – Gain inspiration and learn from top streamers' journeys. Understand legal considerations, ethical standards, and practical tips for long-term success.
- **Conclusion and Appendices** – Recap key lessons, motivate yourself for the future, and access useful tools, glossaries, platform comparisons, and FAQs to continue growing and improving your skills.

Getting Started: Laying the Foundation for Streaming Success

The world of live streaming is full of opportunities, but success requires the right mindset, tools, and strategies. This book will guide you step-by-step, providing practical advice, inspiring examples, and expert tips to help you thrive in this competitive field. Whether you're looking to grow your audience, monetize your content, or future-proof your streaming career, *HowExpert Guide to Live Streaming* is your go-to resource. Start your journey today, dive into Chapter 1, and let's build your path to live streaming success!

Part 1: Foundations of Live Streaming

Chapter 1: Understanding Live Streaming Basics

Live streaming has revolutionized content creation by enabling real-time interaction with audiences across the globe. In this chapter, we'll dive into the fundamentals of live streaming, its evolution, and its growing significance in entertainment, education, and business. Whether you're a beginner exploring live content or a seasoned creator looking to expand your reach, this chapter provides the foundation you need to succeed.

Live streaming breaks traditional barriers, allowing creators to showcase their skills, connect with audiences, and monetize their content instantly. From gaming streams to professional webinars, the possibilities are endless. This chapter highlights the importance of live streaming and how it has become a dynamic platform for connection and growth.

Key Takeaway: Live streaming is more than a trend—it's a powerful tool for engagement, branding, and building lasting communities.

1.1 What is Live Streaming? An Introduction to Real-Time Content Creation

Live streaming is the process of broadcasting video and audio content in real time over the internet. Unlike pre-recorded videos, live streaming enables immediate interaction with viewers, creating a dynamic and engaging experience. Whether you are a gamer, educator, entrepreneur, or content creator, live streaming offers a unique platform to connect authentically, share expertise, and build a community. This section explores the fundamentals of live streaming, highlights its key advantages, and provides actionable steps to get started.

1. Why Live Streaming Is Popular

Live streaming has gained popularity due to its interactive nature and accessibility. Here's why it continues to grow:

- **Real-Time Engagement:** Viewers can interact instantly through comments, polls, and live Q&A sessions, fostering a sense of connection.

- **Cost-Effective Setup:** Affordable equipment and free streaming software make it easy to produce high-quality content.

- **Global Accessibility:** Live streaming breaks geographical barriers, allowing creators to reach audiences worldwide.

- **Community Building:** Regular broadcasts encourage loyalty, turning viewers into long-term supporters and subscribers.

- **Tip:** Focus on consistency to keep your audience engaged. Schedule streams regularly to build anticipation and retain viewers.

2. Advantages of Live Streaming

Live streaming offers multiple benefits for creators and businesses:

- **Authenticity Over Perfection:** Viewers appreciate unscripted moments that highlight personality, making content feel relatable and genuine.

- **Revenue Opportunities:** Platforms offer monetization options like tips, donations, ads, and subscriptions, enabling creators to generate income.

- **Versatile Content Formats:** Streamers can host interviews, product launches, tutorials, and Q&A sessions, adapting to their audience's preferences.

- **Tip:** Plan diverse formats such as behind-the-scenes tours, product reveals, and challenges to keep your streams fresh and engaging.

3. Example

- **Fitness Streamer's Growth:** A fitness coach hosted live workout sessions, attracting fitness enthusiasts and securing sponsorship deals with sportswear brands.

- **Tech Reviewer's Tutorials:** A tech reviewer streamed live gadget reviews, earning affiliate income and attracting sponsorships from electronics companies.

4. Tips

- **Prioritize Engagement:** Use live polls, Q&A sessions, and shoutouts to interact with viewers directly.

- **Experiment with Themes:** Try out different formats and series to keep content exciting.

- **Track Analytics:** Monitor viewer engagement and adjust content based on performance data.

- **Promote Across Platforms:** Share upcoming streams on social media to attract more viewers.

5. Reflection

- **Content Focus:** What type of content resonates most with your target audience?

- **Interactive Features:** How can you incorporate interactive features to make your live streams more engaging?

6. Exercise

- **Topic Development:** Identify three topics or themes you're passionate about.

- **Content Planning:** Develop ideas for turning these topics into engaging live streams, such as tutorials, live Q&A sessions, or product showcases.

- **Test Your Concept:** Create a 30-second pitch describing your first live stream idea. Test it with three people and gather feedback to refine your concept.

- **Go Live:** Launch your first test stream, apply the feedback, and track engagement metrics to see what works best.

1.2 The Evolution of Live Content Creation: From TV to Digital Platforms

Live streaming has evolved from traditional television broadcasts to interactive digital platforms accessible to anyone with internet access. This transformation has redefined how creators and audiences connect, enabling real-time engagement and global reach.

1. Key Milestones in Live Streaming Evolution

The evolution of live streaming spans decades of technological advancements:

- **Television Broadcasts (1950s–1990s):** Live news, sports, and entertainment were exclusive to TV networks with high production costs.

- **Early Internet Streaming (2000s):** Webcams and live chats pioneered online broadcasts, allowing creators to experiment with digital streaming.

- **Social Media Integration (2010s):** Platforms like **Facebook Live** and **Instagram Live** made streaming accessible to everyone, expanding content possibilities.

- **Gaming Boom (2010s–Present): Twitch** revolutionized gaming streams, turning gamers into influencers and building massive online communities.

- **Mobile Streaming (2020s):** Smartphones and apps like **TikTok Live** enabled creators to stream from anywhere, lowering barriers to entry.

- **Tip:** Learn from each phase of evolution to understand trends and adapt your content to stay relevant.

2. Impact of Digital Platforms

Modern platforms have transformed live streaming in several ways:

- **Democratization of Content:** Affordable equipment and free software make live streaming accessible to all creators.

- **Rise of Influencers:** Anyone can build a personal brand and monetize content through ads, donations, and sponsorships.

- **Marketing Transformation:** Businesses use live streaming for promotions, launches, and product demonstrations, making it a powerful marketing tool.

- **Tip:** Use live streaming as a tool to showcase products, host giveaways, or provide tutorials that resonate with your audience.

3. New Technologies Driving Change

Advances in technology continue to shape live streaming:

- **5G Networks:** Faster internet speeds enable seamless, high-quality streaming with minimal delays.

- **AI Analytics:** AI tools automate subtitles, analyze viewer preferences, and optimize content delivery in real time.

- **Cloud Computing:** Scalable storage and processing power support multi-platform streaming without interruptions.

- **Tip:** Incorporate AI tools to improve engagement and streamline production processes.

4. Example

- **Concert Streaming Boom: Artists like Travis Scott** hosted virtual concerts in platforms like **Fortnite**, merging music and gaming for millions of viewers.
- **Live Product Launches: Apple** regularly uses live streaming for product announcements, generating global buzz and sales.

5. Tips

- **Stay Updated with Trends:** Follow the latest streaming technologies and platform updates.
- **Experiment with Formats:** Use live events, Q&A sessions, and tutorials to connect with audiences.
- **Optimize for Mobile:** Ensure your streams are mobile-friendly to maximize reach.
- **Invest in Technology:** Upgrade tools and software as new technologies emerge.

6. Reflection

- **Content Comparison:** List three ways modern live streaming differs from traditional broadcasting.
- **Engagement Strategies:** How can you apply interactive features like polls and live chat to modernize your streams?

7. Exercise

- **Research Top Streamers:** Identify three successful streamers. What makes them unique, and how do they engage their audiences?
- **Analyze Formats:** Study different formats they use—gaming, Q&A, or tutorials—and develop ideas for your own streams.
- **Test Features:** Incorporate at least one new tool or feature inspired by your research into your next stream.

1.3 Why Live Streaming Matters: Entertainment, Education, and Beyond

Live streaming is more than entertainment—it's a versatile tool for teaching, marketing, and building communities. From gamers and educators to entrepreneurs and influencers, creators use live streaming to connect with audiences, deliver value, and grow their reach. This section explores the key applications of live streaming, highlights case studies, and provides actionable strategies for blending entertainment, education, and engagement.

1. Explore Key Applications of Live Streaming

Live streaming serves a wide range of purposes across industries. Here's how creators are using it effectively:

- **Entertainment:** Gamers, musicians, and comedians captivate audiences with performances, live gameplay, and interactive shows.

- **Education:** Teachers and coaches deliver webinars, tutorials, and lessons that engage students in real time.

- **Marketing and Sales:** Businesses host live product launches, demonstrations, and Q&A sessions to boost sales and showcase offerings.

- **Community Building:** Activists, hobbyists, and influencers use live streaming to build supportive networks, rally causes, and share ideas.

- **Tip:** Incorporate interactive polls, chat features, and giveaways to keep your audience engaged and invested.

2. Real-World Case Studies

Successful creators and businesses have leveraged live streaming to achieve growth and impact:

- **Gaming Streamer Success:** Streamer **DrLupo** grew a massive audience through gaming marathons and charity streams, raising millions for causes.

- **Entrepreneurs' Marketing Success:** Small businesses boosted product sales by hosting live demos and Q&A sessions on **Facebook Live**, generating instant buyer engagement.

- **Educational Content Expansion:** Language instructors used **YouTube Live** to deliver classes worldwide, combining interactive lessons with recorded content for replay value.

3. Example

- **Fitness Instructor's Growth:** A fitness coach attracted thousands of viewers through live workout sessions, eventually offering memberships and premium training plans for revenue growth.
- **Music Creator's Audience Engagement:** A musician built a global audience by streaming live concerts and offering behind-the-scenes songwriting sessions, leading to merch sales and ticketed events.

4. Tips

- **Repurpose Content:** Save and edit live streams into shorter highlights for promotion and replay.
- **Engage Through Interaction:** Include polls, Q&A, and giveaways to keep audiences invested.
- **Experiment with Formats:** Test educational webinars, interviews, and product demos to see what resonates.
- **Track Feedback:** Monitor comments and analytics to refine content strategies.

5. Reflection

- **Content Approach:** How can you combine entertainment and education to create valuable live streams?
- **Content Themes:** What topics or themes could you teach, demonstrate, or promote through live streaming?

6. Exercise

- **Content Ideas:** Draft three ways you can use live streaming for educational or promotional purposes.
- **Stream Planning:** Plan a sample outline for your first stream, including interactive segments like Q&A or live polls.
- **Test Session:** Test one idea in a short live session and gather feedback to refine your approach.

1.4 Types of Live Streams: Gaming, IRL, Educational, and Professional

Live streaming content spans multiple formats, offering creators opportunities to connect with diverse audiences. By understanding these formats, you can tailor your streams to suit your niche, engage viewers effectively, and maximize impact. This section explores the most popular live stream categories and provides examples and tips to help you create compelling content.

1. Gaming Streams: Engage with Interactive Playthroughs and Challenges

Gaming streams dominate platforms like Twitch and YouTube Live, offering entertainment and tutorials for gaming enthusiasts.

- **Tutorials and Walkthroughs:** Teach strategies, tips, and solutions to help players improve skills and complete levels.

- **Competitions and Challenges:** Host tournaments and engage viewers with competitive matches, leaderboards, and live commentary.

- **Tip:** Use overlays and alerts to showcase high scores, chat highlights, and subscriber milestones.

2. IRL (In Real Life) Streams: Share Experiences and Lifestyle Content

IRL streams focus on personal experiences and daily activities, allowing creators to showcase their lives in unique ways.

- **Travel Vlogs:** Take viewers on adventures to different destinations, sharing live tours and cultural insights.

- **Fitness and Cooking Demos:** Provide real-time workouts, cooking tutorials, and wellness tips.

- **Tip:** Use portable setups like smartphones and stabilizers for smooth, professional-quality streams on the go.

3. Educational Streams: Teach Skills and Share Knowledge

Educational streams focus on learning and development, helping viewers expand their knowledge in real time.

- **Webinars and Workshops:** Offer training sessions, coaching, and lessons on specialized topics.

- **Q&A Sessions:** Answer audience questions to provide immediate value and build trust.

- **Tip:** Add downloadable worksheets or resources to complement lessons and improve audience retention.

4. Professional Streams: Build Authority and Network

Professional live streams attract businesses, professionals, and industry experts looking to share insights and expand networks.

- **Interviews and Networking Events:** Highlight expert opinions and panel discussions to build authority.

- **Corporate Webinars:** Educate employees, stakeholders, or clients on strategies and trends.

- **Tip:** Promote streams in advance to maximize attendance and engagement.

5. Example

- **Gaming Streamer Success:** A gamer built a following by streaming daily challenges and teaching tips for competitive games, leading to brand sponsorships.

- **Travel Vlogger Growth:** A travel vlogger streamed live tours of historic sites, building a global audience and attracting tourism partnerships.

- **Language Coach Impact:** A language coach gained international students by hosting free grammar lessons and conversation practice sessions.

- **Tech Startup Demo:** A tech startup hosted live product demos, securing investor interest and media coverage.

6. Tips

- **Diversify Formats:** Combine gaming, IRL, and educational elements to appeal to multiple audiences.

- **Plan Ahead:** Develop outlines and schedules to maintain consistency and professionalism.

- **Test Features:** Use polls, challenges, and giveaways to boost interaction.

- **Promote Across Platforms:** Share teasers and highlights to attract more viewers.

7. Reflection

- **Stream Format:** Which type of live stream best suits your goals and audience?

- **Format Combination:** How can you combine formats to create a unique and engaging experience?

8. Exercise

- **Content Planning:** Plan three content ideas for each category (gaming, IRL, educational, and professional).

- **Stream Outlines:** Write outlines for two streams, including titles, themes, and key talking points.

- **Test Session:** Record a test stream for one idea and review the feedback to refine your approach.

1.5 Understanding Audience Expectations: Building Value from Day One

Successful live streaming depends on building trust and retaining viewers through consistent quality, interaction, and value. Audiences expect more than entertainment—they look for reliability, engagement, and connection. Meeting these expectations helps transform casual viewers into dedicated followers who actively support your channel. This section explores audience expectations and proven strategies to build loyalty from the start.

1. Deliver Consistency and Quality

Audiences appreciate streams that follow a predictable schedule and maintain high production standards. Meeting these expectations creates reliability and builds anticipation for future broadcasts.

- **Consistency:** Establish regular streaming times so viewers know when to tune in.

- **Quality Production:** Invest in clear audio, crisp visuals, and stable internet to deliver professional streams.

- **Tip:** Use countdown timers and pre-stream reminders to build excitement and increase attendance.

2. Focus on Engagement and Interaction

Engagement is key to retaining viewers. Audiences value real-time interaction, making them feel involved and appreciated.

- **Chat Engagement:** Respond to comments, highlight viewer questions, and thank participants for joining.
- **Polls and Giveaways:** Use interactive tools to make streams fun and rewarding.
- **Tip:** Incorporate shoutouts and giveaways to reward loyal viewers and build excitement.

3. Offer Exclusive Content for Subscribers

Exclusive perks encourage subscriptions and reward loyalty. Providing bonus content gives viewers an incentive to stay engaged.

- **Subscriber Perks:** Offer badges, custom emotes, and VIP access to private streams.
- **Behind-the-Scenes Content:** Share exclusive insights, previews, or tutorials reserved for subscribers.
- **Tip:** Promote exclusives as part of your channel's growth strategy to boost subscriber retention.

4. Foster a Community-Centric Focus

Strong communities keep viewers returning. By creating a welcoming and inclusive environment, you strengthen viewer loyalty.

- **Encourage Interaction:** Ask viewers questions, share stories, and involve them in decisions.
- **Celebrate Milestones:** Recognize subscriber anniversaries, donations, and community achievements.
- **Tip:** Build community platforms outside streaming, like Discord or Facebook groups, to deepen connections.

5. Example

- **Fitness Streamer Example:** A fitness instructor scheduled weekly live classes at the same time, creating a habit for viewers to join and interact regularly.

- **Gaming Interaction Example:** A streamer hosted live polls during gameplay, letting viewers influence decisions and feel part of the action.
- **Cooking Streamer Example:** A cooking streamer offered private Q&A sessions for subscribers, deepening relationships and building a loyal community.

6. Tips

- **Set Reminders:** Use notifications to keep audiences informed about upcoming streams.
- **Reward Engagement:** Highlight top fans or participants to make them feel valued.
- **Expand Community Spaces:** Build external platforms for continued interaction outside streams.
- **Plan Rewards Ahead:** Offer contests, giveaways, and subscriber perks to increase retention.

7. Reflection

- **Engagement Focus:** How will you keep your audience engaged and returning to your streams?
- **Loyalty Features:** What features or incentives can you add to build viewer loyalty?

8. Exercise

- **Weekly Content Plan:** Develop a weekly content plan with engagement strategies, including chat activities, polls, and giveaways.
- **Subscriber Rewards:** Brainstorm three exclusive perks or rewards to offer subscribers and integrate them into your streaming schedule.
- **Test Features:** Incorporate one new engagement tool or feature and monitor audience response.

Conclusion: Laying the Foundation for Success

Live streaming is more than just broadcasting—it's about creating meaningful connections, delivering consistent value, and engaging viewers authentically. By focusing on quality, interaction, and community building, you can establish trust and loyalty that will sustain your growth as a streamer.

Chapter 1 Review: Understanding Live Streaming Basics

Chapter 1 introduces the fundamentals of live streaming, explaining how it has transformed content creation by enabling real-time interaction and engagement with global audiences. It highlights the role of live streaming in entertainment, education, and business, and provides insights into the tools and strategies creators need to succeed.

1.1 What is Live Streaming? An Introduction to Real-Time Content Creation

- **Definition and Purpose:** Live streaming is the process of broadcasting video and audio in real time, enabling creators to connect authentically and engage directly with audiences.

- **Practical Uses:** Popular for gaming, tutorials, webinars, and product launches, offering creators immediate interaction and feedback.

1.2 The Evolution of Live Content Creation: From TV to Digital Platforms

- **From TV to Digital Platforms:** Live streaming has evolved from traditional TV broadcasts to accessible platforms like **Twitch**, **YouTube**, and **TikTok Live**.

- **Technological Growth:** Advances in mobile devices, high-speed internet, AI tools, and cloud computing have made streaming more affordable, flexible, and scalable.

1.3 Why Live Streaming Matters: Entertainment, Education, and Beyond

- **Practical Applications:** Live streaming supports teaching, marketing, entertainment, and community-building, making it a versatile tool for creators and businesses.

- **Real-World Examples:** Influencers like **Ninja** and entrepreneurs have used live streaming to grow audiences, market products, and monetize content effectively.

1.4 Types of Live Streams: Gaming, IRL, Educational, and Professional

- **Gaming Streams:** Focus on walkthroughs, tutorials, and live competitions, appealing to gaming enthusiasts.

- **IRL (In Real Life) Streams:** Showcase lifestyle content, including travel vlogs, fitness demos, and cooking tutorials.

- **Educational Streams:** Offer webinars, coaching sessions, and interactive lessons for learning-focused content.

- **Professional Streams:** Feature interviews, presentations, and business discussions to connect with professional audiences and build authority.

1.5 Understanding Audience Expectations: Building Value from Day One

- **Consistency and Interaction:** Viewers expect regular schedules, high-quality visuals, and interactive features like polls, giveaways, and Q&A sessions.

- **Building Loyalty:** Encouraging viewer participation, offering exclusive content, and responding to comments helps foster trust and community growth.

Chapter 2: Choosing the Right Platform

Choosing the right platform is one of the most critical decisions for live streamers. Each platform has its strengths, target audiences, and features that cater to specific needs. Whether you're a gamer, entrepreneur, educator, or artist, understanding the differences between platforms can help you maximize reach, engagement, and monetization potential.

This chapter explores the top live streaming platforms, compares their features, and helps you identify the best fit for your content goals. By the end, you'll have a clear roadmap to choose a platform aligned with your vision and audience.

2.1 Use Twitch to Build a Thriving Gaming Community

Twitch dominates the live streaming world, offering powerful tools to grow audiences, foster engagement, and generate income. While it began as a platform for gamers, Twitch now supports music, art, and IRL (In Real Life) streams, making it a versatile choice for creators. This section explores how to maximize Twitch's features, overcome challenges, and build a profitable streaming channel.

1. Engage Viewers with Interactive Features

Twitch provides advanced tools to captivate viewers and keep them coming back for more:

- **Live Chat and Emotes:** Use Twitch's chat and custom emotes to create interactive experiences and foster real-time connections.
- **Extensions and Polls:** Add overlays, polls, and mini-games to make streams interactive and fun.
- **Chatbots:** Set up chatbots for automated greetings, trivia games, and quick responses to keep your chat active and engaging.

2. Unlock Revenue Streams with Monetization Tools

Twitch offers multiple ways to earn revenue while scaling your audience:

- **Subscriptions and Bits:** Offer exclusive perks through subscriptions and allow fans to donate Bits (virtual currency) to support your content.

- **Ads and Sponsorships:** Monetize with ads and collaborate with brands for sponsorship deals.

3. Expand Your Reach with Growth Tools

Twitch offers built-in features to help you grow your audience and build lasting connections:

- **Raids and Hosting:** Collaborate with other streamers by hosting or raiding channels to share audiences.
- **Clips and Highlights:** Encourage viewers to share clips of memorable moments to increase visibility.

4. Overcome Challenges and Stand Out

Twitch's popularity means streamers must work harder to stand out:

- **High Competition:** Millions of streamers compete for attention, so creating unique content and branding is critical.
- **Niche Limitations:** Non-gaming content may require extra creativity to gain traction.
- **Keywords and Titles:** Use compelling stream titles, tags, and keywords to improve discoverability and attract niche audiences.

5. Example

- **Pokimane Example:** Built a diversified income stream through sponsorships, merchandise, and exclusive subscriber content.
- **Ninja Example:** Used collaborative events and raids to grow his audience, securing partnerships and boosting visibility.

6. Tips

- **Engagement Tips:** Incorporate interactive elements like polls, trivia, and chat commands to keep viewers engaged.
- **Monetization Tips:** Offer incentives such as badges, exclusive content, and shoutouts for subscribers.
- **Growth Tips:** Promote your streams on social media and collaborate with other creators to expand visibility.

7. Reflection

- **Tailor Your Content to Your Audience:** Analyze your target audience's preferences and create streams that cater to their interests and needs to keep them engaged.

- **Make Streams Interactive and Memorable:** Incorporate features like polls, games, and Q&A sessions to make streams stand out and keep viewers coming back.

8. Exercise

- **Set Up Your Twitch Profile:** Design your Twitch profile with customized logos, banners, and overlays to reflect your brand identity.

- **Explore Audience Engagement Tools:** Familiarize yourself with the Creator Dashboard and experiment with tools like polls, alerts, and emotes to improve interaction.

- **Plan and Test Your Stream:** Organize your first stream, incorporating interactive elements and testing technical settings to ensure smooth performance.

2.2 Use YouTube Live to Expand Reach and Build Evergreen Content

YouTube Live is a versatile platform for creators looking to combine live streaming with pre-recorded content to maximize long-term visibility. Its strength lies in discoverability through SEO and the ability to repurpose live streams into evergreen content that continues generating views and income long after the stream ends. This section explores how to leverage YouTube Live's features, optimize growth, and build lasting value.

1. Maximize SEO for Discoverability

YouTube Live gives creators access to powerful SEO tools to attract organic traffic and grow visibility:

- **Search Rankings:** Streams and videos rank on both Google and YouTube, making content easily searchable.

- **Keyword Optimization:** Use keywords in titles, descriptions, and tags to boost visibility.

- **Detailed Metadata:** Include timestamps, captions, and transcripts to improve searchability and viewer experience.

2. Unlock Multiple Monetization Streams

YouTube Live provides flexible options to help creators earn revenue while growing their audience:

- **Super Chats and Stickers:** Allow viewers to make paid comments during streams, increasing engagement and income.

- **Channel Memberships:** Offer exclusive perks like badges, emojis, and members-only streams.

- **Ad Revenue and Sponsorships:** Earn through ads and collaborations with brands.

3. Repurpose Content for Evergreen Growth

YouTube Live's ability to save streams as videos allows creators to build a library of evergreen content:

- **Video-on-Demand (VOD):** Recordings stay accessible for repeat views, continuing to generate revenue.

- **Playlists and Tutorials:** Organize live streams into playlists for structured learning or themed content.

- **Highlight Reels:** Edit and re-upload highlights or shorter clips to cater to viewers who prefer quick content.

4. Example

- **Tech Reviews:** MKBHD (Marques Brownlee) uses live streams for product launches and interactive Q&As to engage audiences and grow his following.

- **Financial Coaching:** Graham Stephan combines pre-recorded content with live financial Q&A sessions to boost his income and audience engagement.

5. Tips

- **Optimize Keywords:** Plan SEO strategies for titles, descriptions, and tags to boost visibility.

- **Promote Streams Early:** Schedule and share streams in advance to attract a larger audience.

- **Test New Formats:** Mix live Q&As, tutorials, and themed streams to keep content fresh.

- **Track Performance:** Analyze metrics to identify trends and refine your approach.

6. Reflection

- **SEO Optimization:** How can you optimize your YouTube streams for SEO to improve visibility and attract more viewers?

- **Evergreen Content Creation:** What types of evergreen content can you create by repurposing your live streams?

7. Exercise

- **Plan YouTube Live Series:** Plan a series of YouTube Live streams and outline target keywords to boost discoverability.

- **Write SEO-Optimized Scripts:** Write a script for one stream, including SEO-optimized titles, tags, and descriptions.

- **Repurpose Past Content:** Edit and upload highlights from your past streams to create evergreen content.

2.3 Use Facebook Live to Build Community-Driven Engagement

Facebook Live offers streamers a unique opportunity to connect with audiences through a social network designed for sharing experiences and building communities. It excels at leveraging existing followers, groups, and events for deeper engagement. This section explores how to maximize Facebook Live's features, grow your community, and drive engagement.

1. Leverage Built-In Social Connections

Facebook Live integrates seamlessly with profiles, pages, and groups, making it ideal for targeted audience engagement:

- **Existing Network Integration:** Reach followers directly through your profile or business page to keep streams visible.

- **Group-Based Interaction:** Share live streams in specific groups for niche-focused engagement and higher interaction rates.

- **Event Hosting Features:** Use events to schedule streams, promote launches, or host fundraisers.

2. Monetize with Facebook's Revenue Tools

Facebook Live provides several monetization options for streamers looking to generate income:

- **Stars and Fan Subscriptions:** Allow viewers to support you with virtual gifts and monthly subscriptions.
- **Ad Breaks:** Integrate ads into live broadcasts to earn revenue during streams.
- **Fundraisers and Events:** Collect donations directly through fundraising tools integrated with streams.

3. Build Stronger Communities Through Groups and Events

Facebook's focus on community building allows creators to establish deeper connections with their audience:

- **Private Groups:** Offer exclusive content to members, building loyalty and engagement.
- **Live Polls and Q&A Sessions:** Keep audiences involved through interactive features.

4. Overcome Challenges and Maximize Reach

While Facebook Live is highly accessible, success depends on staying visible and adapting to platform updates:

- **Algorithm Changes:** Organic reach may fluctuate, so consistent posting and engagement strategies are essential.
- **Casual Content Expectations:** Audiences may prefer informal streams, requiring balance between casual and professional styles.
- **Content Testing:** Test different formats like tutorials, interviews, and behind-the-scenes content to see what resonates most.

5. Example

- **BuzzFeed Tasty Example:** Uses interactive cooking demos to generate millions of views and revenue through ads and shares.

- **Small Business Demo Example:** Entrepreneurs host product demonstrations and drive real-time sales through Q&A sessions and promotions.

6. Tips

- **Engagement Tips:** Announce streams in advance and encourage RSVPs to build anticipation.

- **Promotion Tips:** Use cross-posting to share streams across multiple pages or groups for broader reach.

- **Content Tips:** Promote streams within groups and use polls to collect feedback or ideas for future content.

7. Reflection

- **Leverage Groups and Events for Growth:** Identify ways to use Facebook groups and events to grow and engage your audience through targeted interactions.

- **Create Interactive Content for Engagement:** Develop ideas for polls, Q&A sessions, or giveaways to encourage participation and sharing.

8. Exercise

- **Plan a Facebook Live Event:** Outline promotional steps, including posts in groups and paid ads to boost visibility.

- **Write a Stream Script:** Prepare a script that includes interactive elements like polls, giveaways, or Q&A sessions to increase engagement.

- **Analyze Post-Event Results:** Review analytics after the event to identify trends and areas for improvement in future streams.

2.4 Explore Emerging Platforms to Expand Your Audience

Several emerging platforms are gaining traction and offering unique opportunities for niche markets, viral trends, and professional branding. These platforms cater to creators looking for greater freedom, new audiences, and specialized engagement tools. This section highlights key features, strategies, and ways to experiment with these platforms to grow your presence.

1. Use Kick and Rumble for Flexible Monetization

Kick and Rumble are gaining popularity among creators seeking freedom from traditional content policies and higher revenue splits:

- **Gaming and Unfiltered Content:** Both platforms attract creators who focus on gaming, discussions, and unfiltered content that may not fit mainstream standards.

- **Flexible Monetization Models:** With higher revenue splits than major platforms, Kick and Rumble appeal to creators looking for better earnings control.

2. Use TikTok Live for Viral Trends and Younger Audiences

TikTok Live excels at short-form content, making it ideal for engaging younger audiences and leveraging viral trends:

- **Trend-Driven Appeal:** TikTok's algorithm prioritizes short, impactful content, offering rapid visibility for live streams.

- **Interactive Tools:** Features like gifts, stickers, and live Q&As boost real-time engagement and interaction.

3. Use LinkedIn Live for Professional Branding and Networking

LinkedIn Live is perfect for professionals, businesses, and thought leaders focused on corporate content and industry expertise:

- **Professional Branding:** Establish credibility by hosting webinars, thought leadership presentations, and training sessions.

- **Networking Opportunities:** Target a professional audience for discussions, interviews, and virtual networking events.

4. Example

- **TikTok Example:** Creators host live challenges and tutorials to tap into trends and boost follower growth.

- **LinkedIn Example:** Companies use LinkedIn Live for product launches, employee Q&As, and thought leadership panels.

5. Tips

- **Monetization Tips:** Test experimental content that may not align with traditional guidelines to find niche audiences.

- **Engagement Tips:** Incorporate trending music, hashtags, and challenges to maximize visibility.

- **Networking Tips:** Share live events in LinkedIn groups and newsletters to increase attendance and nurture leads.

6. Reflection

- **Match Platforms to Your Goals:** Which emerging platform aligns best with your content style and audience goals? Evaluate the tools and audiences each platform supports.

- **Adapt Strategies for Growth:** How can you adapt your content strategy to fit the unique tools and audiences of these platforms to maximize growth and engagement?

7. Exercise

- **Create Platform-Specific Content:** Choose one emerging platform and create a short live stream focused on engaging your target audience.

- **Measure Performance Metrics:** Track engagement metrics such as comments, shares, and views to assess performance.

- **Refine Strategies Based on Feedback:** Adjust your content and test again based on audience feedback to improve results.

2.5 Platform Comparisons: Features, Monetization, and Audience Reach

Choosing the right platform is essential for maximizing reach, engagement, and revenue. Each platform offers distinct features and caters to different audiences, making it important to align your content strategy with the platform's strengths. This section provides an overview to help you make informed decisions.

1. Feature Breakdown

Each platform specializes in unique features, offering tailored tools for creators:

- **Twitch:** Best for gamers and niche communities, featuring emotes, chat integrations, and extensions for real-time engagement.

- **YouTube Live:** Ideal for evergreen and educational content with SEO tools, long-term storage, and video-on-demand options.

- **Facebook Live:** Focused on social engagement through groups, events, and casual interactions, perfect for community building.
- **Emerging Platforms:** Platforms like Kick, Rumble, TikTok Live, and LinkedIn Live cater to niche creators, offering tools for experimental, professional, and viral content.

2. Monetization Models

Platforms provide different revenue streams, so consider how each option aligns with your goals:

- **Twitch:** Subscriptions, Bits, ads, and affiliate programs provide recurring income for consistent streamers.
- **YouTube Live:** Super Chats, memberships, ad revenue, and sponsorships allow flexible income from live and evergreen content.
- **Facebook Live:** Stars, fan subscriptions, ad breaks, and fundraiser tools focus on community-based support.
- **Emerging Platforms:** Kick and Rumble offer higher revenue splits, while TikTok Live and LinkedIn emphasize engagement-driven growth and professional branding.

3. Audience Reach and Growth Potential

Understanding audience demographics and growth potential ensures better targeting and engagement:

- **Twitch:** Attracts gaming enthusiasts and niche communities seeking interactive experiences.
- **YouTube Live:** Appeals to educational, entertainment, and DIY audiences with strong SEO and discovery features.
- **Facebook Live:** Focuses on personal connections, casual audiences, and community-driven groups and events.
- **Emerging Platforms:** Ideal for niche markets, viral trends, and professional networking through specialized tools and growing audiences.

4. Example

- **Twitch Example:** Creators use Bits and subscriptions for audience support, building steady income through recurring payments.

- **YouTube Example:** Streamers leverage ad revenue and memberships to generate passive income long after a live stream ends.

5. Tips

- **Content Tips:** Match your content type to platform strengths, whether it's gaming, tutorials, social engagement, or professional branding.
- **Cross-Streaming Tips:** Test cross-streaming tools to broadcast on multiple platforms simultaneously and maximize visibility.
- **Optimization Tips:** Track algorithm updates and optimize keywords and descriptions to stay visible and competitive.

6. Reflection

- **Identify Key Features and Goals:** Compare platforms and list the top three features most important to you for content strategy and audience growth.
- **Match Platform Strengths to Your Goals:** Determine which platform best matches your goals for audience engagement and monetization.

7. Exercise

- **Create a Comparison Chart:** Develop a pros-and-cons chart for each platform, highlighting features, monetization, and audience reach.
- **Test Engagement Strategies:** Stream short content on one platform and track engagement metrics like views, shares, and comments to analyze performance.
- **Refine Content Approach:** Evaluate results and make adjustments to improve performance based on audience feedback.

Conclusion: Choosing Your Platform for Success

Evaluate the strengths of each platform based on your goals. With the right platform, you can maximize engagement, build a community, and grow monetization opportunities. Test platforms to refine your strategy and start streaming confidently today!

Chapter 2 Review: Choosing the Right Platform

Chapter 2 focuses on the importance of selecting the right **streaming platform** to match your content goals and audience. It evaluates popular platforms, their features, and monetization options while providing strategies for identifying the best fit for growth and engagement.

2.1 Twitch: The Pioneer of Live Streaming for Gamers

- **Twitch for Gaming** - Known for its focus on gaming and interactive content, Twitch is ideal for gamers and niche communities.

- **Community Engagement Tools** - Features like emotes, chat extensions, and live reactions foster a highly interactive experience.

- **Monetization Options** - Offers subscriptions, bits (donations), and ads for earning revenue.

2.2 YouTube Live: A Versatile Platform for All Creators

- **YouTube for Education** - Suitable for tutorials, webinars, and evergreen content, combining live and pre-recorded videos.

- **SEO Advantages** - Built-in search optimization allows videos to rank in search results, boosting discoverability.

- **Multiple Revenue Streams** - Includes ads, memberships, super chats, and sponsorships.

2.3 Facebook Live: Community-Driven Content and Engagement

- **Facebook for Social Reach** - Leverages existing social networks and groups to connect with viewers.

- **Event Hosting Tools** - Allows event scheduling, group shares, and targeted audience promotion.

- **Monetization Features** - Supports stars (donations), ads, and subscriptions for income generation.

2.4 Emerging Platforms: Kick, Rumble, TikTok Live, and LinkedIn Live

- **Kick and Rumble for Flexibility** - Emerging platforms offering higher revenue splits and fewer restrictions.

- **TikTok for Viral Content** - Focused on short-form and trend-based streams for younger audiences.

- **LinkedIn for Professionals** - Ideal for webinars, networking, and business-related live events.

2.5 Platform Comparisons: Features, Monetization, and Audience Reach

- **Twitch for Gamers and Communities** - Focuses on gaming and interactive niches.

- **YouTube for Versatility** - Combines live and pre-recorded videos for broader visibility.

- **Facebook for Social Engagement** - Emphasizes group interactions and events for community growth.

- **Emerging Platforms for Niche Audiences** - Offer flexibility and unique opportunities for growth.

2.6 Matching Your Content to Platforms: Finding the Best Fit for Growth

- **Gaming Streams on Twitch** - Tailored for competitive and casual gaming.

- **Educational Streams on YouTube** - Ideal for tutorials and long-form lessons.

- **Community-Focused Content on Facebook** - Builds engagement through groups and shared events.

- **Short-Form Trends on TikTok** - Captures younger audiences with quick, interactive content.

Chapter 2 highlights the importance of evaluating platform features, audience demographics, and monetization options to find the best fit for your content strategy. By aligning your goals with the right platform, you can maximize engagement, growth, and revenue potential. The next chapter delves into essential equipment for creating professional-quality streams.

Chapter 3: Essential Equipment for Streaming Success

Equipping yourself with the **right hardware** is the foundation of **streaming success**. Whether you're starting with a **budget-friendly setup** or investing in **professional equipment**, having the proper tools ensures your streams look and sound **polished and professional**. This chapter covers **must-have hardware**, **budget-friendly setups**, **advanced gear**, **device optimization**, and **accessories** to help you create a **high-quality streaming experience** that engages viewers and grows your audience.

3.1 Hardware Must-Haves: Cameras, Microphones, and Lighting

Building a professional-quality stream starts with the right equipment. Viewers expect sharp visuals and clear audio, so investing in high-quality cameras, microphones, and lighting will help you stand out and create a polished broadcast. This section explores essential hardware to level up your streaming setup.

1. Cameras for High-Quality Video

Selecting the right camera ensures sharp visuals and engaging video quality:

- **Webcams for Beginners:** Models like Logitech C920 and Razer Kiyo provide affordable HD video with plug-and-play ease, perfect for new streamers.

- **DSLR and Mirrorless Cameras:** Advanced options like Sony A7 IV and Canon EOS M50 offer cinematic visuals and adjustable lenses for professional content.

- **Action Cameras for Mobility:** Devices like GoPro Hero10 are ideal for dynamic, on-the-go streaming and outdoor events.

- **PTZ Cameras for Versatility:** Pan-tilt-zoom cameras provide multi-angle views and smooth motion control for studio setups.

2. Microphones for Crystal-Clear Audio

High-quality audio ensures viewers stay engaged without distractions:

- **USB Microphones for Simplicity:** Models like Blue Yeti and HyperX QuadCast deliver excellent sound quality with plug-and-play functionality, ideal for beginners.

- **XLR Microphones for Professional Sound:** Options like Shure SM7B produce studio-quality audio when paired with an audio interface, perfect for advanced setups.

- **Lavalier Microphones for Mobility:** Wireless, clip-on mics are great for interviews, fitness streams, and presentations requiring mobility.

- **Headset Microphones for Gamers:** Models like HyperX Cloud II combine clear voice communication with comfort, making them ideal for gaming streams.

3. Lighting for Visibility and Atmosphere

Proper lighting enhances visual quality and sets the tone for streams:

- **Ring Lights for Facial Clarity:** Affordable and portable, ring lights provide even illumination for close-up shots.

- **Softbox Lights for Diffused Lighting:** Larger setups eliminate shadows and create balanced, professional lighting.

- **LED Panels for Custom Effects:** Adjustable colors and brightness allow creative lighting options that match your theme.

- **Key and Fill Lights for Cinematic Effects:** Layered lighting setups add depth and professionalism to visuals.

4. Example

- **Gaming Stream Setup:** A gaming creator upgraded to a DSLR camera and ring light, earning sponsorships by showcasing products.

- **Fitness Stream Setup:** A fitness trainer used a lavalier microphone and softbox lighting to deliver polished workout sessions, increasing subscriptions.

- **Cooking Stream Setup:** A chef integrated overhead cameras and LED panels for tutorials, attracting cooking enthusiasts and partnerships.

5. Tips

- **Cameras:** Invest in a capture card like Elgato Cam Link for DSLR-quality streams. Test different angles for the best look.

- **Microphones:** Use pop filters or foam covers to reduce noise and test audio levels before going live.

- **Lighting:** Position lights at 45-degree angles for even illumination. Use diffusers to soften light and create natural visuals.

6. Reflection

- **Evaluate Your Equipment Needs:** What type of camera, microphone, and lighting setup would best suit your content style?

- **Plan for Professional Upgrades:** How can you improve your current setup to create more professional and engaging streams?

7. Exercise

- **Test Your Setup:** Record a test stream and review video and audio quality to identify areas for improvement.

- **Experiment with Lighting:** Adjust lighting positions and test camera angles for a polished look.

- **Optimize Sound Settings:** Adjust microphone settings and test noise filters to ensure clear audio quality.

3.2 Budget-Friendly Setup Ideas: Start Small, Scale Big

Starting your streaming journey doesn't have to be expensive. With budget-friendly equipment and strategic upgrades, you can create high-quality streams without breaking the bank. This section explores cost-effective tools and DIY enhancements to help you start small and scale up as your audience grows.

1. Minimal Investment for Beginners

Begin your streaming setup with affordable and accessible tools:

- **Built-In Equipment:** Use built-in webcams and laptop microphones to test content ideas before investing in advanced gear.

- **Natural Lighting:** Position your setup near windows to maximize natural light, avoiding the need for costly lighting equipment.

- **Audio First Approach:** Upgrade audio quality before focusing on visuals, as clear sound is often more important to viewers than high-resolution video.

2. Affordable Add-Ons for Quick Improvements

Small upgrades can make a big impact on stream quality without requiring a large investment:

- **USB Microphones:** Models like Samson Q2U and Fifine USB mics deliver excellent audio clarity for under $100.

- **Entry-Level Webcams:** Options like Logitech StreamCam and NexiGo N930AF provide HD visuals and plug-and-play convenience.

- **Clip-On Lights and Tripods:** Affordable ring lights and phone tripods help stabilize video and improve lighting for a more professional look.

3. DIY Enhancements for Professional Touches

Creative and inexpensive solutions can help you achieve professional results without advanced equipment:

- **Backdrop Solutions:** Use curtains, printed designs, or DIY green screens to create clean, customizable backgrounds.

- **Lighting Hacks:** Combine desk lamps with wax paper or shower curtains as diffusers to soften harsh lighting and create a balanced glow.

- **Soundproofing Tips:** Hang blankets or foam panels on walls to improve sound insulation and reduce echo.

4. Example

- **Cooking Streamer Setup:** A cooking streamer started with a built-in webcam, desk lamps for lighting, and a $50 microphone. As the channel grew, they added a ring light and upgraded to a DSLR camera for higher-quality visuals.

- **Fitness Instructor Growth:** A fitness coach streamed workouts using natural light and a phone tripod before scaling up to wireless microphones and studio lights, improving production quality.

5. Tips

- **Prioritize Audio Quality:** Clear sound matters more than visuals, especially for beginners.

- **Test Tools Before Upgrading:** Evaluate budget options before committing to premium gear.

- **Reuse Household Items:** Repurpose everyday objects for soundproofing, lighting, and background effects.

- **Focus on Scalability:** Make gradual upgrades as your audience and revenue grow.

6. Reflection

- **Maximize Budget-Friendly Options:** Are you making the most of budget-friendly options to improve your stream quality?

- **Identify Low-Cost Improvements:** What low-cost upgrades could you make today to improve visuals, lighting, or audio performance?

7. Exercise

- **Prioritize Equipment Needs:** Create a wishlist of equipment upgrades, prioritizing items with the biggest impact on stream quality.

- **Evaluate Test Streams:** Record a test stream using your current setup and evaluate areas needing improvement in lighting, camera angles, or audio clarity.

- **Implement Affordable Upgrades:** Make one affordable upgrade this week and measure its impact on your next live stream.

3.3 Advanced Gear: Elevating Your Production Quality

For experienced streamers, advanced tools provide cinematic visuals and studio-quality sound that enhance production value and deliver a polished, professional experience. This section explores high-end cameras, audio systems, and multi-camera setups to take your streams to the next level.

1. Professional Cameras for Crisp Video

Upgrade your visuals with high-quality cameras designed for professional content creation:

- **4K and 6K Cameras:** Models like Canon EOS R5 and Blackmagic Pocket Cinema Camera deliver ultra-HD resolution for sharp, cinematic visuals.

- **Capture Cards:** Tools like Elgato Cam Link 4K connect DSLR and mirrorless cameras for professional-grade output.

- **PTZ Cameras (Pan-Tilt-Zoom):** Cameras such as Logitech PTZ Pro 2 enable smooth transitions and multi-angle views for versatile setups.

2. Audio Interfaces and Mixers for Superior Sound

Achieve studio-quality audio with advanced microphones and mixing tools:

- **Audio Interfaces:** Devices like Focusrite Scarlett 2i2 optimize sound for XLR microphones, ensuring crystal-clear audio.

- **Mixers:** Tools like GoXLR Mini balance multiple sound inputs and add effects for richer broadcasts.

- **Noise Filters and Pop Filters:** Accessories reduce background noise and vibrations for cleaner sound quality.

3. Multi-Camera Setups for Dynamic Visuals

Enhance engagement with multiple camera angles and seamless transitions:

- **Camera Switchers:** Devices like ATEM Mini Pro allow smooth switching between angles, mimicking TV-quality production.

- **Wide and Close-Up Shots:** Use wide shots for context and close-ups for emphasis to create visual variety.

4. Example

- **Gaming Streamer Setup:** A gaming streamer upgraded to multi-camera angles and 4K video, boosting professionalism and attracting sponsorship deals.

- **Cooking Stream Setup:** A cooking streamer used wide shots for preparation steps and close-ups for plating, enhancing viewer interaction and clarity.

5. Tips

- **Cameras:** Pair cameras with wide-angle lenses for cinematic effects and use external batteries for uninterrupted streams.

- **Audio Tools:** Add compression and equalizers to fine-tune audio clarity and dynamics.

- **Lighting and Effects:** Sync transitions with graphics to create smooth, dynamic visuals for professional-quality streams.

6. Reflection

- **Enhance Production Quality:** What advanced features could enhance your production quality and improve audience engagement?

- **Leverage Multi-Camera Setups:** How can multi-camera setups or audio enhancements elevate your brand and professionalism?

7. Exercise

- **Create an Upgrade Plan:** Outline a step-by-step upgrade plan for adding advanced cameras or audio tools to your setup.

- **Test Transitions and Audio Mixing:** Test multi-camera transitions and audio mixing to refine your workflow.

- **Analyze Viewer Impact:** Record a sample session using advanced gear and analyze its impact on viewer engagement and feedback.

3.4 Optimizing Devices for Streaming: PCs, Consoles, and Mobile Devices

Optimizing your devices ensures smooth performance, stability, and high-quality streams. Whether you're streaming from a PC, console, or mobile device, choosing the right tools and configurations can make a significant impact on your production quality. This section explores ways to enhance performance across different setups.

1. Optimize PCs for High-Performance Streaming

PCs are ideal for professional streaming due to their customization and processing power:

- **High-Speed Processors:** Systems with Intel i7 or AMD Ryzen 7 processors and at least 16GB of RAM ensure lag-free performance and multitasking.

- **Graphics Cards:** NVIDIA RTX series and AMD Radeon RX GPUs handle HD video streaming, 3D effects, and advanced rendering for smooth visuals.
- **Cooling Systems:** Prevent overheating during long sessions by adding fans or liquid cooling systems for stability and durability.

2. Enhance Console Streaming Tools

Consoles provide user-friendly tools, making them great for gaming streams and quick setups:

- **Built-In Features:** PlayStation and Xbox allow direct streaming with simple setups, ideal for beginners.
- **Capture Cards:** Tools like Elgato HD60 S and AverMedia Live Gamer Portable enable overlays, transitions, and custom layouts for professional production.

3. Stream Flexibly with Mobile Devices

Mobile devices make streaming portable and accessible for on-the-go content creators:

- **Streaming Apps:** Apps like Streamlabs Mobile and Prism Live Studio provide customizable overlays and effects.
- **Accessories:** Stabilizers, tripods, and external microphones improve video and audio quality during mobile streams.

4. Example

- **PC Setup Example:** A gaming streamer upgraded to a Ryzen 9 processor and RTX 4080 GPU with an SSD setup, improving performance and reducing lag, attracting higher viewer retention.
- **Mobile Stream Example:** A travel vlogger used a gimbal stabilizer and external microphone to create high-quality mobile streams, growing their audience with portable, real-time content.

5. Tips

- **PC Tips:** Regularly update drivers, optimize settings in streaming software, and use SSDs for faster processing.
- **Console Tips:** Connect external microphones for better sound and sync directly with platforms like Twitch.

- **Mobile Tips:** Test network speeds before streaming and carry portable chargers to avoid interruptions.

6. Reflection

- **Evaluate Your Device Performance:** Are your devices optimized for performance and stability during streams?
- **Upgrade Opportunities:** What upgrades could improve your video, audio, or connectivity?

7. Exercise

- **Test Current Setup:** Test your current setup for speed, audio, and video quality.
- **Identify Improvements:** Identify areas needing improvement and outline specific upgrades for devices, drivers, or software settings.
- **Run Test Stream:** Stream a test session and analyze feedback to refine your setup.

3.5 Accessories That Improve Performance: Tripods, Green Screens, and More

Accessories can significantly improve production quality, streamline workflow, and add creative flexibility to your streaming setup. Investing in the right tools helps you deliver professional results and engage your audience more effectively. This section explores essential accessories that enhance stability, visuals, and control.

1. Stabilizers and Mounts for Professional Angles

Stable camera and microphone positioning is crucial for professional-looking streams:

- **Tripods and Boom Arms:** Keep cameras and microphones steady, reducing vibrations and ensuring sharp visuals and clear audio.
- **Flexible Mounts:** Adjustable setups allow dynamic angles and creative shots, perfect for demonstrations, tutorials, and product showcases.

2. Green Screens and Backdrops for Custom Visuals

Green screens and backdrops enhance visual appeal and enable creative effects:

- **Virtual Effects:** Green screens allow you to replace backgrounds with custom images, animations, or themed visuals.
- **Foldable Backdrops:** Lightweight and portable options provide visual consistency without requiring permanent installations.

3. Stream Decks and Audio Controls for Workflow Efficiency

Advanced control tools improve production quality and allow for seamless transitions and adjustments:

- **Quick Commands:** Devices like Elgato Stream Decks provide customizable buttons for switching scenes, triggering effects, and controlling overlays in real time.
- **Audio Controls:** Mixers and audio interfaces like GoXLR allow precise adjustments, multi-input management, and sound effects integration.

4. Example

- **Cooking Stream Setup:** A cooking streamer used green screens to create themed kitchen backgrounds, improving visual consistency and attracting sponsors.
- **Gaming Streamer Efficiency:** A gamer integrated a stream deck for faster scene transitions and effects, improving production speed and viewer engagement.

5. Tips

- **Mounts and Stability:** Use motorized gimbals or pan-tilt heads for smooth movement during live broadcasts.
- **Green Screen Setup:** Combine green screens with OBS Studio or Streamlabs overlays for professional scenes and transitions.
- **Stream Deck Preparation:** Pre-program buttons for sound effects, transitions, and animations to simplify production tasks.

6. Reflection

- **Streamline Workflow and Visual Appeal:** What accessories would streamline your workflow and enhance visual appeal?
- **Improve Interactivity and Dynamics:** Which tools could make your streams more interactive and dynamic?

7. Exercise

- **Prioritize Accessory Upgrades:** Make a priority list of accessories to improve visuals, stability, and workflow efficiency.

- **Test and Evaluate Enhancements:** Test new accessories, such as tripods or stream decks, to refine your setup and evaluate their impact.

- **Practice Session Review:** Record a short practice session using enhancements and review audience feedback to identify further improvements.

Conclusion: Building a Professional Setup for Streaming Excellence

Chapter 3 highlights the importance of **professional equipment** to produce **high-quality streams** that attract and retain audiences. It covers **budget-friendly setups** for beginners, **advanced tools** for experienced streamers, and **accessories** that improve **efficiency** and **performance**. The next chapter delves into **streaming software and tools** to help creators maximize production quality and engagement.

Chapter 3 Review: Essential Equipment for Streaming Success

Chapter 3 explores the essential equipment needed to create high-quality live streams, focusing on tools that improve visuals, audio, and overall production value. It highlights strategies for building a budget-friendly setup, upgrading to advanced gear, optimizing devices, and adding accessories to streamline workflows and enhance performance.

3.1 Hardware Must-Haves: Cameras, Microphones, and Lighting

- **Cameras for High-Quality Video** - Options range from affordable webcams like Logitech C920 for beginners to professional DSLR and mirrorless cameras for cinematic visuals. Action cameras and PTZ setups provide flexibility for dynamic or studio-based streams.

- **Microphones for Clear Audio** - Recommendations include USB mics for simplicity, XLR mics for studio-level sound, and lavalier mics for hands-free mobility.

- **Lighting for Visual Enhancement** - Ring lights, softbox lighting, and LED panels create a polished look by eliminating shadows and enhancing brightness.

3.2 Budget-Friendly Setup Ideas: Start Small, Scale Big

- **Minimal Investment Options** - Beginners can start with built-in microphones and natural lighting before upgrading.

- **Affordable Add-Ons** - Budget-friendly improvements include USB microphones, entry-level webcams, and clip-on lights for quick quality boosts.

- **DIY Enhancements** - Creators can use curtains for backdrops or desk lamps as inexpensive lighting solutions.

3.3 Advanced Gear: Elevating Your Production Quality

- **High-End Cameras and Capture Cards** - Tools like 4K and 6K cameras and Elgato Cam Link 4K improve video quality and professional integration.

- **Audio Interfaces and Mixers** - Devices such as Focusrite Scarlett 2i2 optimize sound mixing for multi-input setups.

- **Multi-Camera Setups** - Switching between angles adds dynamic visuals and studio-level transitions.

3.4 Optimizing Devices for Streaming: PCs, Consoles, and Mobile Devices

- **PC Optimization** - High-performance processors, graphics cards, and cooling systems ensure smooth streaming.

- **Console Integration** - Built-in streaming features or capture cards add flexibility for console gamers.

- **Mobile Streaming Apps** - Platforms like Streamlabs Mobile make on-the-go streaming accessible.

3.5 Accessories That Improve Performance: Tripods, Green Screens, and More

- **Tripods and Stabilizers** - Improve camera stability and positioning.

- **Green Screens and Backgrounds** - Enable customized visuals for overlays and effects.

- **Stream Decks** - Streamline scene transitions and sound effects with quick-access controls.

Chapter 3 provides a comprehensive guide to choosing the right equipment for both budget-conscious beginners and professional streamers looking to scale their production. It emphasizes affordable tools, advanced gear, and practical accessories to enhance visuals, audio, and workflow efficiency. This foundation prepares creators to deliver high-quality streams and sets the stage for integrating software and tools covered in the next chapter.

Chapter 4: Streaming Software and Tools

The right software and tools can transform an ordinary stream into an extraordinary experience. Whether you're just starting out or looking to optimize your setup, this chapter will guide you through essential streaming software, branding tools, automation features, plugins, and mobile apps to make your broadcasts professional, engaging, and seamless.

4.1 Getting Started with OBS Studio and Streamlabs

Broadcasting software is the foundation of a professional live stream, enabling creators to design layouts, manage transitions, and engage audiences effectively. OBS Studio and Streamlabs are two of the most popular platforms, offering powerful features to meet a variety of needs. This section explores both tools and provides actionable tips to help you optimize your streaming experience.

1. OBS Studio: Customize and Control Your Streams

OBS Studio is free, open-source software designed for creators who want complete control over their streaming setup.

- **Flexible and Free Features:** OBS Studio allows advanced customization without additional costs, making it ideal for professional-quality streams.

- **Scene and Source Management:** Organize multiple layouts, transitions, and visual sources for polished production.

- **Plugins and Extensions:** Expand functionality with plugins for virtual cameras, animations, and interactive overlays.

- **Cross-Platform Support:** OBS works on Windows, macOS, and Linux, offering compatibility for all systems.

2. Streamlabs: Simplify Setup and Engagement

Streamlabs is a user-friendly, feature-rich platform designed for creators seeking simplicity and convenience.

- **Built-In Widgets and Alerts:** Pre-designed tools for donations, chat overlays, and subscriber notifications simplify engagement.

- **Drag-and-Drop Customization:** Easily create layouts and overlays without coding or design expertise.

- **Cloud Backup and Syncing:** Save your layouts in the cloud for portability and quick recovery.

- **Mobile Integration:** Stream directly from your phone with the **Streamlabs Mobile App**, perfect for creators on the go.

3. Tips

- **OBS Tips:**

  - Use plugins like **StreamFX** for 3D effects, dynamic transitions, and visual filters to enhance production quality.

  - Assign **hotkeys** for quick scene changes and smoother live performance during broadcasts.

- **Streamlabs Tips:**

  - Use the **Theme Library** to quickly design branded overlays that match your style.

  - Enable **Streamlabs' chatbot** to automate viewer interaction with commands and responses.

4. Example

- **Gaming Streamer Success:** A gamer integrated OBS Studio plugins for custom transitions and interactive alerts, improving viewer retention and attracting sponsors.

- **Lifestyle Streamer Growth:** A travel vlogger used Streamlabs' mobile app and pre-built overlays for smooth, professional travel streams, growing an international audience.

5. Reflection

- **Customization Needs:** Do you prefer the advanced customization of OBS Studio or the simplicity of Streamlabs?

- **Content Focus:** How can your chosen platform support your streaming goals and audience engagement?

6. Exercise

- **Build a Stream Setup:** Create a multi-scene layout using OBS Studio with at least three transitions and test the flow.

- **Design Overlays:** Use Streamlabs' drag-and-drop tools to create a custom overlay, incorporating alerts and widgets.

- **Test and Optimize:** Record practice streams on both platforms, analyze feedback, and refine settings to maximize performance.

- **Take Action Now:** Optimize your broadcasting software today—test layouts, overlays, and scenes to deliver high-quality, engaging streams that captivate viewers!

4.2 Customizing Overlays, Alerts, and Themes for Branding

Branding is essential for making your streams memorable. Overlays, alerts, and themes give your stream a professional and cohesive look, helping to establish your identity and attract viewers. This section explores how to create visuals that reflect your style and enhance engagement.

1. Enhance Visual Appeal with Overlays

Overlays structure your stream and reinforce branding consistency:

- **Static Overlays:** Use logos, frames, and panels to create polished visuals that highlight your identity.

- **Animated Overlays:** Add movement with animations to grab attention and make streams more dynamic.

- **Custom Designs:** Tools like Canva, Photoshop, and StreamElements allow you to design overlays tailored to your theme and niche.

2. Boost Engagement with Real-Time Alerts

Alerts provide instant feedback to viewers, encouraging interaction and participation:

- **Follower and Donation Alerts:** Acknowledge new followers, subscribers, and donations instantly to build excitement.

- **Custom Sounds and Animations:** Use unique audio effects and animations to reinforce branding and make alerts stand out.

- **Event Lists:** Highlight recent activity, such as top donors or new subscribers, to motivate audience involvement.

3. Establish Brand Identity with Themes

Themes set the visual tone for your stream and make it easily recognizable:

- **Pre-Made Themes:** Use templates from Streamlabs or OWN3D for quick and consistent branding setups.

- **Custom Branding:** Develop unique layouts, fonts, and colors that reflect your personality and niche.

- **Platform Consistency:** Maintain cohesive visuals across multiple platforms, including Twitch, YouTube, and Facebook Live, to strengthen recognition.

4. Example

- **Overlay Example:** A gaming streamer used custom overlays featuring animated frames and logo watermarks to reinforce their brand and attract sponsors.

- **Alert Example:** A charity streamer designed custom donation alerts with sound effects and animations, boosting contributions during fundraising events.

- **Theme Example:** A music creator used seasonal themes and colors to align streams with holidays, increasing viewer engagement during themed events.

5. Tips

- **Overlay Tips:** Match overlay colors, fonts, and styles to your niche to create a cohesive brand image. Test overlay visibility on different devices to ensure clarity across screens.

- **Alert Tips:** Create themed alerts for special events like charity streams or giveaways to increase viewer interest. Incorporate chatbot commands that trigger alerts automatically during key moments.

- **Theme Tips:** Update themes seasonally or during promotions to keep content fresh and engaging. Collect feedback from viewers about theme updates to refine your brand identity.

6. Reflection

- **Leverage Branding for Engagement:** How can custom branding set your stream apart and improve viewer engagement?

- **Align Visuals with Your Identity:** What visual elements best reflect your niche and personality?

7. Exercise

- **Design a Sample Overlay:** Use tools like Canva or Photoshop to create an overlay with colors and fonts that match your brand.

- **Test Alerts and Themes:** Implement and test custom alerts and themes during a live stream, evaluating their impact on engagement.

- **Refine Branding Based on Feedback:** Collect viewer feedback and adjust overlays, alerts, and themes to optimize branding and performance.

- **Build Your Brand Identity:** Focus on creating visuals that reflect your style and enhance viewer engagement to make your stream professional and recognizable.

4.3 Automation and Multi-Streaming Tools for Efficiency

Automation saves time and multi-streaming expands reach, helping you manage your stream efficiently while connecting with broader audiences. These tools simplify workflows, maximize visibility, and improve engagement. This section explores strategies to enhance your streaming process through automation and multi-platform broadcasting.

1. Save Time with Automation Features

Automation tools reduce repetitive tasks, allowing you to focus on content creation and audience interaction:

- **Chat Bots:** Tools like Nightbot and StreamElements moderate chats, automate responses, and run giveaways, ensuring organized and interactive chat rooms.

- **Scheduling Tools:** Pre-schedule streams, social media posts, and announcements to maintain consistency, build anticipation, and keep followers informed.

- **Pre-Recorded Content:** Platforms like OBS and Restream let you stream pre-recorded videos as live broadcasts, offering flexibility while maintaining audience engagement.

2. Expand Reach with Multi-Streaming Platforms

Multi-streaming platforms allow you to broadcast simultaneously across multiple platforms, broadening your reach and impact:

- **Restream.io:** Stream to Twitch, YouTube, and Facebook Live simultaneously, maximizing exposure without extra effort.

- **StreamYard:** A user-friendly multi-streaming platform with built-in branding tools, overlays, and split-screen features ideal for interviews and collaborations.

- **Analytics Tools:** Platforms like Streamlabs and Restream offer viewer metrics, providing insights to analyze performance, improve engagement, and refine content strategies.

3. Example

- **Automation Example:** A streamer used Nightbot to manage chat moderation, share donation links, and run giveaways, improving organization and audience participation.

- **Multi-Streaming Example:** An educational creator streamed lessons simultaneously on Twitch, YouTube, and Facebook Live using Restream.io, tripling audience reach and engagement.

4. Tips

- **Automation Tips:** Use chatbots to welcome viewers, share links, and run giveaways automatically. Schedule countdown timers and reminders to build anticipation and increase attendance.

- **Multi-Streaming Tips:** Test multi-streaming platforms to find the most effective ones for engagement. Customize overlays and branding to create consistent visuals across platforms while tailoring content for each audience.

5. Reflection

- **Leverage Automation for Efficiency:** Are you using automation tools to save time and focus more on content and engagement?

- **Expand Your Audience with Multi-Streaming:** How can multi-streaming help you grow your audience and expand your visibility?

6. Exercise

- **Set Up Chatbots:** Automate greetings, links, and responses using Nightbot or StreamElements to streamline interactions.

- **Test Scheduling Tools:** Schedule at least one pre-recorded stream to test automation tools and evaluate viewer engagement.

- **Explore Multi-Streaming Options:** Test multi-streaming platforms to compare performance metrics, identify audience preferences, and refine your content strategy.

- **Streamline Your Workflow:** Develop a checklist to optimize automation tools and streamline your workflow, ensuring consistency and efficiency across platforms.

4.4 Plugins and Extensions to Enhance Viewer Experience

Plugins and extensions make streams more interactive, engaging, and entertaining, encouraging viewers to stay involved. This section explores tools that improve interaction, streamline workflows, and elevate production value.

1. Engage Audiences with Interactive Plugins

Interactive plugins keep viewers entertained and involved, making streams more dynamic:

- **Polls and Games:** Add trivia, polls, and giveaways to spark engagement and participation during streams.

- **Music Requests:** Let viewers request songs to create a personalized experience and enhance audience enjoyment.

- **Emotes and Stickers:** Use animated reactions and stickers to make chats lively and visually appealing.

2. Boost Efficiency with Productivity Plugins

Productivity plugins simplify workflows, improve efficiency, and ensure smoother streaming operations:

- **Stream Deck Integrations:** Customize commands and shortcuts for quick scene changes, sound effects, and transitions.

- **Hotkeys and Shortcuts:** Use programmable keys to streamline actions like muting audio, changing overlays, or triggering alerts.

- **Analytics Extensions:** Tools like StreamElements provide performance insights and engagement data to optimize future streams.

3. Example

- **Interactive Plugin Example:** A variety streamer used polls and giveaways to keep viewers engaged, resulting in higher retention and increased follower growth.

- **Productivity Plugin Example:** A gaming creator integrated Stream Deck for quick scene transitions and sound effects, improving efficiency and professionalism during broadcasts.

4. Tips

- **Interactive Plugin Tips:** Integrate chatbot plugins to automate polls and giveaways. Highlight top contributors in real time with leaderboards to encourage participation and rewards.

- **Productivity Plugin Tips:** Use timer plugins for countdowns and scheduled breaks to maintain engagement. Test plugins before going live to ensure smooth performance and compatibility.

5. Reflection

- **Enhance Interaction with Plugins:** Which plugins could boost interaction and engagement in your streams?

- **Streamline Workflows with Productivity Tools:** How can productivity plugins help you streamline your workflow and improve efficiency?

6. Exercise

- **Test Interactive Plugins:** Install one interactive plugin, such as polls or emotes, and test its impact during a live broadcast.

- **Experiment with Productivity Tools:** Set up a productivity plugin like Stream Deck integrations and experiment with shortcuts to improve stream management.

- **Analyze Plugin Performance:** Review viewer responses and metrics after testing plugins to refine your approach and boost engagement further.

4.5 Mobile Streaming Apps for Flexibility and Portability

Mobile streaming apps provide the flexibility to go live from anywhere, making them ideal for events, travel, outdoor activities, or IRL (In Real Life) content. With the ability to broadcast on the go, mobile streaming apps enable creators to capture spontaneous moments and engage audiences in real time. This section explores key mobile tools and features for flexible streaming.

1. Use Streamlabs Mobile App for Quick Setup

Streamlabs Mobile App simplifies mobile streaming with easy-to-use features designed for both beginners and experienced creators:

- **Quick Setup:** Go live in minutes with pre-built templates, customizable widgets, and intuitive controls.
- **On-Screen Tools:** Add alerts, overlays, and donation goals directly within the app to keep streams interactive and engaging.
- **Integrated Chat Features:** Monitor chat in real time to respond instantly to audience questions and comments.

2. Leverage Larix Broadcaster for Professional Mobile Streams

Larix Broadcaster is ideal for creators seeking advanced mobile streaming features and professional-quality broadcasts:

- **RTMP Streaming:** Connect to platforms that support RTMP connections, including Twitch, YouTube, and Facebook Live.
- **Professional Settings:** Adjust bitrates, resolutions, and codecs to optimize quality based on connection speeds and audience preferences.
- **Multistream Capability:** Stream to multiple platforms simultaneously to expand reach and visibility.

3. Example

- **Event Coverage Example:** A content creator used Streamlabs Mobile App to live stream a music festival, engaging viewers with interactive overlays and live chats.

- **Travel Stream Example:** A travel vlogger used Larix Broadcaster with stabilizers and external microphones to produce professional-quality mobile streams from remote locations.

4. Tips

- **Streamlabs Tips:** Test your stream's layout and connection quality before going live to avoid interruptions. Use mobile-friendly overlays and widgets for a seamless viewing experience on smaller screens.

- **Larix Tips:** Test bitrate and resolution settings before streaming to ensure stable performance and smooth playback. Use external microphones and stabilizers to improve sound and video quality during outdoor or mobile streams.

5. Reflection

- **Enhance Content Variety with Mobile Streams:** How can mobile streaming add variety and spontaneity to your content?

- **Improve Mobile Stream Quality:** What tools or features could improve the quality and professionalism of your mobile streams?

6. Exercise

- **Mobile App Testing:** Test a mobile app like Streamlabs or Larix Broadcaster by streaming an outdoor scene or event.

- **Performance Evaluation:** Evaluate the performance of overlays, alerts, and audio quality during the broadcast.

- **Engagement Analysis:** Analyze viewer engagement metrics and feedback to identify areas for improvement and refine your mobile streaming approach.

Conclusion

Streaming software and tools are the foundation for creating professional, engaging content. OBS Studio and Streamlabs provide versatile options for setup and customization, while branding elements, automation tools, and plugins enhance quality and interaction. Mobile apps allow flexibility, enabling you to stream anytime, anywhere. With these strategies, you're ready to elevate your production value and create memorable live experiences. The next chapter will focus on planning impactful content to sustain growth and audience retention.

Chapter 4 Review: Streaming Software and Tools

Chapter 4 explores the essential software and tools needed to enhance live streaming production, improve efficiency, and create an engaging viewer experience. It covers popular streaming programs, customization options, automation tools, and mobile apps, providing streamers with practical strategies to optimize their workflow and deliver professional-quality streams.

4.1 Getting Started with OBS Studio and Streamlabs

- **OBS Studio for Flexibility** - A free, open-source software that supports custom layouts, multi-scene setups, and third-party plugins for advanced customization.

- **Streamlabs for Ease of Use** - An all-in-one tool with built-in overlays, alerts, and donation tracking, ideal for beginners and casual streamers.

- **Cross-Platform Compatibility** - Both tools are compatible with Windows, Mac, and Linux, ensuring broad accessibility.

4.2 Customizing Overlays, Alerts, and Themes for Branding

- **Overlays for Visual Appeal** - Incorporate logos, animations, and frames to reinforce brand identity.

- **Alerts for Engagement** - Use pop-ups for followers, subscribers, and donations to acknowledge audience support.

- **Themes for Professional Design** - Pre-made templates offer easy customization for a polished look, while custom themes allow unique branding.

4.3 Automation and Multi-Streaming Tools for Efficiency

- **Automation Features** - Tools like StreamElements and Streamlabs Cloudbot handle alerts, moderation, and chat commands to simplify management.

- **Multi-Streaming Services** - Platforms such as Restream.io and Castr allow streaming to multiple platforms simultaneously, maximizing reach and engagement.

- **Scheduling and Notifications** - Built-in scheduling tools notify audiences about upcoming streams, ensuring better attendance.

4.4 Plugins and Extensions to Enhance Viewer Experience

- **Chat Widgets and Games** - Interactive plugins like polls, games, and leaderboards encourage viewer participation.

- **Custom Widgets for Branding** - Tools like Streamlabs Widgets allow custom alerts and animated transitions to enhance presentation.

- **Music and Sound Effects** - Licensed music libraries and soundboards create atmosphere and keep streams engaging.

4.5 Mobile Streaming Apps for Flexibility and Portability

- **Streamlabs Mobile** - Allows streaming from smartphones with overlays and alerts for on-the-go content creation.

- **Prism Live Studio** - Offers real-time effects, filters, and music integration for mobile streaming.

- **Twitch and YouTube Mobile Apps** - Enable direct streaming to platforms with built-in analytics.

Chapter 4 provides streamers with the tools and strategies needed to customize their streams, automate processes, and expand their reach through multi-streaming and mobile flexibility. By implementing the right software and tools, creators can deliver high-quality broadcasts while staying efficient and engaging. The next chapter explores content planning strategies to help streamers develop engaging and consistent programming.

Part 2: Content Creation and Engagement

Chapter 5: Planning Your Content Like a Pro

Great content doesn't happen by accident—it's carefully planned, structured, and executed. Planning your content like a pro involves defining your niche, building consistency, crafting engaging ideas, and leveraging trends to stay relevant. This chapter will guide you step-by-step through the process of organizing and refining your content strategy, ensuring each live stream is impactful and keeps viewers coming back for more.

5.1 Finding Your Niche: Defining Themes and Styles

Choosing the right niche is essential for attracting the right audience and establishing a loyal following. Successful streamers focus on themes and styles that resonate with their passion while appealing to a specific viewer base. This section explores how to identify your niche, align content with audience needs, and refine your streaming style.

1. Discover Your Passion and Expertise

Building content around topics you enjoy and excel at increases consistency and authenticity:

- **Evaluate Your Interests:** Focus on subjects you genuinely enjoy discussing or demonstrating and can sustain long-term. Passion-driven content is easier to maintain and attracts like-minded viewers.

- **Identify Strengths:** Highlight unique skills, talents, or specialized knowledge that set you apart from others. Consider topics where you already have expertise or a competitive edge.

- **Research Popular Categories:** Explore high-performing niches like gaming, cooking, tutorials, fitness, and talk shows to identify opportunities.

2. Match Audience Needs and Trends

Understanding your audience and delivering value tailored to their needs increases retention and growth:

- **Analyze Trends and Search Data:** Tools like Google Trends and Twitch categories can help identify popular topics and audience demands.

- **Provide Solutions or Entertainment:** Decide whether your goal is to educate, entertain, or inspire viewers, then craft your content accordingly.

- **Engage with Communities:** Participate in forums and social media to learn what audiences are discussing and requesting.

3. Refine Your Content Style

Experimenting with formats and themes helps you create a unique identity that resonates with viewers:

- **Live Tutorials:** Teach skills step-by-step, focusing on education and hands-on value.

- **Challenge Streams:** Engage audiences with interactive challenges, games, and competitions.

- **Storytelling Formats:** Share personal anecdotes or scripted narratives to keep viewers hooked.

4. Tips

- **Brainstorm Ideas:** List hobbies, talents, and interests that can translate into engaging content.

- **Test Niches:** Stream short sessions in different categories to gauge audience interest before committing.

- **Observe Trends:** Follow successful streamers to discover ideas and learn best practices.

- **Develop Signature Styles:** Create catchphrases, themes, or segments to make your streams memorable.

5. Example

- **Gaming Streamer Success:** A gamer built a following by streaming daily challenges and teaching tips for competitive games, leading to brand sponsorships.

- **Fitness Influencer Growth:** A fitness streamer combined live workout tutorials with Q&A sessions, attracting fitness enthusiasts and growing their subscriber base.

- **Cooking Channel Engagement:** A cooking streamer gained popularity by showcasing quick recipes and meal prep ideas, complemented by audience polls to select weekly themes.

6. Reflection

- **Sustain Long-Term Content:** What topics or themes excite you enough to sustain long-term content creation?
- **Stand Out in Your Niche:** How can your expertise or style stand out in a crowded niche?

7. Exercise

- **Brainstorm Niches:** List three potential niches and write a short pitch for each, explaining why they suit your strengths and interests.
- **Test Your Niche:** Host a sample stream focused on one niche and analyze viewer engagement.
- **Refine and Improve:** Review audience feedback and performance metrics to determine whether the niche resonates with your audience and shows growth potential.

5.2 Building a Content Calendar: Consistency is Key

Consistency builds trust, helps viewers anticipate your streams, and boosts algorithm visibility. A content calendar organizes ideas, keeps you on schedule, and reduces last-minute stress. This section explores how to plan themes, schedule effectively, and remain adaptable while maintaining consistency.

1. Plan Weekly and Monthly Themes

Organizing streams around consistent themes keeps viewers engaged and coming back for more:

- **Weekly Focus Topics:** Assign themes like "Motivation Mondays" or "Friday Game Night" to create predictable and exciting programming.
- **Seasonal Content:** Incorporate holidays, events, and trends to make streams timely and relevant.
- **Recurring Segments:** Develop signature segments, such as Q&A sessions, tutorials, or giveaways, to establish routine expectations.

2. Schedule and Optimize Streaming Times

Scheduling streams at the right time maximizes viewership and engagement:

- **Prime Streaming Hours:** Analyze audience analytics to determine peak viewing times and adjust schedules to match audience availability.

- **Time Management Tools:** Use platforms like Trello, Asana, or Google Calendar to organize tasks, set reminders, and track deadlines.

- **Consistency Over Frequency:** Focus on delivering consistent, high-quality streams instead of overwhelming viewers with too many sessions.

3. Balance Structure with Flexibility

A successful content calendar balances preparation with adaptability to capture trends and spontaneous opportunities:

- **Mix Live and Pre-Recorded Content:** Plan pre-recorded segments as filler episodes or backups in case of scheduling conflicts.

- **Adapt to Trends:** Leave space for spontaneous streams based on breaking news, viral challenges, or viewer requests.

- **Evaluate and Adjust:** Review analytics regularly to identify trends and fine-tune schedules for better performance.

4. Tips

- **Create Themed Days:** Use ideas like "Tutorial Tuesdays" or "Feedback Fridays" to build consistency and engagement.

- **Post Social Media Reminders:** Build anticipation with countdowns and updates before streams.

- **Batch-Plan Content:** Outline monthly themes in advance to save time and reduce last-minute stress.

- **Schedule Breaks for Balance:** Plan occasional breaks to prevent burnout while staying connected with your audience.

5. Example

- **Gaming Calendar Example:** A gaming streamer planned a weekly schedule with themes like "Multiplayer Mondays" and "Challenge Fridays," maintaining consistency and increasing viewership by 30%.

- **Fitness Stream Example:** A fitness creator used seasonal challenges, like "30-Day Workout Challenges," to keep viewers motivated and engaged throughout the month.

6. Reflection

- **Maintain Viewer Engagement:** Are you streaming consistently enough to keep viewers engaged?

- **Optimize Calendar for Trends:** How can you optimize your calendar to align with viewer habits and trends?

7. Exercise

- **Content Calendar Planning:** Create a one-month content calendar, including themes, stream titles, and potential dates.

- **Analytics Testing:** Use analytics to select prime streaming times and test different schedules to see what resonates best.

- **Backup Episode Preparation:** Plan two pre-recorded backup episodes to ensure consistency even during unexpected disruptions.

5.3 Crafting Engaging Stream Ideas: Themes, Challenges, and Special Events

The most successful streams are creative, engaging, and interactive. Planning diverse ideas keeps viewers entertained and encourages participation. This section covers strategies for building themes, creating challenges, and hosting special events that captivate your audience.

1. Develop Unique Themes and Topics

Creating thematic streams establishes structure and keeps content fresh:

- **Story-Based Streams:** Build narratives with cliffhangers to keep viewers invested and eager for the next episode.

- **Educational Streams:** Offer tutorials, how-tos, or Q&A sessions to provide value and establish authority in your niche.

- **Lifestyle and Behind-the-Scenes Content:** Share personal stories, workflows, or creative processes to build authenticity and connection.

2. Introduce Challenges and Competitions

Challenges add excitement and encourage participation, turning viewers into active contributors:

- **Audience Participation Games:** Engage viewers with trivia, polls, and interactive mini-games that promote real-time involvement.

- **Giveaways and Contests:** Offer prizes or rewards for participation in challenges, boosting engagement and excitement.

- **Milestone Rewards:** Celebrate milestones with giveaways or exclusive perks for dedicated followers.

3. Host Special Events and Collaborations

Special events and guest appearances add novelty and attract new audiences:

- **Milestone Celebrations:** Host virtual parties to celebrate follower counts, anniversaries, or fundraising goals.

- **Guest Appearances:** Collaborate with other streamers or influencers to expand reach and cross-promote audiences.

- **Theme Nights or Series:** Plan recurring events like "Throwback Thursdays" or "Challenge Fridays" to establish consistency while keeping ideas flexible.

4. Example

- **Gaming Challenges:** A gaming streamer gained rapid growth by hosting interactive challenges, such as viewer-vs-streamer matches and trivia contests.

- **Trivia Nights:** Another creator boosted engagement with themed trivia nights and prizes, encouraging viewers to invite friends and build excitement.

5. Tips

- **Brainstorm Creative Ideas:** List out unique topics, formats, and collaborations to keep streams engaging.

- **Leverage Trends:** Incorporate trending topics, games, or memes to stay relevant and attract new viewers.

- **Engage with Viewers in Real Time:** Use tools like polls and chat overlays to boost interaction and personalize experiences.

- **Test and Analyze Results:** Track engagement metrics to identify which ideas resonate most with your audience.

6. Reflection

- **Incorporate Enjoyable Elements:** What types of streams do you enjoy watching? How can you incorporate those elements into your own content?

- **Excite Your Audience:** Which challenges or special events would excite your audience and encourage participation?

7. Exercise

- **Idea Generation:** Brainstorm 10 stream ideas, including themes, interactive challenges, and collaborations.

- **Audience Test:** Test one idea that includes audience participation and analyze feedback and engagement metrics.

- **Event Planning:** Plan a themed event or giveaway and outline steps to promote it effectively before going live.

5.4 Scripting and Improvisation Techniques for Impactful Content

Balancing preparation with spontaneity is key to keeping streams engaging and authentic. Whether fully scripted or improvised, having a framework ensures smooth delivery while allowing room for flexibility. This section explores scripting techniques, improvisation tips, and strategies to create compelling content.

1. Use Scripting Techniques for Structure

Effective scripts add clarity and flow without feeling robotic:

- **Outline Key Points:** Map out main topics, transitions, and segment breaks to keep streams organized.

- **Write Hooks and Introductions:** Start strong with compelling hooks, questions, or bold statements to grab attention immediately.

- **Prepare Calls to Action:** Include prompts for likes, follows, and shares throughout the stream to boost engagement.

2. Apply Improvisation Tips for Natural Delivery

Improvisation keeps streams lively and helps maintain authenticity:

- **Practice Thinking on Your Feet:** Role-play scenarios to improve confidence when handling unexpected moments.

- **Engage with Chat in Real Time:** React to questions, comments, and suggestions to keep streams interactive and dynamic.

- **Recover from Mistakes Smoothly:** Turn errors into jokes or lessons to maintain momentum and humor.

3. Combine Scripted and Improvised Elements

Blending structure and spontaneity ensures balance:

- **Scripted Openings and Closings:** Use scripts for introductions and conclusions to set the tone and wrap up effectively.

- **Improvised Q&A Sessions:** Dedicate portions of the stream for unscripted interactions, adding spontaneity.

- **Segment Flexibility:** Plan segments but allow time for unexpected moments or viewer-led activities.

4. Example

- **Talk-Show Format:** A talk-show streamer combined a scripted intro with unscripted audience Q&A sessions, striking a perfect balance between polish and spontaneity.

- **Gaming Walkthroughs:** A gamer used scripted tutorials for clarity while improvising reactions during gameplay to keep the energy high.

5. Tips

- **Prepare Talking Points:** Write flexible outlines instead of word-for-word scripts to maintain authenticity.

- **Practice Transitions:** Rehearse moving between topics or activities to avoid awkward pauses.

- **Use Cue Cards or Prompts:** Keep quick reminders nearby to stay on track without losing spontaneity.

- **Balance Segments:** Mix pre-planned segments with free-flowing conversations to keep content dynamic.

6. Reflection

- **Balance Preparation and Spontaneity:** Are your streams too scripted or too improvised? How can you balance preparation and spontaneity?

- **Improve Delivery Techniques:** What techniques can you use to make your delivery feel more natural and engaging?

7. Exercise

- **Script Outline Preparation:** Write a script outline for your next stream, including key points, introductions, and closing remarks.

- **Improvisation Testing:** Leave 30% of your schedule open for improvisation and test how it impacts viewer engagement.

- **Performance Review:** Record and review your performance to identify areas for improvement in transitions and delivery.

5.5 Leveraging Trends and News to Stay Relevant

Staying up-to-date with trends and current events keeps your content fresh and appealing. Timely topics can attract new viewers, increase engagement, and position you as a relevant voice in your niche. This section explores tools and strategies for identifying and leveraging trends effectively.

1. Use Trend Research Tools

Tracking trends helps you identify popular topics and themes that resonate with audiences:

- **Google Trends:** Track search patterns and rising keywords to find trending topics.

- **Social Media Hashtags:** Follow hashtags on platforms like Twitter, Instagram, and TikTok to spot viral challenges and conversations.

- **Platform Analytics:** Monitor trending categories and streams on Twitch, YouTube, and Facebook Live for content ideas.

2. Capitalize on Viral Moments

Leveraging viral content can boost visibility and attract new audiences:

- **React Streams:** Share live reactions to breaking news, viral videos, or memes to engage viewers and spark conversations.

- **Trend Adaptations:** Put a unique spin on trending topics to make them relevant to your niche. For example, a cooking streamer could recreate trending recipes with their own twist.

- **Timely Collaborations:** Partner with other creators to participate in viral challenges or events, multiplying exposure.

3. Balance Trends with Evergreen Content

While trends provide spikes in visibility, evergreen content sustains long-term growth:

- **Mix Formats:** Alternate between trend-based streams and timeless topics like tutorials, FAQs, or skill-building sessions.

- **Repurpose Content:** Convert live reactions or trend discussions into highlight reels or shorts to maintain relevance after the trend fades.

- **Adapt Quickly:** Be ready to pivot and integrate trends without losing focus on your core message.

4. Example

- **Live Reactions to Viral Trends:** A fitness streamer gained visibility by reacting to viral workout challenges and creating their own versions, encouraging audience participation.

- **News Commentary Streams:** A tech streamer discussed breaking news about product launches, attracting viewers interested in updates and reviews.

5. Tips

- **Monitor Trends Daily:** Stay active on platforms to catch trends early and act fast.

- **Prepare Content Quickly:** Timeliness matters, so prepare graphics and overlays in advance for fast deployment.

- **Blend Trends with Your Style:** Add your personality or expertise to trending topics to stand out.

- **Analyze Performance Metrics:** Track views, shares, and comments to evaluate the impact of trend-based streams.

6. Reflection

- **Incorporate Trends Effectively:** How often do you incorporate trends into your content?

- **Balance Relevance and Longevity:** Are you balancing trending and evergreen material effectively to maintain relevance and longevity?

7. Exercise

- **Trend Analysis:** Pick one current trend and design a live stream around it.

- **Performance Evaluation:** Test viewer reactions and track engagement metrics to evaluate its impact.

- **Content Repurposing:** Create a follow-up plan to repurpose successful trend-based content into highlights or short clips for ongoing visibility.

Conclusion

Planning your content like a pro transforms random ideas into a cohesive strategy that builds viewer loyalty and growth. By finding your niche, staying consistent with a content calendar, and balancing scripted and spontaneous elements, you'll deliver streams that stand out. Don't forget to leverage trends and interactive tools to keep your content relevant and engaging. In the next chapter, we'll dive into building a unique brand identity that strengthens your connection with your audience.

Chapter 5 Review: Planning Your Content Like a Pro

Chapter 5 provides a strategic guide for streamers to plan their content effectively. It focuses on selecting a niche, building a content calendar, creating engaging stream ideas, and leveraging trends to maintain relevance. Streamers will learn how to keep their streams consistent and captivating, ensuring long-term audience engagement.

5.1 Finding Your Niche: Defining Themes and Styles

- **Discovering Your Passion and Expertise** - Streamers are encouraged to focus on topics they enjoy and are knowledgeable about, ensuring sustainable and authentic content creation.

- **Matching Audience Needs** - By using tools like Google Trends, streamers can identify what their audience is interested in, tailoring their content to meet viewer demands.

- **Refining Content Style** - Streamers are advised to explore various formats, such as tutorials, challenges, or storytelling, to define a style that best engages their target audience.

5.2 Building a Content Calendar: Consistency is Key

- **Planning Weekly and Monthly Themes** - Consistent themes, like "Motivation Mondays" or "Fitness Fridays," help create a regular streaming schedule, building anticipation and loyalty among viewers.

- **Scheduling and Timing** - Analyzing audience activity to identify peak streaming times ensures maximum engagement and growth.

- **Balancing Structure with Flexibility** - While maintaining a content calendar is essential, streamers should leave room for adapting to trending topics and spontaneous content to keep their streams fresh.

5.3 Crafting Engaging Stream Ideas: Themes, Challenges, and Special Events

- **Themes and Topics** - Streamers are encouraged to try various content types, such as educational streams or behind-the-scenes footage, to keep their content diverse and engaging.

- **Challenges and Competitions** - Interactive games, challenges, and polls foster audience participation and increase engagement.

- **Special Events and Collaborations** - Hosting special events or collaborating with other creators can expand reach and attract new viewers.

5.4 Scripting and Improvisation Techniques for Impactful Content

- **Scripting Techniques for Structure** - Streamers are advised to use basic scripts with key points and hooks to ensure a smooth flow and maintain viewer interest.

- **Improvisation Tips for Natural Delivery** - Engaging with live chat and adapting to real-time feedback helps keep the stream authentic and dynamic.

5.5 Leveraging Trends and News to Stay Relevant

- **Trend Research Tools** - Streamers can use tools like Google Trends to stay informed about trending topics, ensuring their content remains relevant.

- **Capitalizing on Viral Moments** - Reacting to viral moments or news helps streamers stay current and attract new viewers.

Chapter 5 provides streamers with essential strategies for planning and delivering consistent, engaging content. By defining a niche, scheduling streams, and incorporating trends, streamers can build a loyal audience and create dynamic, impactful broadcasts. The next chapter will explore building a unique brand identity.

Chapter 6: Building Your Brand Identity

Building a strong brand identity is essential for standing out in the competitive world of live streaming. Your brand is more than just visuals—it's the message, personality, and connection you build with your audience. This chapter explores how to create a professional and memorable brand through logos, visual consistency, storytelling, and taglines. By the end of this chapter, you'll have the tools to establish a unique identity that resonates with viewers.

Key Takeaway: A well-defined brand identity attracts viewers, builds trust, and leaves a lasting impression.

6.1 Designing Logos, Banners, and Thumbnails for Recognition

Visual branding elements like logos, banners, and thumbnails are the first impression viewers have of your stream. These visuals need to be eye-catching, memorable, and aligned with your content style. This section covers how to create visual assets that strengthen brand recognition and attract viewers.

1. Craft a Recognizable Logo

A strong logo builds identity and helps viewers instantly recognize your stream:

- **Simplicity Matters:** Keep designs clean, scalable, and easy to recognize.
- **Color Psychology:** Use colors that reflect your tone—bright for fun and energy, dark for sophistication and professionalism.
- **Versatility:** Ensure logos look good in various sizes and formats, from profile icons to banners.

2. Build Consistent Banners and Thumbnails

Banners and thumbnails create a cohesive look across your profiles and videos:

- **Channel Banners:** Highlight your streaming schedule, social media handles, and a tagline that defines your brand.
- **Thumbnails:** Use bold text, high-contrast images, and recognizable fonts to stand out in crowded feeds.
- **Video Frames and Overlays:** Customize your visuals to match your niche, whether it's gaming, tutorials, or lifestyle content.

3. Leverage Branding Tools for Professional Designs

Modern tools simplify the process of designing high-quality visuals:

- **Graphic Design Tools:** Platforms like Canva, Adobe Express, and Figma offer templates for beginners and advanced users.

- **AI Logo Makers:** Services like Looka and Tailor Brands generate logo ideas quickly, allowing customization based on your preferences.

- **Custom Illustration Services:** Hire freelance designers for unique, personalized branding elements.

4. Example

- **Gaming Streamer Redesign:** A gaming streamer redesigned their thumbnails with brighter colors and bold fonts, increasing click-through rates by 30%. Over six months, this led to higher visibility and a 20% rise in subscriptions.

- **Educational Channel Branding:** A tutorial-focused streamer used custom banners to emphasize their schedule and expertise, resulting in stronger brand recognition and better viewer retention.

5. Tips

- **Test Color Schemes:** Experiment with colors to match your tone and niche.

- **Use Templates for Consistency:** Pre-made designs save time and create a unified look.

- **Highlight Key Information:** Include schedules, handles, and taglines in banners to reinforce branding.

- **Refresh Visuals Regularly:** Update visuals to reflect changes in branding or seasonal themes.

6. Reflection

- **Reflect Content Style and Personality:** How can your visuals reflect your content style and personality?

- **Optimize for Platforms and Devices:** Are your logos and thumbnails optimized for visibility across different devices and platforms?

7. Exercise

- **Draft Logo Designs:** Sketch a rough logo idea or create a draft using a free design tool like Canva.

- **Template Creation:** Design one banner and one thumbnail template for future streams.

- **Feedback Testing:** Test the visuals across platforms and collect feedback from viewers to refine designs.

6.2 Consistency Across Platforms: Unified Look and Messaging

Consistency in branding builds trust and helps viewers recognize you across multiple platforms. A unified look reinforces credibility and ensures your audience can easily find and follow you anywhere.

1. Establish Unified Design Elements

Align visual elements to create a seamless brand experience:

- **Color Schemes and Fonts:** Use the same colors and typography across all platforms to maintain consistency.

- **Profiles and Bios:** Align messaging with similar descriptions, taglines, and links to reinforce identity.

- **Content Templates:** Design overlay templates for streams, highlight reels, and thumbnails to create a cohesive visual style.

2. Adopt a Multi-Platform Approach

Expanding across platforms increases reach and audience engagement:

- **Cross-Promotion:** Link all your platforms in descriptions and bios to encourage viewers to follow you everywhere.

- **Content Adaptation:** Tailor posts to each platform while keeping branding elements consistent.

- **Scheduling Syncs:** Maintain similar posting schedules across platforms to reinforce consistency.

3. Build Platform-Specific Variations

Customize designs while preserving branding identity for different platforms:

- **YouTube Headers vs. Twitch Panels:** Adjust layouts to suit platform-specific requirements without losing core visual identity.

- **Stories vs. Posts:** Adapt graphics for Instagram stories, TikTok clips, or YouTube thumbnails to fit formats and viewer preferences.

- **Short-Form and Long-Form Content:** Repurpose highlights for short clips and maintain consistent visual elements.

4. Example

- **Fitness Streamer Expansion:** A fitness streamer unified their look across Instagram, YouTube, and Twitch, boosting follower crossover by 40%. Customizing banners for each platform maintained consistency while adapting for each audience.

- **Gaming Streamer Alignment:** A gaming creator optimized their overlays and thumbnails for both YouTube and Twitch, improving recognition and viewership retention.

5. Tips

- **Audit Branding Across Platforms:** Regularly review designs, bios, and links for consistency.

- **Repurpose Content Strategically:** Adapt videos and graphics for each platform without losing branding elements.

- **Use Templates for Quick Adjustments:** Create adaptable designs that can be customized quickly.

- **Monitor Analytics:** Track engagement to measure how branding affects visibility and adjust as needed.

6. Reflection

- **Maintain Consistency Across Platforms:** Does your current branding look consistent across platforms?

- **Adapt Designs for Different Formats:** How can you adapt visuals to fit different formats while staying true to your brand?

7. Exercise

- **Branding Audit:** Review all your social profiles and make a checklist to align visuals and messaging.

- **Design Updates:** Create platform-specific banners or thumbnails that follow your branding style.

- **Engagement Testing:** Test consistency by sharing content across platforms and analyzing viewer responses.

6.3 Establishing Trust and Authenticity with Viewers

Trust is the foundation of a loyal audience. Building authenticity helps viewers connect with you on a deeper level, turning casual viewers into dedicated followers. This section outlines practical strategies to establish trust and showcase authenticity in your streams.

1. Be Genuine and Relatable

Audiences appreciate creators who are real and transparent:

- **Show Personality:** Let viewers see your real self, including humor, quirks, and even imperfections.

- **Share Stories:** Talk about personal challenges, wins, and lessons to create emotional connections.

- **Stay Consistent:** Be true to your style and messaging across all platforms to reinforce credibility.

2. Engage Regularly to Build Relationships

Frequent interaction creates a sense of community:

- **Respond to Comments:** Answer questions and acknowledge regular viewers by name to build rapport.

- **Polls and Feedback:** Use polls and surveys to involve your audience in content planning and decision-making.

- **Exclusive Perks:** Offer shoutouts or exclusive content for loyal viewers to make them feel valued.

3. Build Transparency Through Openness

Being open about your process and progress fosters trust:

- **Behind-the-Scenes Footage:** Share raw moments like setting up your equipment, rehearsing content, or brainstorming ideas.

- **Progress Updates:** Celebrate milestones and share personal goals to inspire and connect with your audience.

- **Acknowledging Mistakes:** Address errors openly and use them as teachable moments to build credibility.

4. Example

- **Lifestyle Streamer Journey:** A lifestyle streamer shared personal struggles and celebrated small wins with followers, earning empathy and donations to support their content journey. Within six months, this authenticity doubled their engagement rate.

- **Fitness Trainer Growth:** A fitness streamer documented their progress toward personal fitness goals, motivating viewers to join challenges and improving viewer retention.

5. Tips

- **Ask for Input Regularly:** Show that viewer opinions matter by incorporating their suggestions into streams.

- **Celebrate Successes Together:** Highlight milestones and thank your audience for their support.

- **Be Transparent About Goals:** Share your aspirations and keep viewers updated on progress.

- **Use Humor and Vulnerability:** Balance lightheartedness with sincerity to keep interactions relatable.

6. Reflection

- **Share Personal Insights:** What personal stories or insights can you share to connect with your audience?

- **Strengthen Viewer Relationships:** How can you make your streams more interactive to build stronger relationships?

7. Exercise

- **Personal Story Practice:** Write down three personal anecdotes that align with your content theme and practice sharing them on your next stream.

- **Engagement Activity:** Test a poll or survey to gather viewer feedback and incorporate suggestions into your next stream.

- **Transparency Review:** Record and review a segment focused on transparency to evaluate its impact on engagement.

6.4 Storytelling Techniques: Making Connections Through Narratives

Effective storytelling captivates audiences and keeps them invested in your journey. Stories add emotion, relatability, and authenticity, transforming streams into memorable experiences. This section explores strategies for incorporating storytelling into your content.

1. Develop Your Brand Story

A strong narrative builds connections and gives your content a purpose:

- **Origins and Mission:** Share why you started streaming, what motivates you, and the goals behind your content.

- **Milestones and Growth:** Highlight key achievements, lessons learned, and turning points that shaped your journey.

- **Behind-the-Scenes Moments:** Offer insights into your preparation process or personal challenges to build transparency.

2. Incorporate Stories into Streams

Integrating narratives during broadcasts keeps audiences engaged:

- **Real-Time Reactions:** Share personal reactions to live events, audience interactions, or unexpected moments.

- **Interactive Segments:** Create polls and ask viewers to contribute ideas or feedback that shape the storyline.

- **Daily Highlights:** Recap funny, exciting, or emotional moments from previous streams to build continuity.

3. Leverage Emotional Hooks to Build Connections

Emotions make stories memorable and relatable:

- **Personal Challenges and Triumphs:** Highlight obstacles you've overcome to inspire and connect with viewers.

- **Inspirational Stories:** Motivate viewers with anecdotes about personal growth, success, or future aspirations.
- **Audience-Centered Content:** Share stories involving your viewers—celebrate their contributions or showcase their impact on your stream.

4. Example

- **Artistic Storytelling:** An artist streamer narrated their creative process during live painting sessions, making viewers feel part of the artwork's creation. They later auctioned completed pieces, generating both income and engagement.
- **Fitness Progress Journals:** A fitness streamer documented their weight loss journey, inspiring viewers to join challenges and celebrate milestones together.

5. Tips

- **Prepare Story Outlines:** Draft story points in advance to maintain flow while leaving room for improvisation.
- **Use Visual Cues:** Incorporate overlays, photos, and clips to support visual storytelling.
- **Engage with Viewers' Stories:** Encourage audience members to share their experiences and respond to them during streams.
- **Repurpose Content:** Turn successful story segments into highlight reels or social media snippets.

6. Reflection

- **Enhance Relatability Through Stories:** How can storytelling make your streams more relatable and memorable?
- **Inspire Through Experiences:** What personal experiences or milestones could inspire or motivate your audience?

7. Exercise

- **Story Outline Practice:** Outline a short personal story to weave into your next stream.
- **Delivery Rehearsal:** Practice delivering it with emotional hooks and audience prompts.

- **Engagement Test:** Test the story's impact by tracking engagement metrics and viewer feedback.

6.5 Creating Catchy Taglines and Memorable Themes

A strong tagline can define your brand and make it instantly recognizable. Paired with memorable themes, it reinforces your identity and attracts a loyal audience. This section explores how to craft compelling taglines and build themes that resonate.

1. Craft a Catchy Tagline

A tagline captures the essence of your brand in a few memorable words:

- **Keep It Short and Impactful:** Aim for 5–7 words that are easy to remember.

- **Highlight Value:** Emphasize what makes your content unique—whether it's humor, expertise, or inspiration.

- **Use Wordplay or Rhythm:** Add fun, rhyme, or alliteration to make it catchy.

2. Build Themes Around Your Tagline

Consistent themes make your content more engaging and recognizable:

- **Stream Titles:** Reinforce branding with creative series names tied to your tagline.

- **Recurring Segments:** Plan themed events like "Tech Talk Tuesdays" or "Motivation Mondays" to create routine and anticipation.

- **Visual Branding:** Match colors, fonts, and overlays to reflect your tagline's tone.

3. Expand Brand Themes with Promotions

Promotions and campaigns amplify your message and attract new viewers:

- **Hashtag Campaigns:** Develop custom hashtags for promotions and contests to increase visibility.

- **Special Events:** Host marathons, giveaways, or themed challenges to reinforce your brand identity.

- **Merchandise and Products:** Create branded merchandise that highlights your tagline and themes.

4. Example

- **Gordon Ramsay's Branding:** Celebrity chef Gordon Ramsay's tagline "Perfection on Every Plate" reinforces his reputation for culinary expertise and high standards, tying seamlessly into his TV shows, books, and cooking challenges.

- **Ninja's Gaming Identity:** Popular gamer Ninja uses his tagline "Victory Awaits" to promote competitive gaming content, challenges, and tutorials, creating a high-energy, aspirational brand.

5. Tips

- **Focus on Audience Appeal:** Test taglines and themes to ensure they resonate with your target audience.

- **Stay Flexible:** Update slogans and themes as your content evolves.

- **Incorporate Taglines in Graphics:** Reinforce branding by including your tagline in overlays, thumbnails, and banners.

- **Promote Everywhere:** Use your tagline consistently across platforms and promotional materials.

6. Reflection

- **Define Your Message Clearly:** What message do you want your tagline to convey?

- **Align with Brand Identity:** Does your tagline align with your brand's personality and goals?

7. Exercise

- **Brainstorm Taglines:** Brainstorm three potential taglines and test them with friends or followers.

- **Design Graphics:** Design sample graphics incorporating your tagline.

- **Evaluate Branding Impact:** Host a themed stream or event to evaluate audience response to your branding strategy.

Conclusion: Crafting a Memorable Brand

Building your brand identity is a vital step in growing your live streaming presence. By designing logos, maintaining consistency, establishing authenticity, leveraging storytelling, and crafting catchy taglines, you can create a memorable and trustworthy brand that keeps viewers coming back.

Final Exercise: Create a checklist summarizing your branding plan, including visuals, messaging strategies, stories, and themes. Use it to review and refine your identity as you grow.

Use the reflections and exercises in this chapter to refine your identity and set yourself apart in the competitive world of live streaming.

Chapter 6 Review: Building Your Brand Identity

Chapter 6 highlights the importance of creating a strong brand identity for streamers. A well-defined brand helps attract viewers, build trust, and establish long-lasting connections. This chapter provides actionable steps to build a memorable brand through logos, consistency, storytelling, and catchy taglines.

6.1 Designing Logos, Banners, and Thumbnails for Recognition

- **Logos: Crafting a Recognizable Symbol** - Streamers should keep logo designs simple, versatile, and aligned with their content's tone. Colors should reflect the brand's personality—bright for fun, dark for sophistication.

- **Banners and Thumbnails: Building Consistency** - Banners and thumbnails should be consistent across platforms. Using bold text and high-contrast images makes thumbnails eye-catching and easy to recognize.

- **Enhancing Recognition with Branding Tools** - Tools like Canva, Adobe Spark, and AI-driven platforms like Looka help create professional-quality designs quickly and efficiently.

6.2 Consistency Across Platforms: Unified Look and Messaging

- **Unified Design Elements** - Maintaining the same color schemes, fonts, and profiles across all platforms strengthens a consistent brand identity.

- **Multi-Platform Approach** - Cross-promotion between platforms like Twitch, YouTube, and Instagram helps increase visibility. Content should be adapted for each platform while maintaining branding consistency.

- **Building Platform-Specific Variations** - Customize content to suit each platform, such as designing platform-specific YouTube headers or Instagram stories, ensuring brand consistency while tailoring for each audience.

6.3 Establishing Trust and Authenticity with Viewers

- **Be Genuine** - Streamers should show their true personality and share personal stories to build trust and connect with their audience.

- **Engage Regularly** - Consistently responding to comments and asking for feedback helps build a sense of community.

- **Build Transparency** - Sharing behind-the-scenes content and progress updates helps foster deeper connections with viewers, making them feel involved.

6.4 Storytelling Techniques: Making Connections Through Narratives

- **Developing Your Brand Story** - Streamers should share their origin story and mission to create an emotional connection with viewers.

- **Incorporating Stories into Streams** - Sharing real-time reactions and interactive segments allows viewers to feel involved in the content.

6.5 Creating Catchy Taglines and Memorable Themes

- **Crafting a Catchy Tagline** - A tagline should be short, memorable, and highlight the streamer's unique value.

- **Building Themes Around Your Tagline** - Streamers can reinforce their brand by using creative stream titles, recurring segments, and hashtags aligned with their tagline to encourage viewer retention.

Chapter 6 equips streamers with the tools to develop a strong and memorable brand identity. By focusing on visuals, authenticity, storytelling, and consistency, streamers can set themselves apart in the competitive live streaming world.

Chapter 7: Technical Setup and Optimization

Setting up a technically sound and optimized streaming environment is crucial for delivering high-quality, professional broadcasts. From configuring software to troubleshooting problems, this chapter will equip you with the knowledge to ensure smooth and reliable streams. It also covers strategies to handle pressure and unexpected failures, helping you maintain confidence during live broadcasts.

Key Takeaway: A well-optimized and reliable setup is the backbone of any successful streaming career.

7.1 Setting Up Software, Internet Speed, and Backup Systems

A strong foundation begins with setting up the right software, internet connection, and backup systems to minimize disruptions. Ensuring reliable performance helps you maintain professionalism and keep viewers engaged.

1. Streaming Software Essentials

Reliable streaming software forms the backbone of any broadcast:

- **OBS Studio (Open Broadcaster Software):** A free, powerful, and customizable tool for streaming and recording.

- **Streamlabs OBS:** A beginner-friendly version of OBS with pre-built themes, widgets, and overlays.

- **XSplit Broadcaster:** Ideal for professional-grade features like scene transitions, multi-camera setups, and advanced editing tools.

2. Internet Connection Requirements

A stable internet connection ensures smooth, high-quality streams:

- **Upload Speed Recommendations:** At least 5 Mbps for 720p HD and 10 Mbps for 1080p Full HD streaming.

- **Stability Over Speed:** Use a wired Ethernet connection to reduce latency and packet loss.

- **Speed Testing Tools:** Tools like Speedtest.net and Fast.com monitor performance before going live.

3. Backup Systems and Redundancy

Having fail-safe systems prevents downtime and technical disruptions:

- **Secondary Internet Connection:** Mobile hotspots or backup ISPs act as fail-safes for sudden outages.

- **Power Backups:** Use uninterruptible power supplies (UPS) to prevent shutdowns during power failures.

- **Backup Streaming Software:** Pre-configure secondary software, such as vMix or Restream, to switch seamlessly during emergencies.

4. Example

- **Professional Gamer Setup:** Ninja maintains a dual-internet connection with wired Ethernet and mobile hotspot backups, ensuring zero interruptions during high-stakes tournaments.

- **Tech Reviewer Preparation:** Marques Brownlee (MKBHD) uses UPS devices and pre-configured streaming software to handle unexpected technical issues, preserving production quality.

5. Tips

- **Test Equipment Weekly:** Regular testing prevents unexpected failures.

- **Invest in High-Quality Routers:** Use dual-band routers with beamforming technology for stronger signals.

- **Simulcast for Wider Reach:** Broadcast on multiple platforms simultaneously to increase audience growth.

- **Monitor Metrics:** Track upload speeds and network stability throughout each session.

6. Reflection

- **Improve Internet Stability:** What steps can you take to improve your internet speed and stability?

- **Prepare for Emergencies:** Are your backup systems prepared to handle sudden outages or failures?

7. Exercise

- **Speed Test Analysis:** Run a speed test and analyze the results.

- **Backup Plan Creation:** Create a backup plan including secondary internet options, power backups, and software redundancies.

- **Emergency Simulation:** Test a full-stream simulation using all primary and backup systems to ensure smooth transitions during emergencies.

7.2 Optimizing Audio and Video for Quality Streaming

A polished stream depends on professional audio and video quality. This section covers optimization techniques for both, ensuring a smooth and visually appealing broadcast.

1. Optimize Audio for Crystal-Clear Sound

High-quality audio improves viewer experience and engagement:

- **Microphone Settings:** Adjust gain, noise suppression, and filters to remove background noise.

- **Audio Mixing Software:** Tools like Voicemeeter and Adobe Audition allow multi-channel mixing for advanced setups.

- **Testing Sound Levels:** Perform pre-stream tests to balance volume, reduce clipping, and maintain consistency.

2. Enhance Video Quality for Professional Streams

Clear visuals attract viewers and make streams more engaging:

- **Resolution and Bitrate Settings:**
  - **720p:** 3000–5000 Kbps for smooth streaming.
  - **1080p:** 6000 Kbps or higher for high-definition clarity.

- **Frame Rates:**
  - **30 FPS:** Suitable for casual streams.
  - **60 FPS:** Ideal for fast-paced gaming or action streams.

- **Lighting Adjustments:** Test brightness, shadows, and angles to eliminate poor visuals and create a polished look.

3. Fine-Tune Encoder Settings for Performance

Encoders process video data and impact stream quality:

- **Hardware Encoding (NVENC/QuickSync):** Optimized for performance and ideal for lower-end PCs.

- **Software Encoding (x264):** Provides better quality but requires more CPU power, suited for high-performance systems.

4. Example

- **Lilly Singh's Studio Setup:** Lilly Singh balances professional audio using Rode NT1 microphones and crisp visuals with Canon EOS R5 cameras, ensuring engaging talk-show-style live streams.

- **Casey Neistat's Video Quality:** Casey Neistat uses portable DSLRs and high-quality lavalier microphones to maintain top-tier video and audio clarity while streaming dynamic, outdoor content.

5. Tips

- **Monitor Audio with Headphones:** Test in real-time to ensure clarity and avoid echo or distortion.

- **Balance Resolution and Bitrate:** Match settings with internet speeds to prevent lag.

- **Keep Backup Equipment Ready:** Have spare microphones, cameras, and cables to handle emergencies.

- **Test Frequently:** Run test streams before going live to detect and fix issues early.

6. Reflection

- **Deliver Professional Results:** Are your current audio and video settings delivering professional results?

- **Upgrade for Quality:** What upgrades could improve your stream quality?

7. Exercise

- **Test Stream Recording:** Record a short test stream and review the quality.

- **Optimize Settings:** Adjust encoder, lighting, and sound settings based on your test results.

- **Experiment with Overlays:** Experiment with overlays and transitions to refine visual presentation.

7.3 Troubleshooting Tech Issues On the Fly

Technical difficulties are inevitable, but learning to address them quickly keeps streams running smoothly. This section explores common streaming issues, quick fixes, and proactive strategies to minimize disruptions.

1. Common Streaming Issues and Solutions

Identifying and resolving issues swiftly prevents losing viewers:

- **Audio Delays:** Sync audio with video using OBS advanced audio settings or audio filters.

- **Dropped Frames:** Lower bitrate or resolution if bandwidth is unstable, and prioritize wired connections over Wi-Fi.

- **Lagging Video:** Close background applications, clear cache, and upgrade CPU or RAM for better performance.

2. Quick-Fix Tools for Fast Recovery

Use tools and apps designed to detect and solve problems in real time:

- **StreamHealth Monitoring Tools:** Platforms like Twitch Inspector and YouTube Studio detect errors instantly and suggest solutions.

- **Remote Support Apps:** Tools like TeamViewer and AnyDesk allow experts to troubleshoot problems remotely.

- **Diagnostic Tools:** Speedtest.net and OBS logs help identify connection or software-related problems.

3. Proactive Testing to Prevent Failures

Preventive measures ensure smoother broadcasts:

- **Test Streams:** Run private test streams before broadcasting live to check for audio and video sync.

- **Redundancy Tests:** Simulate failures like internet drops or software crashes to practice quick recoveries.

- **Regular Updates:** Keep software, drivers, and firmware updated to avoid compatibility issues.

4. Example

- **Gamer DrLupo's Backup Setup:** DrLupo uses a dual-PC setup to ensure streams continue even if one system fails, minimizing downtime during tournaments.

- **Lifestyle Creator Emma Chamberlain:** Emma uses test streams and backup lighting to ensure seamless delivery when recording live Q&A sessions, adapting quickly to tech problems.

5. Tips

- **Label Equipment:** Organize cables and devices to speed up troubleshooting.

- **Record Test Streams:** Review recorded tests for audio sync and visual lag issues.

- **Create a Troubleshooting Checklist:** Write steps for fixing common problems like frame drops or delayed audio.

- **Backup Critical Files:** Save overlays, layouts, and assets to the cloud for quick restoration.

6. Reflection

- **Rehearse Troubleshooting Steps:** What troubleshooting steps can you rehearse to avoid panic during failures?

- **Prepare for Emergencies:** Are you prepared with backup tools or devices for emergencies?

7. Exercise

- **Mock Failure Scenario:** Perform a mock failure scenario (e.g., audio delay or internet drop) and practice fixing the issue quickly.

- **Troubleshooting Checklist:** Create and test a troubleshooting checklist.

- **Backup Test Stream:** Record a backup test stream and analyze the performance to make adjustments.

7.4 Backup Plans for Equipment and Network Failures

Preparedness is essential for recovering quickly from technical failures. This section outlines strategies for equipment and network issues to minimize downtime and keep streams running smoothly.

1. Backup Equipment for Quick Recovery

Having backup gear ensures fast swaps during emergencies:

- **Spare Cameras and Microphones:** Pre-configure replacements for immediate use if primary devices fail.

- **Backup Cables and Power Supplies:** Stock extra HDMI cables, chargers, and USB hubs to avoid disruptions caused by damaged wires.

- **Secondary Computers or Devices:** Keep a laptop or mobile device ready as an emergency streaming station.

2. Network Failover Solutions for Stable Streaming

Reliable network backups prevent stream interruptions:

- **Mobile Hotspots:** Use 4G/5G devices as emergency internet connections to avoid downtime.

- **Load Balancers:** Devices like Peplink combine multiple internet sources for uninterrupted streaming by automatically switching networks during failures.

- **Ethernet over Wi-Fi:** Prioritize wired connections for stability, keeping Wi-Fi as a secondary option.

3. Cloud and Remote Backup Tools

Cloud storage and remote access tools provide added security and flexibility:

- **Cloud-Based Recording:** Services like Restream automatically save streams, protecting data in case of software or hardware crashes.

- **Remote Access Software:** Apps like Parsec, TeamViewer, or LogMeIn allow you to manage devices and settings remotely in emergencies.

- **Automatic File Backups:** Sync layouts, overlays, and assets to cloud services like Google Drive or Dropbox for quick recovery.

4. Example

- **Streamer Pokimane's Setup:** Pokimane maintains spare cameras and microphones along with cloud backups, enabling her to resume streams quickly during technical failures.
- **Tech Reviewer Linus Tech Tips:** Linus uses load balancers and mobile hotspots to guarantee uninterrupted streams during large-scale events, maintaining professionalism under pressure.

5. Tips

- **Conduct Regular Tests:** Simulate failures and rehearse backup activation procedures.
- **Organize Backup Kits:** Label equipment and cables to speed up replacements.
- **Invest in Failover Tools:** Configure load balancers and mobile hotspots for network redundancy.
- **Backup Settings and Files:** Save layouts, templates, and stream settings to cloud platforms for instant restoration.

6. Reflection

- **Test and Improve Backups:** How can you test and improve your backup systems?
- **Pre-Configured Devices:** Are your backup devices pre-configured and ready for quick deployment?

7. Exercise

- **Backup Plan Creation:** Create and test a backup plan that includes spare devices and an alternative internet connection.
- **Simulate Emergency Scenarios:** Simulate a power outage or internet failure and practice switching to backup systems.
- **Evaluate Performance:** Evaluate performance and identify areas for improvement based on test results.

7.5 Streaming Under Pressure: Tips for Consistency

Maintaining composure under pressure separates amateur streamers from professionals. This section provides strategies to stay consistent, handle stress, and deliver polished streams even during challenging situations.

1. Mental Preparation for Calm and Focus

Staying mentally prepared boosts confidence and helps reduce stress:

- **Mindfulness Techniques:** Practice deep breathing, short meditations, or visualization exercises to relax before going live.

- **Pre-Stream Rituals:** Develop routines like warm-ups, checklist reviews, or motivational affirmations to ease nerves and boost focus.

2. Managing Unexpected Stress During Streams

Handling crises calmly prevents disruptions and reassures viewers:

- **Delegate Tasks:** Assign moderators to manage chat interactions, troubleshoot technical issues, and enforce rules in real time.

- **Time Management Tools:** Use planners, calendars, and reminder apps to organize tasks and avoid last-minute stress.

- **Break Management:** Schedule short breaks during long streams to re-energize and maintain focus.

3. Technical Preparedness to Minimize Errors

Anticipating issues ensures faster recovery and smoother broadcasts:

- **Hotkeys and Macros:** Use shortcuts to quickly resolve problems, switch scenes, mute audio, or restart overlays without delays.

- **Emergency Alerts:** Prepare visual overlays or banners to notify viewers if technical issues arise, maintaining transparency and professionalism.

- **Backup Systems:** Have backup microphones, cameras, and connections ready for immediate swaps if needed.

4. Example

- **DrLupo's Composure:** DrLupo maintains focus during charity streams by using pre-planned overlays and moderators to handle questions, enabling smooth operations even under pressure.

- **Ali Abdaal's Planning Strategies:** Ali Abdaal uses pre-stream rituals, like journaling and warm-ups, to mentally prepare for long Q&A and tutorial sessions, resulting in consistently polished content.

5. Tips

- **Create Backup Scripts:** Prepare filler topics to cover technical delays or pauses.

- **Practice Offline Scenarios:** Simulate unexpected issues and rehearse solutions.

- **Leverage Moderators:** Train moderators to handle disruptions and technical issues quickly.

- **Hydrate and Breathe:** Keep water nearby and use breathing exercises to reset focus during streams.

6. Reflection

- **Reduce Pressure Strategies:** What strategies can you practice to reduce pressure before and during streams?

- **Optimize Tools and Workflows:** Are your tools and workflows optimized to handle emergencies effectively?

7. Exercise

- **Stress-Test Stream:** Perform a stress-test stream where moderators simulate challenges like sudden internet drops or chat surges.

- **Quick Response Assessment:** Assess how quickly you respond and identify areas for improvement.

- **Ritual and Hotkey Testing:** Refine pre-stream rituals and test hotkey setups for faster reactions under pressure.

Conclusion: Building Confidence Through Preparation

A reliable streaming setup doesn't just come from having the best equipment—it's about preparation, optimization, and troubleshooting skills. By following the techniques in this chapter, you'll be ready to deliver consistent, high-quality broadcasts no matter what challenges arise.

Chapter 7 Review: Technical Setup and Optimization

Chapter 7 focuses on building a reliable and optimized streaming setup to ensure smooth, high-quality broadcasts. It provides tips on software, internet speed, backup systems, audio and video optimization, troubleshooting, and managing pressure, equipping streamers with the knowledge to handle technical challenges and maintain professional performance.

7.1 Setting Up Software, Internet Speed, and Backup Systems

- **Streaming Software Essentials** - OBS Studio, Streamlabs OBS, and XSplit are recommended, each offering unique features such as customization, pre-built themes, and professional-grade capabilities.

- **Internet Connection Requirements** - A stable wired Ethernet connection with at least 5 Mbps for 720p or 10 Mbps for 1080p HD streaming is essential for smooth performance.

- **Backup Systems and Redundancy** - Secondary internet connections, like mobile hotspots, and uninterruptible power supplies (UPS) should be set up to ensure continuity in case of failure.

7.2 Optimizing Audio and Video for Quality Streaming

- **Audio Optimization** - Streamers should adjust microphone settings, use noise suppression, and test sound levels to ensure clear, professional audio.

- **Video Optimization** - Set appropriate resolution (720p: 3000–5000 Kbps, 1080p: 6000 Kbps) and frame rates (30 FPS for casual streams, 60 FPS for fast-paced content). Proper lighting adjustments are also crucial for clear visuals.

- **Encoder Settings** - Streamers should choose hardware encoding (NVENC) for smoother performance or software encoding (x264) for higher video quality.

7.3 Troubleshooting Tech Issues On the Fly

- **Common Streaming Issues and Solutions** - Streamers should address audio delays, dropped frames, and video lag by adjusting settings or upgrading hardware.

- **Quick-Fix Tools** - StreamHealth Monitoring tools and remote support apps, such as TeamViewer, allow real-time troubleshooting.

- **Proactive Testing** - Running test streams and simulating failures beforehand helps prepare for potential issues.

7.4 Backup Plans for Equipment and Network Failures

- **Backup Equipment** - Having spare cameras, microphones, and cables ready for quick swaps ensures uninterrupted streaming.

- **Network Failover Solutions** - Mobile hotspots and load balancers help maintain a stable connection if the primary internet fails.

- **Cloud and Remote Backup Tools** - Cloud-based services and remote access tools enable efficient recovery during system failures.

7.5 Streaming Under Pressure: Tips for Consistency

- **Mental Preparation** - Mindfulness techniques and pre-stream rituals help streamers stay calm under pressure.

- **Managing Unexpected Stress** - Delegating tasks to moderators and using time management tools reduces stress during live broadcasts.

- **Technical Preparedness** - Hotkeys for quick transitions and emergency alerts ensure smooth operation in case of issues.

Chapter 7 emphasizes the importance of technical preparation and troubleshooting to maintain a seamless streaming experience. By optimizing their setup, testing systems, and managing pressure, streamers can ensure high-quality broadcasts regardless of challenges.

Chapter 8: Audience Interaction and Engagement

Building a strong connection with your audience is the cornerstone of a successful streaming career. Effective engagement not only keeps viewers entertained but also fosters loyalty and long-term growth. This chapter explores proven strategies to interact with your audience, handle negativity, and create an engaging and interactive streaming experience.

Key Takeaway: Consistent audience engagement builds trust, fosters community, and enhances viewer retention.

8.1 Mastering Real-Time Engagement: Best Practices

Engaging with viewers in real time creates a sense of connection and builds relationships that keep them coming back. This section highlights strategies to boost interaction and retain audiences.

1. Active Communication Techniques

Communicating effectively builds rapport and keeps conversations flowing:

- **Welcome New Viewers by Name:** Acknowledge new arrivals to make them feel included. Use chat commands or overlays to highlight their presence.

- **Ask Open-Ended Questions:** Encourage conversation by asking viewers about their thoughts, preferences, and experiences.

- **Respond Quickly to Comments:** Show viewers that their input matters by interacting promptly, thanking them for comments, and addressing their questions.

- **Share Personal Stories:** Build connections through relatable anecdotes, personal insights, and humorous moments that resonate with your audience.

2. Creating an Inclusive Environment

Inclusion encourages viewers to stay engaged and feel valued:

- **Encourage Participation:** Use polls, live Q&A sessions, and call-to-action prompts to keep viewers involved. Highlight viewer comments and questions during streams.

- **Celebrate Milestones:** Recognize follower counts, donations, and subscriber goals to show appreciation. Create special "milestone celebrations" to reward viewer loyalty.

- **Use Visual and Audio Cues:** Add on-screen alerts and sound effects to highlight messages, subscriptions, and donations, making participation feel interactive and valued.

3. Leveraging Feedback for Improvement

Feedback helps refine content and address viewer preferences:

- **Ask for Input:** Poll viewers about potential topics and content directions to involve them in planning.

- **Analyze Chat Behavior:** Use chat logs and analytics tools to assess what topics and activities generate the most engagement.

- **Adjust in Real Time:** Monitor audience reactions and adapt content or tone to maintain interest.

4. Example

- **Cooking Streamer Case Study:** A cooking streamer doubled her engagement rate by incorporating viewer suggestions into recipes live. She also used polls to let the audience pick ingredients, making them feel like active participants.

- **Twitch Gamer Example:** A Twitch gamer hosted trivia challenges between gameplay sessions, rewarding winners with shoutouts and giveaways to boost interaction.

5. Tips

- **Prepare Conversation Starters:** Have questions or topics ready to spark discussions during slower moments.

- **Pin Important Messages:** Highlight key announcements or comments to guide focus.

- **Test Interactive Tools:** Experiment with chatbots, polls, and overlays to keep viewers engaged.

- **Reward Engagement:** Offer shoutouts or small rewards like custom emotes to active participants.

6. Reflection

- **Boost Audience Involvement:** What are three ways you can make your audience feel more involved?

- **Adapt Through Feedback:** How can you adapt your approach based on viewer feedback?

7. Exercise

- **Interactive Segment Planning:** Plan and test an interactive segment, such as a live Q&A, trivia session, or poll.

- **Engagement Metrics Tracking:** Track engagement metrics (comments, reactions, and shares) to analyze effectiveness.

- **Feedback Analysis:** Use feedback forms or polls to refine the segment and repeat it with improvements.

8.2 Handling Negative Comments and Trolls Effectively

Every streamer faces negativity, but handling it professionally ensures a safe and welcoming space for your audience. This section covers strategies to manage negative comments and trolls while maintaining positivity.

1. Establish Clear Rules to Set Boundaries

Preventing negativity starts with defining expectations:

- **Set Chat Guidelines:** Clearly outline acceptable behavior in your stream description, pin rules in the chat, and include automated reminders during streams.

- **Use Moderators:** Assign trusted viewers or team members to enforce rules, manage trolls, and protect the positive atmosphere.

2. Respond Professionally to Negativity

Handling negative comments calmly prevents escalation:

- **Stay Calm and Professional:** Address constructive criticism respectfully while ignoring intentional provocations. Focus responses on positivity.

- **Timeouts and Bans:** Use timeouts for minor offenses and permanent bans for severe violations. Keep moderation consistent and transparent.

- **Redirect Focus:** Shift the conversation back to positive topics to keep the mood upbeat and engaging.

3. Use Moderation Tools for Efficient Control

Automated tools simplify moderation and prevent inappropriate comments:

- **Chat Filters:** Block specific words or phrases to prevent offensive language automatically.

- **Automated Moderation Bots:** Tools like Nightbot or Moobot enforce rules, respond to commands, and maintain chat order.

- **AI-Based Moderation Tools:** Advanced tools like AutoMod filter comments based on sentiment analysis and detect inappropriate behavior early.

4. Example

- **Pokimane's Moderation Strategy:** Pokimane uses automated bots and multiple moderators to enforce rules, creating a positive chat experience while publicly thanking moderators for their efforts.

- **Dr Disrespect's Handling Style:** Dr Disrespect combines humor and strict enforcement to shut down trolls quickly, reinforcing his confident persona and entertaining his audience.

5. Tips

- **Create Moderator Guidelines:** Train moderators to handle specific scenarios and enforce rules fairly.

- **Reward Positive Behavior:** Offer VIP badges or shoutouts to viewers who contribute positively.

- **Turn Negativity into Jokes:** Use humor to disarm trolls without losing control of the chat.

- **Test Tools Before Streaming:** Ensure bots and filters are properly configured to avoid blocking legitimate comments.

6. Reflection

- **Handle Negativity Professionally:** How do you currently handle negativity in your streams?

- **Improve Positivity:** What improvements can you make to create a more welcoming environment?

7. Exercise

- **Update Chat Rules:** Create or update your chat rules and post them prominently in your stream description.

- **Test Moderation Bots:** Test an automated moderation bot and customize its filters for your audience.

- **Train Moderators:** Train moderators on emergency response procedures and review chat logs for patterns to improve handling strategies.

8.3 Building a Loyal Community Through Trust and Fun

A loyal community turns casual viewers into long-term supporters and advocates for your brand. This section explores ways to build trust, foster fun, and create an interactive experience that strengthens viewer loyalty.

1. Build Trust Through Authenticity

Trust is the foundation of any strong community:

- **Be Yourself:** Share personal stories, behind-the-scenes insights, and vulnerable moments to build relatability and authenticity.

- **Consistency is Key:** Stick to regular streaming schedules and deliver on promises to establish reliability and build habits for your audience.

- **Follow Through with Engagement:** Highlight fan contributions, such as artwork, memes, or shoutouts, to deepen connections and show appreciation.

2. Foster Fun and Creativity

Adding entertainment and interactivity keeps streams engaging:

- **Host Themed Streams:** Celebrate holidays, special events, or themed nights to encourage participation and excitement.

- **Include Viewers in Decisions:** Use polls and voting features to let your audience decide stream topics, gameplay moves, or challenges.
- **Collaborate with Other Streamers:** Partner with creators in similar niches to expand reach and merge communities for cross-engagement.

3. Reward Loyalty and Celebrate Achievements

Recognizing and rewarding viewers helps maintain enthusiasm:

- **Milestone Celebrations:** Celebrate follower counts, anniversaries, or subscriber goals with giveaways and shoutouts.
- **Exclusive Perks:** Offer VIP badges, emotes, or private Discord channels for loyal followers.
- **Interactive Contests:** Host art challenges, fitness competitions, or quiz nights with prizes to increase engagement.

4. Example

- **Fitness Streamer's Weekly Challenges:** A fitness streamer hosted weekly challenges and celebrated participants' progress with recognition and giveaways, leading to increased engagement and trust.
- **Gaming Streamer's Interactive Storylines:** A gaming creator built a role-playing experience where viewers shaped the storyline through polls and choices, keeping viewers invested and excited for each session.

5. Tips

- **Engage Off-Stream:** Connect with your audience through social media, Discord, or exclusive groups to maintain relationships outside of live streams.
- **Host Community Nights:** Plan events like movie nights, game tournaments, or AMAs to bond with your audience.
- **Celebrate Viewer Contributions:** Feature fan art, memes, and content submissions on your streams to encourage involvement.
- **Incorporate Inside Jokes:** Build a sense of belonging by creating recurring jokes and phrases unique to your audience.

6. Reflection

- **Enhance Engagement and Fun:** What unique elements can you introduce to make your community more engaging?

- **Reward Loyal Viewers:** How can you reward loyal viewers and keep them excited to participate?

7. Exercise

- **Themed Event Planning:** Plan and promote a themed event for your audience, integrating contests and collaborative activities.

- **Rewards Program Creation:** Create a rewards program that includes badges, giveaways, and exclusive perks.

- **Social Media Strategy:** Develop a social media strategy to stay connected with your community between streams.

8.4 Using Chat Bots and Moderators to Boost Interaction

Chat bots and moderators streamline engagement and improve interaction quality. This section explores tools and strategies to enhance viewer experiences while maintaining a well-organized chat environment.

1. Leverage Chat Bot Features and Tools

Chat bots automate tasks and simplify audience engagement:

- **Automated Welcome Messages:** Greet new viewers and share essential links, schedules, and stream rules.

- **Commands and Shortcuts:** Use pre-set commands for FAQs, donation links, social media handles, and reminders.

- **Giveaways and Contests:** Automate raffles, trivia games, and prize draws to boost participation.

- **Polls and Voting:** Enable polls to involve viewers in content decisions or challenges.

2. Assign Moderators for Effective Management

Moderators help maintain a positive and welcoming atmosphere:

- **Trusted Community Members:** Recruit reliable, active viewers to assist with enforcing rules and handling issues.

- **Training for Moderators:** Provide clear guidelines on rules, commands, and tools to ensure consistent moderation.
- **Emergency Procedures:** Prepare moderators for handling trolls, spam, or sudden disruptions by implementing quick-response plans.

3. Enhance Engagement Through Interaction Tools

Streamlining engagement with bots and moderators increases participation:

- **Custom Responses:** Program bots to answer repetitive questions, freeing time for meaningful conversations.
- **Leaderboard Features:** Highlight top chat participants or donors to encourage competition and interaction.
- **Highlight Viewer Messages:** Use tools to pin important messages and display shoutouts during streams.

4. Example

- **Tech Streamer Efficiency:** A tech-focused streamer used chat bots to deliver quick links to product recommendations and tutorials, boosting viewer satisfaction and saving time.
- **Gaming Creator Case Study:** A gaming streamer ran polls and giveaways through chat bots, encouraging real-time engagement and doubling their average watch time.

5. Tips

- **Customize Commands:** Set up pre-configured responses to FAQs, saving time and streamlining interactions.
- **Monitor Bot Performance:** Regularly test and update bot features to match evolving audience needs.
- **Empower Moderators:** Provide them with tools and authority to handle disruptions quickly and effectively.
- **Track Engagement Data:** Use analytics from bots to identify what commands or features viewers engage with most.

6. Reflection

- **Improve Efficiency with Bots:** How can chat bots improve efficiency and engagement in your streams?

- **Equip Moderators Effectively:** Are your moderators equipped with the right tools and training to manage your chat effectively?

7. Exercise

- **Bot Configuration Testing:** Test a chat bot in your stream and configure commands for frequently asked questions and giveaways.

- **Engagement Activity Analysis:** Host a poll or contest using a bot feature and analyze engagement metrics to assess performance.

- **Moderator Training Review:** Review moderator feedback to refine procedures and update training materials as needed.

8.5 Creating Interactive Polls, Games, and Contests

Interactive elements add excitement and engagement, encouraging viewers to participate actively. Incorporating polls, games, and contests makes streams more dynamic and fun while fostering a sense of community. This section explores strategies for using these tools effectively to boost participation and strengthen viewer connections.

1. Use Polls and Voting Systems for Engagement

Polls keep viewers involved and make streams feel collaborative:

- **Live Polls on Twitch and YouTube:** Let viewers vote on stream topics, gameplay decisions, or content direction.

- **Feedback Polls:** Collect viewer opinions to guide future content planning and improvements.

- **Decision-Based Polls:** Use polls during interactive streams, such as choosing game strategies or plot developments.

- **Tip:** Announce poll results live to build excitement and recognize viewer participation.

2. Host Games and Challenges to Boost Participation

Games and challenges create fun, competitive environments:

- **Trivia Quizzes:** Host quizzes with prizes like exclusive emotes, merchandise, or shoutouts.

- **Viewer Challenges:** Let viewers submit fun challenges for live completion, such as speed runs, special skills, or improvisational tasks.

- **Mini-Games:** Integrate chat-based games like scavenger hunts or virtual races using bot features.

- **Tip:** Offer points systems or badges for participants to track and celebrate their progress.

3. Organize Contests and Giveaways for Incentives

Contests and giveaways reward participation and build excitement:

- **Prize Drawings:** Offer giveaways tied to milestones, such as subscriber goals or anniversaries.

- **Creative Contests:** Encourage submissions for artwork, memes, or content ideas. Showcase winning entries live for recognition.

- **Community Challenges:** Set collective goals (e.g., follower count) and reward the entire audience with giveaways or events.

- **Tip:** Clearly define eligibility, timelines, and judging criteria to maintain trust.

4. Example

- **Art Streamer Example:** An artist held live sketch requests and allowed viewers to vote on themes, boosting engagement and showcasing audience preferences.

- **Music Creator Example:** A musician ran song cover contests, letting viewers vote for the best performances and rewarding winners with signed merchandise.

5. Tips

- **Schedule Events in Advance:** Promote contests and games ahead of time to maximize participation.

- **Use Bots for Automation:** Streamline entries, reminders, and prize distributions using chat bots.

- **Reward Loyalty:** Offer recurring contests for long-time viewers to keep them engaged.

- **Leverage Social Media:** Announce contests and games on social platforms to attract new participants.

6. Reflection

- **Boost Viewer Engagement:** How can contests and challenges complement your content and increase viewer engagement?

- **Understand Audience Preferences:** What themes or activities resonate most with your audience?

7. Exercise

- **Plan and Test Events:** Plan and run a live poll or contest in your next stream.

- **Analyze Participation Metrics:** Track participation metrics, such as votes, comments, and shares, to evaluate success.

- **Refine Interactive Formats:** Test different interactive formats and refine based on viewer feedback.

Conclusion: Cultivating Audience Engagement for Long-Term Success

Audience interaction is the key to building a loyal and supportive community. By mastering real-time engagement, handling negativity, leveraging tools, and adding interactive elements, you can create a dynamic and welcoming environment. Use the strategies in this chapter to strengthen your connections and keep your audience coming back for more!

Chapter 8 Review: Audience Interaction and Engagement

Chapter 8 explores the vital role of audience interaction in building a successful streaming career. It provides strategies for fostering a strong connection with viewers, handling negativity, and creating an engaging experience that encourages viewer loyalty and long-term growth.

8.1 Mastering Real-Time Engagement: Best Practices

- **Active Communication Techniques** - Welcoming new viewers by name, asking open-ended questions, and responding quickly to comments create a sense of connection and inclusion. Sharing personal stories helps make the stream more relatable.

- **Creating an Inclusive Environment** - Encourage participation through polls, live Q&A sessions, and milestone celebrations. Visual and audio cues, like on-screen alerts, further enhance engagement.

- **Leveraging Feedback for Improvement** - Asking for viewer input and analyzing chat behavior allows streamers to tailor content to boost engagement.

8.2 Handling Negative Comments and Trolls Effectively

- **Establishing Clear Rules** - Streamers should set clear chat guidelines and use moderators to maintain a positive atmosphere. Automated reminders help enforce rules during streams.

- **Responding to Negativity** - Stay calm and professional by addressing constructive criticism respectfully and ignoring intentional provocations. Redirect focus to positive discussions.

- **Tools for Moderation** - Using chat filters, automated bots, and AI-based tools helps manage negativity and maintain a safe space for viewers.

8.3 Building a Loyal Community Through Trust and Fun

- **Building Trust Through Authenticity** - Streamers should be themselves, share personal stories, and remain consistent to build trust with their audience.

- **Fostering Fun and Creativity** - Hosting themed streams, collaborating with other creators, and allowing viewers to participate in decisions helps build a loyal community.

- **Engaging with Viewers** - Regular interaction and recognition of fan contributions, such as fan art or shoutouts, strengthens connections.

8.4 Using Chat Bots and Moderators to Boost Interaction

- **Chat Bot Features and Tools** - Bots can automate welcome messages, giveaways, and polls to enhance engagement.

- **Assigning Moderators** - Trusted viewers can help manage chat and ensure smooth operation during streams. Training moderators is essential for effective management.

- **Emergency Procedures** - Moderators should be prepared to handle disruptions and enforce chat rules quickly.

8.5 Creating Interactive Polls, Games, and Contests

- **Polls and Voting Systems** - Live polls help involve viewers in stream decisions and provide valuable feedback.

- **Games and Challenges** - Trivia quizzes and viewer-submitted challenges engage viewers and make streams more interactive.

- **Contests and Giveaways** - Reward viewers with prizes for participating in challenges and contests, encouraging continued interaction.

Audience engagement is key to building loyalty and fostering a positive community. By mastering real-time interaction, managing negativity, and using interactive tools, streamers can create a dynamic environment that keeps viewers coming back.

Part 3: Growth and Monetization Strategies

Chapter 9: Growing Your Audience

Building and expanding your audience is one of the most vital aspects of live streaming success. The larger and more engaged your viewership, the greater your chances of sustaining growth, monetizing effectively, and building a long-lasting brand. This chapter provides actionable strategies to increase visibility, leverage collaborations, host events, optimize SEO, and network within the industry to reach new audiences and retain loyal fans.

9.1 Leveraging Social Media Marketing for Visibility

Social media platforms are essential tools for increasing visibility and attracting viewers to your streams. A well-planned marketing strategy can help you expand your reach and create a buzz around your content. This section explores ways to leverage social media for growth and engagement.

1. Choose the Right Social Media Platforms

Different platforms cater to unique audiences and content styles:

- **Instagram and TikTok:** Perfect for short, engaging highlights, teasers, and behind-the-scenes content.

- **Twitter (X):** Ideal for quick updates, promotions, and building real-time conversations with followers.

- **Facebook:** Best for promoting community groups and events to a broader audience.

- **YouTube Shorts and Reels:** Excellent for creating viral content to capture attention and funnel viewers to live streams.

- **Tip:** Tailor content formats to match each platform's strengths. Use vertical videos for TikTok and Reels, and focus on interactive polls and questions for Instagram Stories.

2. Develop Content Strategies for Social Media Growth

Content variety and consistency drive engagement:

- **Repurpose Stream Highlights:** Clip your best moments and post them as short videos to attract attention.

- **Post Consistently:** Create a content calendar for daily or weekly updates to keep your profile active and visible.

- **Engage Through Stories and Polls:** Use interactive tools like polls, Q&As, and countdowns to build hype and encourage participation.

- **Hashtag Strategies:** Use trending and niche-specific hashtags to increase discoverability and connect with relevant audiences.

- **Tip:** Cross-promote your streams by embedding teaser clips and countdowns on multiple platforms to maximize reach.

3. Example

- **Fitness Streamer Example:** A fitness streamer gained 10,000 new followers in one month by posting TikTok workout highlights and redirecting viewers to live Q&A sessions on Twitch. She boosted engagement by sharing polls about fitness challenges and using hashtags like #WorkoutLive and #FitnessChallenge.

- **Gaming Creator Example:** A gamer grew their audience by posting daily highlights of clutch plays on Instagram Reels, building momentum for live tournaments streamed on YouTube.

4. Tips

- **Analyze Engagement Metrics:** Use analytics tools like Instagram Insights or TikTok Analytics to track performance and adjust strategies.

- **Collaborate with Influencers:** Partner with social media influencers to tap into new audiences.

- **Optimize Posting Times:** Post during peak activity hours to maximize visibility.

- **Encourage Shares and Tags:** Prompt viewers to share clips and tag friends to broaden exposure.

5. Reflection

- **Align Platforms with Audience Goals:** What social media platforms best align with your target audience?

- **Refine Content Strategies:** How can you refine your content strategies to increase reach and engagement?

6. Exercise

- **Social Media Planning:** Create a week-long social media posting schedule, including highlights, countdowns, and polls.

- **Analyze Engagement Results:** Test engagement results and track follower growth to refine your approach.

- **Optimize Visibility:** Experiment with video formats and hashtags to optimize visibility and reach.

9.2 Collaborating with Streamers for Shared Growth

Collaborations can exponentially increase your exposure by tapping into other streamers' audiences. Partnering with creators in similar niches fosters mutual growth and expands reach. This section explores strategies for finding partners and building effective collaborations.

1. Find the Right Collaborators

Choosing the right partners ensures aligned audiences and meaningful collaborations:

- **Look for Complementary Niches:** Partner with streamers whose audiences share common interests with yours to ensure relevance.

- **Engage Before Collaboration:** Follow, comment, and share their content to establish rapport and build relationships before reaching out.

- **Target Influencers and Rising Streamers:** Connect with both established creators and those on the rise to diversify your collaborations and grow with new audiences.

- **Tip:** Use social platforms like Discord, Twitter (X), and LinkedIn to network with potential collaborators and start conversations.

2. Explore Creative Collaboration Ideas

Collaborations can take many forms, adding value to both audiences:

- **Co-Streaming Events:** Stream games, discussions, or competitions together to attract shared viewership.

- **Guest Appearances:** Host interviews or guest spots to introduce each other's audiences and build cross-channel visibility.

- **Cross-Promotions:** Swap shoutouts or host giveaways that require viewers to follow both creators to enter.

- **Shared Series:** Develop themed content, such as multi-episode collaborations or joint tutorials, to keep audiences engaged over time.

3. Example

- **Gaming Collaboration Example:** Two streamers collaborated on a "Battle Royale Showdown" event, attracting over 15,000 viewers combined. Both gained followers through mutual shoutouts and giveaway incentives.

- **Lifestyle Influencers Example:** A fitness coach and nutrition expert created a joint health-focused series, combining workouts and meal prep tutorials, resulting in shared audiences and increased engagement.

4. Tips

- **Start Small:** Test collaborations with short events before committing to long-term partnerships.

- **Coordinate Marketing:** Promote collaborations in advance through social media, emails, and countdowns.

- **Evaluate Results:** Analyze growth metrics like follower count, views, and engagement to assess performance.

- **Stay Professional:** Use clear agreements to define roles, expectations, and timelines.

5. Reflection

- **Complementary Content Ideas:** What type of creators would complement your content style and audience?

- **Adding Variety Through Collaborations:** How can collaborations add variety and excitement to your streams?

6. Exercise

- **Research Collaborators:** Identify three potential collaborators and research their content.

- **Draft Partnership Proposals:** Draft outreach messages proposing partnership ideas for events or giveaways.

- **Plan Collaborative Events:** Plan a short collaborative event and track audience growth and engagement to refine your strategy.

9.3 Hosting Events, Giveaways, and Challenges to Boost Viewership

Hosting interactive events and giveaways creates excitement and attracts both new and returning viewers. This section explores ways to plan engaging activities that build momentum and increase viewership.

1. Types of Events That Engage Viewers

Interactive events encourage participation and create memorable experiences:

- **Special Streams and Marathons:** Plan themed streams, such as holiday specials, 24-hour marathons, or game tournaments to captivate audiences.

- **Giveaways and Contests:** Offer prizes like merchandise, gift cards, or shoutouts for contest winners to drive excitement.

- **Viewer Challenges:** Let viewers suggest tasks or challenges to complete live, making them feel involved in the content creation process.

- **Live Competitions:** Organize trivia games, scavenger hunts, or talent showcases to increase interaction.

2. Plan Effective Events for Maximum Impact

Preparation and promotion ensure success:

- **Promote in Advance:** Announce events on all platforms to build hype and anticipation. Use countdown timers and teaser clips to grab attention.

- **Engage During Events:** Use interactive tools like polls, chat games, and reward systems to keep participants involved.

- **Follow Up Post-Event:** Post highlights, thank-you messages, and polls to recap the event and maintain viewer engagement.

- **Tip:** Use tools like Gleam.io or StreamElements to automate giveaway entries and winner selections.

3. Example

- **Cooking Streamer Example:** A cooking streamer increased her average viewership by 200% after hosting a "Mystery Ingredient Challenge" where viewers voted on ingredients in real time, making the process highly interactive.

- **Gaming Streamer Example:** A gamer attracted thousands of viewers by hosting a "Battle Royale Showdown" with prizes for top players, driving competition and excitement.

4. Tips

- **Test Smaller Events First:** Start with mini-challenges or small giveaways to build confidence and measure results.

- **Use Themes and Holidays:** Plan events around seasonal themes or trending topics to stay relevant.

- **Collaborate for Impact:** Partner with other streamers to expand reach and create larger-scale events.

- **Analyze Metrics Post-Event:** Review viewership stats, chat engagement, and social shares to optimize future events.

5. Reflection

- **Identify Viewer Preferences:** What types of events resonate most with your audience?

- **Tailor Engagement Tools:** How can giveaways and challenges be tailored to match your brand?

6. Exercise

- **Event Planning Strategy:** Plan and schedule an interactive event, including promotional posts, prizes, and follow-up content.

- **Test Engagement Tools:** Test engagement tools like polls, chat games, and automated giveaways.

- **Analyze Event Metrics:** Analyze results to refine strategies for future events.

9.4 SEO Optimization and Keywords for Better Discovery

Search Engine Optimization (SEO) helps new viewers find your content through search engines and platform recommendations. Optimizing keywords and stream details increases visibility and attracts relevant audiences. This section explores practical strategies for leveraging SEO to grow your audience.

1. Conduct Effective Keyword Research

Identifying the right keywords is the foundation of SEO. Focus on terms your target audience is searching for to increase reach and engagement.

- **Trending Keywords:** Use tools like **Google Keyword Planner** and **TubeBuddy** to find trending terms in your niche.

- **Long-Tail Keywords:** Incorporate phrases like *"live gameplay tutorial"* or *"live Q&A about streaming equipment"* to attract targeted viewers.

- **Tag Optimization:** Add relevant tags to titles, descriptions, and metadata to match viewer searches.

- **Tip:** Review competitor keywords and analyze trending streams to stay competitive.

2. Write SEO-Friendly Titles and Descriptions

Your title and description should grab attention while being optimized for search engines.

- **Engaging Titles:** Use action-oriented phrases like *"Watch Now"* or *"Learn How"* to spark curiosity.

- **Keyword-Rich Descriptions:** Integrate primary and secondary keywords naturally to highlight your content's value.

- **Call-to-Action Links:** Include links to related videos, playlists, or social profiles to keep viewers engaged.

- **Tip:** Update titles and descriptions after streams end to optimize for long-term discovery.

3. Use Hashtags and Tags for Better Reach

Tags and hashtags improve visibility on platforms like **YouTube**, **Twitch**, and **Facebook Live**.

- **Relevant Tags:** Include keywords like **#livestreaming** or **#streamingsetup** to target your niche.

- **Trending Hashtags:** Research and use trending hashtags to appear in recommendations and trending sections.

- **Platform-Specific Tags:** Adapt strategies to platform preferences, such as Twitch Categories or YouTube Tags.

- **Tip:** Combine broad and niche hashtags for broader reach and targeted visibility.

4. Example

- **Gaming Stream Example:** A streamer optimized their title with *"Watch Now: Fortnite Tips & Tricks for Beginners"* and added tags like **#FortniteTips** and **#GamingLive**, increasing their discoverability.

- **Educational Stream Example:** A creator used *"Live Q&A: How to Set Up Streaming Equipment (Step-by-Step Guide)"* to attract tech-savvy viewers searching for tutorials.

5. Tips

- **Track Keywords Regularly:** Monitor keyword performance using analytics tools to refine your SEO strategy.

- **Balance Keywords and Engagement:** Focus on both keyword optimization and engaging content to retain viewers.

- **Experiment with Keywords:** Test variations in tags and titles to identify what resonates best with your audience.

- **Utilize Analytics Tools:** Use built-in analytics from **YouTube Studio** and **Twitch Dashboard** to measure keyword effectiveness.

6. Reflection

- **Analyze Keywords for Your Niche:** What keywords best describe your niche and audience preferences?

- **Enhance Discoverability with Hashtags:** How can you incorporate trending hashtags and keywords into your next stream?

7. Exercise

- **Research Keywords:** Use a keyword planner to research trending terms related to your niche.

- **Draft SEO Titles:** Create three SEO-friendly titles for upcoming streams based on your keyword research.

- **Analyze Results:** Test updated descriptions and metadata after your next stream and track the results using analytics tools.

9.5 Networking and Building Relationships in the Industry

Networking is a cornerstone of success in the live streaming industry. Building strong connections can lead to collaborations, sponsorships, and audience growth, ensuring long-term sustainability. This section explores strategies for expanding your network and strengthening industry relationships.

1. Build Industry Connections

Establishing relationships with fellow creators, influencers, and brands can open doors to new opportunities:

- **Attend Events and Conventions:** Participate in industry events like **TwitchCon**, **VidCon**, and **PAX** to meet creators, influencers, and sponsors. Face-to-face interactions often lead to collaborations and sponsorship deals.

- **Engage in Online Communities:** Join **Discord groups**, **Reddit forums**, and **Facebook groups** focused on streaming. Actively contribute to discussions, share insights, and demonstrate expertise to build credibility.

- **Leverage Social Media Platforms:** Follow and interact with creators and brands on **LinkedIn**, **Twitter**, and **Instagram** to establish relationships and stay informed about industry trends.

2. Build Strong Relationships with Your Audience

Creating a loyal community around your content strengthens viewer retention and engagement:

- **Exclusive Groups and Memberships:** Offer private **Discord channels**, **Facebook groups**, or **Patreon tiers** for top supporters to create a sense of exclusivity.

- **Interactive Events:** Host **meet-and-greets**, **giveaways**, or **Q&A sessions** to connect with your audience and make them feel valued.

- **Audience Collaboration:** Involve viewers in streams through **shoutouts**, **polls**, or **contests** to increase participation.

3. Partner with Influencers and Sponsors

Collaborating with influencers and brands amplifies visibility and adds credibility:

- **Cross-Promotions:** Partner with other creators for **co-hosted streams**, **interviews**, or **challenges** to expand reach.

- **Secure Sponsorships:** Approach brands that align with your niche. Highlight your **audience demographics** and **analytics** to showcase your value.

- **Create Value-Driven Proposals:** Present clear benefits for sponsors, such as **targeted marketing campaigns** and **unique content opportunities**.

4. Example

- **TwitchCon Success Story:** A streamer connected with a game developer at **TwitchCon**, leading to a **sponsorship deal** and **early access** to new game content.

- **Discord Growth Hack:** A creator used **exclusive Discord groups** to retain top fans, increasing **viewer loyalty** and **tips**.

- **Cross-Promotion Boost:** Two streamers collaborated on a **charity event**, doubling **viewership** and attracting **media coverage**.

5. Tips

- **Follow Up Quickly:** Reach out after events with **personalized messages** to keep connections active.

- **Provide Value First:** Offer **assistance**, **insights**, or **shoutouts** to establish trust before asking for collaborations.

- **Track Networking Progress:** Maintain a **contact list** with details about meetings, shared interests, and next steps.

- **Leverage LinkedIn for Growth:** Use **LinkedIn** to showcase your profile and connect directly with potential sponsors or collaborators.

6. Reflection

- **Expand Networking Opportunities:** What events or online communities can you join to expand your network?

- **Grow Through Collaboration:** How can you use exclusive groups or collaborations to grow your audience?

7. Exercise

- **Explore New Communities:** List **three industry events** or **online communities** to join this month.

- **Draft Outreach Messages:** Create a **networking message** to introduce yourself and offer value to a potential contact.

- **Track Networking Progress:** Develop a **contact tracker** to monitor connections and follow-ups.

Conclusion: Building Momentum for Long-Term Growth

Growing your audience requires consistency, creativity, and strategic planning. By leveraging social media, collaborations, events, SEO, and networking, you can attract and retain viewers. Use the tips and tools in this chapter to expand your reach and solidify your streaming career.

Chapter 9 Review: Growing Your Audience

Chapter 9 focuses on strategies to grow and engage your audience, a key factor in achieving long-term success in live streaming. It covers leveraging social media, collaborating with other streamers, hosting events, optimizing SEO, and networking to expand your reach and retain loyal fans.

9.1 Leveraging Social Media Marketing for Visibility

- **Choosing the Right Social Media Platforms** - Instagram and TikTok are ideal for posting highlights and behind-the-scenes content, while Twitter and Facebook are best for real-time updates and community engagement.

- **Content Strategies for Social Media Growth** - Repurpose stream highlights, maintain a consistent posting schedule, engage with viewers through polls and stories, and use trending hashtags to boost visibility.

9.2 Collaborating with Streamers for Shared Growth

- **Finding the Right Collaborators** - Partnering with streamers in complementary niches helps expand your reach. Building relationships through engagement on social media can lead to effective collaborations.

- **Creative Collaboration Ideas** - Co-stream events, guest appearances, and cross-promotions through shoutouts and giveaways can significantly increase exposure and attract new viewers.

9.3 Hosting Events, Giveaways, and Challenges to Boost Viewership

- **Types of Events That Engage Viewers** - Special streams, giveaways, and viewer challenges create excitement and attract both new and returning viewers.

- **Planning Effective Events** - Promoting events in advance, using interactive tools during streams, and following up with highlights and thank-you messages keeps viewers engaged and encourages participation.

9.4 SEO Optimization and Keywords for Better Discovery

- **Keyword Research for Streams** - Using tools like Google Keyword Planner to identify trending terms and optimize stream titles, descriptions, and tags helps improve discoverability.

- **SEO-Friendly Titles and Descriptions** - Streamers should include action words and relevant keywords in their titles and descriptions to increase their chances of being found by new viewers.

9.5 Networking and Building Relationships in the Industry

- **Industry Connections** - Engaging with conventions or joining online communities like Discord and Reddit allows streamers to network and collaborate with others in the industry.

- **Building Relationships with Viewers** - Offering exclusive groups for top supporters can deepen viewer connections and foster loyalty.

Growing your audience requires a combination of strategic planning and consistent execution. By using social media, collaborating with others, hosting engaging events, optimizing SEO, and networking effectively, streamers can expand their reach and build a loyal, long-term following.

Chapter 10: Audience Retention and Analytics

Retaining viewers is just as important as attracting them. A loyal audience fuels long-term growth, monetization opportunities, and community building. This chapter explores how to analyze viewer behavior, create engagement strategies, plan repeat-worthy content, and use surveys and polls to shape streams that resonate with your audience.

10.1 Understanding Viewer Behavior with Data Insights

Understanding viewer behavior through data insights is essential for improving streams, retaining audiences, and increasing engagement. This section explores how to analyze key metrics, leverage analytics tools, and apply insights to refine your content strategy.

1. Track Key Audience Metrics

Monitoring audience behavior helps identify trends and optimize content performance:

- **Viewer Count Trends:** Observe peak viewing times and patterns to schedule streams effectively.

- **Average Watch Time:** Measure session durations to pinpoint drop-off moments and improve content pacing.

- **Engagement Rate:** Evaluate chat activity, comments, and reactions to gauge interaction levels.

- **Retention Rate:** Track returning viewers to assess audience loyalty and satisfaction.

- **Conversion Rates:** Analyze follows, subscriptions, and donations to measure content impact.

2. Use Analytics Tools for Performance Optimization

Analytics tools provide valuable insights to refine your approach and monitor progress:

- **Twitch Insights and Stream Reports:** Track views, followers, and chat activity to evaluate growth.

- **YouTube Studio Analytics:** Review impressions, click-through rates, and audience demographics to optimize marketing.

- **Google Analytics:** Measure website traffic and cross-platform engagement for broader performance insights.

- **Streamlabs and OBS Reports:** Monitor technical metrics like bitrate and dropped frames to maintain stream quality.

3. Apply Data Insights to Content Strategy

Incorporating data-driven strategies improves viewer engagement and content quality:

- **Adjust Content Timing:** Schedule streams during peak hours to reach larger audiences.

- **Introduce Interactive Features:** Add polls, giveaways, and Q&A sessions to increase participation.

- **Develop Themed Content:** Focus on recurring topics or themes identified as popular to build consistency and audience anticipation.

4. Example

- **Poll Integration Boosted Watch Time:** A gaming streamer added polls at the 15-minute mark, increasing average watch time by 35% in one month.

- **Tutorial Focus Doubled Followers:** A tech streamer shifted focus to instructional content, attracting a broader audience and doubling followers.

- **Music Requests Increased Retention:** A music streamer introduced live song requests, improving retention rates by 20%.

5. Tips

- **Focus on Audience Behavior:** Use viewer data to identify patterns and experiment with scheduling or formats to optimize engagement.

- **Test Different Content Approaches:** Compare thumbnails, titles, and descriptions using A/B testing to refine discoverability.

- **Analyze Demographics Regularly:** Adjust content to match audience shifts and evolving preferences.

- **Experiment with Features:** Incorporate polls, giveaways, and themed events to build participation and loyalty.

6. Reflection

- **Analyze Trends and Patterns:** What patterns or trends do your current analytics reveal about viewer behavior?

- **Tailor Strategy Based on Data:** How can you tailor your content strategy based on data insights?

7. Exercise

- **Review Analytics Reports:** Review your most recent analytics report and identify one area to optimize (e.g., scheduling, engagement, or content themes).

- **Create and Test Plans:** Create an action plan to test new features or formats and track results over two weeks.

10.2 Improving Retention with Engagement Strategies

Engagement is key to keeping viewers interested and invested in your streams. Strategies that involve direct interaction create memorable experiences and foster loyalty. This section explores techniques to enhance engagement and strengthen connections with your audience.

1. Use Real-Time Interaction Techniques

Live interaction creates immediate connections and keeps viewers engaged:

- **Shoutouts and Acknowledgments:** Welcome new viewers by name and publicly thank subscribers and donors to make them feel valued.

- **Interactive Q&A Sessions:** Respond to live questions to build rapport and encourage participation.

- **Gamification Elements:** Use chat games, challenges, and rewards to keep viewers active and entertained.

- **Subscriber-Only Content:** Offer exclusive perks, such as behind-the-scenes access, private streams, or custom emotes, to build loyalty.

2. Engage Your Community Beyond Streams

Extending engagement outside your streams helps maintain interest and strengthen relationships:

- **Social Media Follow-Ups:** Share highlights, polls, and updates across platforms to keep your audience connected.

- **Community Recognition Programs:** Celebrate milestones, such as top fans, subscriber anniversaries, and giveaways to show appreciation.

- **Collaborative Content Planning:** Let viewers vote on challenges, themes, or future content ideas to make them feel involved.

3. Example

- **Fitness Streamer's Poll Success:** A fitness streamer introduced weekly subscriber-only polls, allowing viewers to vote on workout themes. This approach increased retention by 40% within one month.

- **Game Streamer's Challenge Integration:** A game streamer created weekly challenges with leaderboard rankings and prize giveaways, boosting chat activity and subscriber numbers.

- **Art Streamer's Collaborative Projects:** An art streamer let viewers vote on elements of a live drawing session, improving engagement and repeat attendance.

4. Tips

- **Automate Engagement with Tools:** Use chatbots like StreamElements or Nightbot to automate welcome messages, polls, and alerts.

- **Personalize Interactions:** Address viewers by name and acknowledge their contributions regularly to build stronger connections.

- **Encourage Participation:** Add interactive elements like polls, giveaways, and trivia games to encourage audience involvement.

- **Highlight Viewer Contributions:** Showcase fan art, comments, or suggestions during streams to celebrate audience input.

5. Reflection

- **Assess Current Strategies:** Which engagement strategies have been most successful for you so far?

- **Explore New Techniques:** What new techniques can you introduce to improve participation?

6. Exercise

- **Test Engagement Methods:** Test two new engagement methods (e.g., polls, giveaways, or games) in your next stream.

- **Analyze Impact:** Track participation metrics and analyze the impact on viewer retention.

10.3 Building Long-Term Relationships Beyond Streaming

Strong relationships with viewers lead to a loyal fan base and sustained growth. This section focuses on creating deeper connections that extend beyond live sessions and foster long-term loyalty.

1. Create Exclusive Spaces for Interaction

Private and exclusive spaces provide a sense of belonging and keep viewers engaged outside of live streams.

- **Discord Servers:** Build private communities where members can chat, participate in polls, and access exclusive content.

- **Subscriber-Only Chats:** Offer dedicated spaces for exclusive discussions and deeper interactions with your audience.

- **Loyalty Programs:** Reward top viewers with badges, gifts, and public recognition to make them feel valued and appreciated.

2. Personalize Communication

Personalizing your communication helps strengthen relationships and encourages viewer loyalty.

- **Social Media and Emails:** Send updates, thank-you messages, and special offers to keep your audience informed and appreciated.

- **Fan Spotlights:** Feature viewer-generated content, such as artwork or memes, during streams to celebrate their creativity.

- **Direct Interactions:** Provide personalized shoutouts, voice messages, or video responses for top supporters to make connections more meaningful.

3. Example

- **Artist Streamer's VIP Discord Success:** An artist streamer created a Discord VIP group for paid subscribers, resulting in a 25% increase in subscription revenue within three months.

- **Gaming Creator's Loyalty Program:** A gaming creator implemented a badge and reward system for long-term subscribers, boosting retention and encouraging new subscriptions.

- **Music Streamer's Fan Spotlight:** A music streamer featured fan song requests and shoutouts, strengthening viewer bonds and driving higher participation rates.

4. Tips

- **Use Membership Platforms:** Platforms like **Patreon** allow you to create membership tiers with personalized perks for your supporters.

- **Offer Unique Rewards:** Provide custom badges, shoutouts, or early access to content as exclusive rewards for loyal viewers.

- **Encourage Community Building:** Foster interaction among fans by hosting group activities, contests, and collaborative projects.

- **Celebrate Milestones:** Recognize anniversaries, subscriber goals, and community achievements to build excitement and connection.

5. Reflection

- **Reward Systems:** What systems can you set up to reward and retain loyal viewers?

- **Personal Connections:** How can you make your interactions more personal and engaging?

6. Exercise

- **Create a VIP Group:** Create a VIP group or exclusive channel and promote it to your audience this week.

- **Test a Loyalty Program:** Develop a loyalty program or badge system and test it over the next month to track engagement and retention.

10.4 Content Planning That Encourages Repeat Visits

Creating content that keeps viewers coming back is vital for retention. Consistency, structure, and creative planning help build habits for viewers to tune in regularly. This section explores proven strategies to increase engagement and foster loyalty.

1. Develop Content Themes and Series

Themed content and recurring series create structure and anticipation, encouraging repeat visits.

- **Weekly Shows:** Establish recurring series like "Motivation Mondays" or "Tech Talk Fridays" to create habits and expectations.

- **Seasonal Events:** Plan streams around holidays, trending topics, or special occasions to add excitement and relevance.

- **Tutorial Series:** Offer step-by-step guides or multi-part lessons to keep viewers invested and returning for new installments.

- **Challenge-Based Themes:** Introduce interactive challenges or competitions to promote audience participation and maintain interest.

2. Schedule Consistently for Engagement

Consistency in scheduling builds trust and helps viewers integrate your streams into their routines.

- **Fixed Streaming Times:** Develop a consistent schedule so viewers know exactly when to tune in and plan accordingly.

- **Advance Promotions:** Use countdowns, highlight reels, and teaser trailers across social media to generate anticipation and excitement.

- **Surprise Pop-Ups:** Occasionally host unannounced, spontaneous streams to create surprise and add freshness to your content.

- **Content Calendars:** Utilize tools like **Notion**, **Trello**, or **Google Calendar** to plan and visualize your content schedule effectively.

3. Example

- **Gaming Streamer Boosted Viewership:** A gaming streamer increased viewership by 30% with a weekly "Boss Battle Friday" theme, promoted through Discord chats and social posts.

- **Tech Creator's Tutorial Series:** A tech creator developed a 10-part streaming setup tutorial series, attracting consistent viewers looking for step-by-step guidance.

- **Seasonal Events Engagement:** A lifestyle streamer hosted themed holiday streams, resulting in spikes in attendance and higher engagement during seasonal promotions.

4. Tips

- **Organize with Planning Tools:** Use planners like **Notion** or **Trello** to schedule streams, organize themes, and track ideas.

- **Promote Consistently:** Post reminders and teasers on social media to build anticipation for upcoming content.

- **Experiment with Content Formats:** Test recurring series, tutorials, and pop-up streams to determine what resonates best with your audience.

- **Track Performance:** Use analytics tools to monitor performance and refine content strategies based on viewer behavior.

5. Reflection

- **Content Ideas for Recurring Series:** What content ideas can you develop into recurring series to attract repeat visits?

- **Scheduling Improvements:** How can you improve consistency and promotions to boost anticipation and engagement?

6. Exercise

- **Develop a Two-Week Plan:** Create a two-week streaming schedule with themes, recurring events, and special promotions to encourage repeat visits.

- **Analyze Viewer Trends:** Track participation and performance metrics to evaluate the impact of your planning efforts and identify areas for improvement.

10.5 Using Surveys and Polls for Audience Feedback

Feedback helps you understand what viewers enjoy and what improvements they want to see. Surveys and polls create direct communication channels, enabling audience participation and ensuring your content aligns with their preferences.

1. Select Effective Tools for Surveys and Polls

Choosing the right tools makes gathering feedback simple and interactive.

- **Google Forms:** Collect detailed feedback anonymously, allowing viewers to share honest opinions.

- **StrawPoll and Twitch Polls:** Use real-time voting tools during streams for immediate feedback.

- **Instagram and Twitter Polls:** Gather quick insights through social media stories and posts.

- **YouTube Community Polls:** Engage subscribers directly on your channel to measure preferences and reactions.

2. Ask Targeted Questions to Gather Insights

Crafting the right questions provides valuable feedback to improve streams.

- **Content Preferences:** Ask, "What topics do you enjoy most?" to understand favored themes and segments.

- **Engagement Ideas:** Include questions like, "What games or themes should we try next?" to crowdsource creative ideas.

- **Technical Feedback:** Assess quality by asking, "How's the audio and video quality?" to address production issues.

- **Frequency Preferences:** Determine availability by asking, "What days or times work best for you to watch streams?"

3. Example

- **Educator Streamer's Success:** An educator streamer increased viewer satisfaction by 25% after implementing polls that allowed fans to vote on lesson topics.

- **Gaming Poll Impact:** A gaming creator used live polls to select games for streams, resulting in higher engagement and viewer retention.

- **Lifestyle Streamer's Feedback Loop:** A lifestyle streamer adjusted content based on poll results, leading to better alignment with audience preferences and increased participation.

4. Tips

- **Schedule Regular Polls:** Use weekly or monthly polls to maintain ongoing feedback and keep content fresh.

- **Engage Viewers Live:** Conduct polls during streams to boost participation and ensure real-time input.

- **Analyze Results:** Review survey responses and spot patterns to make informed improvements.

- **Incentivize Participation:** Offer shoutouts or small rewards to encourage viewers to complete surveys.

5. Reflection

- **Feedback Questions:** What types of questions can help you improve future streams and meet audience expectations?

- **Content Adjustments:** How can you use survey results to shape your content strategy moving forward?

6. Exercise

- **Create and Share a Survey:** Develop a short survey or poll and share it with your audience through multiple platforms.

- **Apply Viewer Feedback:** Analyze the results and implement at least one suggestion in your next stream to test audience satisfaction.

Conclusion: Turning Viewers into Long-Term Supporters

Retaining viewers is about understanding their needs, creating engaging content, and building meaningful relationships. By leveraging analytics, improving engagement, planning repeatable content, and collecting feedback, you can transform casual viewers into loyal supporters. Implement the tips, tools, and exercises in this chapter to optimize your strategy and sustain long-term growth.

Chapter 10 Review: Audience Retention and Analytics

Chapter 10 emphasizes the importance of retaining viewers to build long-term growth, monetization opportunities, and community building. It explores how to analyze viewer behavior, create engagement strategies, and use surveys to shape content that resonates with your audience.

10.1 Understanding Viewer Behavior with Data Insights

- **Key Metrics to Track** - Monitor viewer count trends, average watch time, engagement rate, retention rate, and conversion rates to understand what keeps your audience engaged.

- **Tools for Analytics** - Use platforms like Twitch Insights, YouTube Studio, and Google Analytics to track performance and identify trends that can inform your content strategy.

10.2 Improving Retention with Engagement Strategies

- **Real-Time Interaction Techniques** - Engage viewers by welcoming them by name, responding to comments, using gamification, and offering subscriber-only content.

- **Community Engagement Beyond Streams** - Use social media to share highlights and host giveaways. Recognize milestones and celebrate loyal viewers to foster engagement.

10.3 Building Long-Term Relationships Beyond Streaming

- **Creating Exclusive Spaces for Interaction** - Build private communities like Discord servers or offer subscriber-only chats to deepen viewer relationships.

- **Personalizing Communication** - Send thank-you messages, feature fan-generated content, and offer personalized shoutouts to top supporters.

10.4 Content Planning That Encourages Repeat Visits

- **Develop Content Themes and Series** - Plan recurring streams, like "Motivation Mondays" or "Tech Talk Fridays," to create consistent content that encourages repeat visits.

- **Scheduling for Consistency** - Use fixed streaming times and advance promotions to build anticipation, and surprise viewers with spontaneous streams.

10.5 Using Surveys and Polls for Audience Feedback

- **Tools for Surveys and Polls** - Use tools like Google Forms, StrawPoll, and Instagram polls to gather feedback on content preferences, engagement ideas, and technical issues.

- **Questions to Include** - Ask about content preferences, themes, and feedback on technical quality to improve future streams.

Retaining viewers involves understanding their needs and continuously delivering engaging content. By using analytics, improving interaction, and gathering feedback, streamers can build loyal communities and sustain long-term growth.

Chapter 11: Monetizing Your Live Streams

Turning your passion for live streaming into a sustainable income is achievable with the right strategies. This chapter explores proven methods for monetizing live streams, from affiliate marketing and donations to merchandise sales, exclusive content, and long-term growth strategies. By the end, you'll have a clear roadmap to diversify income streams, maximize profits, and build financial stability.

11.1 Affiliate Marketing and Sponsored Partnerships

Affiliate marketing and sponsorships are effective ways to generate income while aligning with brands that complement your niche. This section outlines strategies to maximize revenue, build credibility, and form valuable partnerships.

1. Master Affiliate Marketing Basics

Affiliate marketing enables streamers to earn commissions by promoting products or services that resonate with their audience.

- **Join Affiliate Programs:** Sign up for programs like **Amazon Associates**, **Impact Radius**, and **Rakuten Advertising** to start earning commissions.

- **Promote Tools You Use:** Feature products such as ring lights, ergonomic chairs, or streaming software that viewers may find useful.

- **Provide Discount Codes and Links:** Offer exclusive coupon codes or referral links to incentivize purchases and track performance.

- **Test Products Before Promotion:** Share hands-on experiences through demos and reviews to build trust and authenticity.

2. Build Effective Sponsorship Partnerships

Sponsorships create opportunities to collaborate with brands and generate consistent income while providing value to your audience.

- **Find Sponsorship Deals:** Use platforms like **Billo** and **Social Bluebook** to discover partnership opportunities.

- **Negotiate Terms Clearly:** Define deliverables, such as product shoutouts, sponsored segments, or logo placements, to meet expectations.

- **Showcase Value to Sponsors:** Highlight audience demographics, engagement rates, and content analytics to demonstrate ROI.
- **Stay Transparent with Viewers:** Clearly disclose sponsorships to maintain trust and comply with advertising guidelines.

3. Example

- **Beauty Streamer's Partnership Win:** A beauty streamer partnered with a skincare brand and earned $1,500 in commissions by offering an exclusive 15% discount code.
- **Fitness Influencer's Gear Sponsorship:** A fitness creator promoted exercise bands and mats, doubling their affiliate sales through tutorial-based streams.
- **Tech Reviewer's Product Launch:** A tech influencer collaborated with a gadget company, using live unboxing videos and affiliate links to drive sales and engagement.

4. Tips

- **Focus on Relevance:** Choose brands and products that naturally align with your content and audience preferences.
- **Track Results Regularly:** Monitor link clicks, purchases, and engagement rates to optimize strategies.
- **Incorporate Promotions Naturally:** Weave product mentions into content seamlessly rather than forcing promotions.
- **Create Limited-Time Offers:** Highlight time-sensitive discounts to drive urgency and conversions.

5. Reflection

- **Product Fit:** What affiliate products or services align best with your audience's interests?
- **Growth Potential:** How can you tailor your pitches to attract more sponsors and partnerships?

6. Exercise

- **Identify Key Products:** Make a list of five products or brands that complement your niche and audience.

- **Draft an Outreach Email:** Write a professional email pitch highlighting your audience metrics, engagement rates, and sponsorship ideas to secure partnerships.

11.2 Donations, Subscriptions, and Memberships

Monetizing viewer loyalty through tips, subscriptions, and memberships creates recurring revenue and strengthens community bonds. This section explores methods to generate income while rewarding supporters.

1. Collect Direct Donations and Tips

Encouraging direct contributions builds immediate financial support and shows appreciation for loyal viewers.

- **Set Up Tip Links:** Use platforms like **Streamlabs, Ko-fi,** or **PayPal.me** to create easy donation options.

- **Highlight Contributions:** Enable real-time alerts to publicly recognize and celebrate supporters during streams.

- **Encourage Milestones:** Set donation goals with rewards such as personalized shoutouts, exclusive content, or milestone celebrations.

- **Offer One-Time Incentives:** Provide downloadable resources, thank-you videos, or custom graphics as rewards for large tips.

2. Offer Subscriptions and Membership Models

Subscriptions and memberships provide recurring income while offering exclusive perks to build community loyalty.

- **Twitch Subscriptions:** Offer tiered benefits such as badges, emotes, ad-free viewing, and special chat privileges.

- **YouTube Memberships:** Provide perks like exclusive emojis, members-only posts, and live streams to engage subscribers.

- **Patreon and Ko-fi Memberships:** Create monthly tiers for bonus content, private group chats, and behind-the-scenes updates.

- **Custom Platforms:** Develop personalized subscription plans using platforms like **Memberful** or **Buy Me a Coffee** for greater control.

3. Provide Incentives to Reward Subscribers

Adding value encourages sign-ups and builds long-term loyalty.

- **Exclusive Content:** Host subscriber-only streams, tutorials, and Q&A sessions for deeper engagement.

- **Custom Badges and Emotes:** Reward subscribers with visual recognition, such as badges and emojis, to foster identity and inclusion.

- **Giveaways and Contests:** Organize raffles, challenges, or member-only events to incentivize participation and renewals.

- **Early Access and Sneak Peeks:** Provide early access to new content, updates, or limited-edition merchandise.

4. Example

- **Fitness Streamer's Subscriber Growth:** A fitness streamer boosted income by 40% through subscriber-only workout plans and Q&A sessions.

- **Gamer's Exclusive Challenges:** A gaming streamer hosted subscriber-only tournaments, increasing subscriptions and viewer participation.

- **Music Creator's VIP Access:** A musician offered behind-the-scenes songwriting sessions for members, enhancing engagement and building deeper connections.

5. Tips

- **Promote Subscriber Perks Regularly:** Remind viewers of membership benefits during streams and on social media.

- **Bundle Incentives:** Combine exclusive content, giveaways, and badges for higher perceived value.

- **Celebrate Milestones:** Recognize top supporters publicly and offer loyalty rewards to keep subscribers engaged.

- **Test Membership Models:** Experiment with different tiers and benefits to discover what resonates most with your audience.

6. Reflection

- **Subscriber Rewards:** What rewards would motivate your audience to subscribe and stay engaged?

- **Tier Structure:** How can you design membership tiers that balance exclusivity and accessibility?

7. Exercise

- **Design Membership Tiers:** Create three membership tiers with distinct benefits and pricing.

- **Launch and Promote Memberships:** Develop a marketing plan to promote your membership tiers across streams and social platforms.

11.3 Selling Merchandise and Custom Products

Merchandise not only generates income but also reinforces your brand identity. Offering unique products allows you to connect with your audience while building a revenue stream. This section covers strategies for designing, promoting, and selling merchandise effectively.

1. Design Merchandise That Reflects Your Brand

Creating unique designs and customized products strengthens your identity and appeals to your target audience.

- **Create Unique Logos and Designs:** Use tools like **Canva**, **Placeit**, or hire freelance designers on **Fiverr** and **Upwork** to create eye-catching graphics.

- **Choose Print-on-Demand Platforms:** Services like **Teespring**, **Printify**, and **Merch by Amazon** handle production, shipping, and returns.

- **Offer Custom Niche Products:** Develop items specific to your audience, such as gaming gear, workout apparel, art prints, planners, or mugs featuring your branding.

- **Test Samples Before Launch:** Order samples to check quality and ensure designs look professional before promoting them.

2. Promote Merchandise to Drive Sales

Effective promotion ensures that your audience knows about your products and feels motivated to make purchases.

- **Showcase Products Live:** Feature products during streams by wearing branded apparel or demonstrating their use.

- **Offer Discounts and Bundles:** Provide exclusive coupon codes for subscribers and bundle related products for added value.

- **Limited Edition Drops:** Create urgency with seasonal or limited-time releases to encourage immediate purchases.
- **Highlight Customer Reviews:** Share testimonials or user-generated content to build trust and show product quality.

3. Example

- **Cooking Streamer's Holiday Promotion:** A cooking streamer generated $5,000 in sales with branded aprons and recipe books during a holiday-themed sale.
- **Gaming Creator's Custom Gear:** A gamer sold mousepads, controllers, and keychains featuring custom artwork, boosting brand visibility and income.
- **Fitness Influencer's Workout Gear:** A fitness streamer launched a line of branded water bottles and resistance bands, resulting in a 30% increase in sales after live demonstrations.

4. Tips

- **Use Eye-Catching Graphics:** Invest in professional designs to make products visually appealing and aligned with your branding.
- **Bundle Offers for Value:** Combine related products into packages to boost sales and encourage larger purchases.
- **Leverage Social Proof:** Highlight customer photos, reviews, and testimonials to build trust.
- **Track Performance Metrics:** Use analytics from platforms like **Shopify** or **Etsy** to monitor sales and refine marketing strategies.

5. Reflection

- **Audience Fit:** What merchandise fits your niche and resonates most with your audience?
- **Promotion Strategies:** How can you incorporate live demonstrations and seasonal offers into your marketing plan?

6. Exercise

- **Brainstorm Product Ideas:** List three products that align with your brand and audience interests.

- **Create a Sales Plan:** Develop a promotional strategy that includes discounts, giveaways, and social media campaigns to boost sales.

11.4 Leveraging Super Chats and Exclusive Content

Super Chats and exclusive content allow fans to provide direct support while accessing premium materials. This section explores ways to increase viewer engagement and revenue through interactive features and exclusive offerings.

1. Use Super Chats and Viewer Donations

Super Chats and tipping tools enable fans to contribute directly while gaining recognition and interaction.

- **YouTube Super Chats:** Allow fans to pay to pin messages during live streams, ensuring visibility and engagement.

- **Twitch Bits:** Offer tipping features that let viewers cheer and receive shoutouts or badges.

- **Interactive Incentives:** Reward donors with live shoutouts, personalized messages, or the opportunity to request custom challenges.

- **Goal-Oriented Donations:** Set milestones for donation goals and provide rewards such as giveaways, behind-the-scenes content, or on-stream celebrations.

2. Provide Exclusive Content for Members

Exclusive content builds loyalty and encourages fans to subscribe for premium experiences.

- **Early Access Videos:** Reward paying fans with sneak peeks, unreleased content, or behind-the-scenes footage.

- **Downloadable Resources:** Provide useful resources such as guides, templates, checklists, or eBooks.

- **Private Events:** Host member-only streams, interactive Q&A sessions, or small-group workshops to create intimacy.

- **Bonus Content Libraries:** Offer access to exclusive playlists, tutorials, and archives that non-members can't view.

3. Example

- **Travel Streamer's Premium Offers:** A travel streamer boosted earnings by 50% by offering premium travel itineraries and subscriber-only group chats.

- **Tech Creator's Downloadable Guides:** A tech content creator provided detailed setup guides and exclusive tutorials, increasing paid memberships.

- **Fitness Influencer's VIP Sessions:** A fitness streamer offered private workout streams and meal plans, leading to higher subscriber retention rates.

4. Tips

- **Showcase Exclusive Content During Streams:** Regularly promote premium content to remind viewers of its value and encourage sign-ups.

- **Offer Tiered Pricing Options:** Provide multiple membership levels with increasing benefits to appeal to different budgets.

- **Engage with Paying Members:** Build stronger relationships through personalized shoutouts and interactive polls.

- **Highlight Limited-Time Offers:** Create urgency with time-limited access to premium content to drive interest and conversions.

5. Reflection

- **Premium Offer Ideas:** What exclusive content or benefits can you offer to encourage more donations and memberships?

- **Engagement Opportunities:** How can you make premium content more interactive and appealing?

6. Exercise

- **Design a Premium Offer:** Create one premium product or experience, such as a workshop or private stream.

- **Promote Your Offer:** Develop a strategy to market your premium offer during your next broadcast and track audience response.

11.5 Long-Term Income Growth Strategies for Streamers

Building long-term, sustainable income as a streamer involves diversifying revenue streams, investing in relationships with your audience, and staying adaptable to industry changes. This section explores strategies to help you scale your income over time and secure financial stability.

1. Diversifying Revenue Streams for Stability

Relying on a single income source can leave streamers vulnerable. Diversifying income channels ensures steady revenue, even when one fluctuates.

- **Subscriptions and Donations:** Platforms like Twitch and YouTube offer recurring revenue from subscribers. Encourage loyal viewers to become members and offer exclusive perks, such as custom badges or members-only content.

- **Affiliate Marketing:** Promote products relevant to your audience through affiliate links to earn commissions on sales.

- **Merchandising:** Offer branded merchandise like t-shirts or posters to fans. This provides tangible support and generates extra income.

2. Building Strong Partnerships and Sponsorships

As your audience grows, partnerships become a valuable income source.

- **Brand Deals and Sponsored Content:** Partner with companies whose products align with your content. Sponsored streams or videos let you monetize your audience while maintaining content relevance.

- **Collaborations with Creators:** Work with other streamers or influencers to access new sponsorship opportunities and cross-promotion. This can lead to co-branded products or exclusive events.

3. Expanding Into Content Beyond Live Streaming

To achieve long-term growth, streamers should explore content beyond live streams to maximize revenue potential.

- **Creating Evergreen Content:** Repurpose streams into on-demand videos (VODs or tutorials) to generate income long after the stream ends. These videos can also earn ad revenue.

- **Building a Personal Brand:** Establish yourself as an authority in your niche. A strong personal brand can open doors to paid opportunities, such as guest appearances or hosting gigs, and lead to new content avenues like podcasting or YouTube production.

4. Example

- **Merchandise Success:** A gaming streamer built a loyal fan base and launched limited-edition merchandise, creating a reliable income stream outside of ad revenue.

- **Brand Partnership:** A fitness streamer partnered with a well-known athletic brand, promoting exclusive discounts, leading to a long-term sponsorship deal and increased earnings.

5. Tips

- **Diversify Income:** Build multiple income sources, such as memberships, affiliate marketing, and merchandise, to ensure long-term financial stability.

- **Leverage Your Audience:** Actively encourage your audience to support you through tips, memberships, and merchandise.

- **Monitor Trends:** Stay updated on new monetization options, like NFTs or changes to streaming platforms, to keep income flowing.

6. Reflection

- **Diversify Your Streams:** What other income channels could you explore to ensure financial stability in the long term?

- **Evaluate Partnerships:** Which brands could you partner with to boost your income potential?

7. Exercise

- **Create a Revenue Plan:** Outline a strategy for diversifying your income over the next year, including goals for memberships, affiliate marketing, and merchandise.

- **Research Sponsorships:** Identify brands or companies to collaborate with and craft a partnership proposal.

- **Track Growth:** Regularly monitor your income streams, adjusting strategies based on analytics and feedback to optimize earnings.

Conclusion: Turning Streaming into Sustainable Income

Monetizing your live streams is about leveraging multiple income sources—affiliate marketing, subscriptions, merchandise, exclusive content, and scalable strategies. By applying the tools and exercises in this chapter, you can build a profitable streaming career and secure long-term success.

Chapter 11 Review: Monetizing Your Live Streams

Chapter 11 explores strategies for turning live streaming into a sustainable income. It covers affiliate marketing, donations, merchandise sales, exclusive content, and long-term growth strategies to help streamers maximize profits and build financial stability.

11.1 Affiliate Marketing and Sponsored Partnerships

- **Affiliate Marketing Basics** - Join affiliate programs like Amazon Associates or ShareASale to promote products relevant to your niche and earn commissions.

- **Partnering with Sponsors** - Reach out to brands directly or use platforms like Grapevine to connect with sponsors. Demonstrate ROI by highlighting viewer engagement and demographics.

11.2 Donations, Subscriptions, and Memberships

- **Direct Donations and Tips** - Use services like Streamlabs or PayPal for tips and set donation milestones with rewards to encourage contributions.

- **Subscriptions and Membership Models** - Offer tiered benefits on platforms like Twitch and YouTube, or create memberships through Patreon with perks like exclusive content or chats.

- **Incentives for Subscribers** - Provide custom badges, exclusive streams, or giveaways to motivate subscriptions and reward loyal viewers.

11.3 Selling Merchandise and Custom Products

- **Designing Your Merchandise** - Create unique logos and designs, and use print-on-demand platforms like Teespring to handle production and shipping.

- **Promoting Merchandise** - Feature products live, offer subscriber discounts, and create limited edition items to build excitement and drive sales.

11.4 Leveraging Super Chats and Exclusive Content

- **Super Chats and Viewer Donations** - Use platforms like YouTube Super Chats or Twitch Bits to allow fans to support with paid messages or tipping.

- **Exclusive Content for Members** - Offer early access videos, downloadable resources, or member-only events to incentivize donations and paid memberships.

11.5 Long-Term Income Growth Strategies for Streamers

- **Scaling Through Content Repurposing** - Repurpose stream highlights into YouTube clips or tutorials to attract new viewers and monetize evergreen content.

- **Hosting Online Classes and Consulting Services** - Create webinars or coaching programs to share your expertise, offering additional revenue streams.

Monetizing your live streams requires leveraging diverse income sources, including affiliate marketing, subscriptions, merchandise, and exclusive content. By applying these strategies, streamers can build a profitable, sustainable career in the long term.

Chapter 12: Advanced Revenue Streams

Scaling your streaming business requires diversifying income streams and creating long-term, sustainable revenue strategies. This chapter explores advanced monetization techniques such as offering online courses, paid memberships, evergreen content, partnerships, and scaling with teams and agencies. By the end, you'll have the tools to transform your streaming passion into a thriving business.

12.1 Offering Online Classes, Courses, and Consulting Services

Sharing your expertise through courses and consulting is one of the most scalable ways to earn income as a streamer. Whether teaching streaming setups, gaming strategies, or creative skills, online learning provides passive income opportunities and builds authority in your niche.

1. Create Online Courses for Passive Income

Online courses allow you to package your expertise into a structured learning experience.

- **Define Your Niche:** Focus on topics your audience values, such as video editing, live streaming tutorials, or social media growth strategies.

- **Choose Hosting Platforms:** Use tools like **Teachable**, **Udemy**, or **Thinkific** to host and sell your courses.

- **Plan Course Structures:** Organize lessons into modules with videos, worksheets, and quizzes to enhance engagement and retention.

- **Bundle Exclusive Offers:** Add downloadable resources, cheat sheets, or templates to provide extra value for paid students.

- **Pre-Record Lessons:** Create high-quality videos that can be reused and sold repeatedly for passive income.

2. Provide Consulting Services for Personalized Coaching

Consulting services allow you to offer customized advice and build stronger relationships with your audience.

- **1-on-1 Coaching:** Offer tailored strategies for stream setup, branding, monetization, or content growth.
- **Group Workshops:** Host live sessions covering niche topics, such as SEO strategies, audience building, or advanced editing techniques.
- **Tiered Packages:** Develop different pricing levels with increasing value, including VIP packages for premium access.
- **Follow-Up Support:** Provide post-session resources, such as email templates or feedback forms, to maintain value beyond consultations.

3. Example

- **Gaming Streamer's Community Course:** A gaming streamer created a course on building Twitch communities, earning $12,000 in passive income within three months while offering premium coaching calls.
- **Fitness Creator's Virtual Training Program:** A fitness creator launched structured workout programs with tiered pricing, combining self-paced videos with live group coaching.
- **Tech Consultant's Branding Workshop:** A tech expert hosted branding workshops for new streamers, attracting businesses and solo creators looking to grow online.

4. Tips

- **Leverage Case Studies:** Include real-world examples and success stories in lessons to make content relatable and actionable.
- **Engage with Students:** Offer Q&A sessions or community forums to provide ongoing support and feedback.
- **Market Your Expertise:** Promote courses and services through streams, social media, and email marketing campaigns.
- **Offer Early-Bird Discounts:** Create urgency and attract early sign-ups with limited-time pricing offers.

5. Reflection

- **Teaching Opportunities:** What expertise can you teach to your audience that provides value and scalability?
- **Coaching Ideas:** How can you structure coaching programs to appeal to different audience segments?

6. Exercise

- **Create a Course Outline:** Develop a 5-module course outline focusing on a niche topic your audience values.

- **Set Pricing Options:** Create tiered pricing for coaching sessions or packages, and test them with your audience for feedback.

12.2 Creating Paid Membership Tiers and Special Content

Membership programs provide predictable monthly revenue while rewarding loyal fans with exclusive perks and content. This section explores how to design, promote, and scale membership programs to strengthen audience engagement and income.

1. Design Membership Tiers with Value

Creating tiered memberships allows you to offer flexible options for different budgets and levels of interest.

- **Basic Tier ($5/month):** Provide access to private chats, member-only polls, and custom badges for recognition.

- **Mid-Tier ($15/month):** Include bonus live streams, interactive Q&A sessions, and behind-the-scenes content.

- **Premium Tier ($30+/month):** Offer personalized shoutouts, exclusive gifts, private coaching sessions, or VIP access to special events.

- **Bundle Benefits:** Combine multiple perks in higher tiers to increase perceived value and encourage upgrades.

2. Choose Platforms for Membership Programs

Selecting the right platform simplifies managing subscriptions and delivering rewards.

- **Patreon and Ko-fi:** Popular platforms for managing memberships, offering flexible pricing, and distributing exclusive content.

- **YouTube Memberships:** Integrated directly into YouTube channels, providing emojis, badges, and private content options.

- **Twitch Subscriptions:** Built-in tiers for emotes, badges, ad-free viewing, and subscriber-only chat features.
- **Custom Websites:** Develop personalized membership programs through platforms like **Memberful** or **Podia** for greater control.

3. Promote Membership Programs Effectively

Consistent promotion drives sign-ups and maintains interest.

- **Highlight Benefits During Streams:** Display visuals and breakdowns of membership tiers and rewards to attract interest.
- **Offer Limited-Time Bonuses:** Provide early access, exclusive merch, or special discounts for new members to boost sign-ups.
- **Leverage Testimonials:** Feature reviews and feedback from existing members to showcase value and credibility.
- **Engage Subscribers in Content Decisions:** Use polls to let members vote on content ideas, rewards, or special events.

4. Example

- **Fitness Streamer's Membership Growth:** A fitness streamer boosted memberships by 50% in three months by adding workout plans, meal guides, and private coaching for subscribers.
- **Gaming Creator's VIP Access:** A gamer offered exclusive game tutorials and subscriber-only tournaments, doubling subscriptions within two months.
- **Lifestyle Influencer's Behind-the-Scenes Perks:** A lifestyle influencer created premium tiers with early access to vlogs and personal Q&A sessions, attracting long-term members.

5. Tips

- **Focus on Value:** Ensure that each tier offers clear, unique rewards that justify the price.
- **Test New Perks Regularly:** Experiment with new benefits like polls, shoutouts, and giveaways to keep programs fresh.
- **Promote Across Platforms:** Use social media, email newsletters, and streams to consistently promote membership options.

- **Reward Loyalty:** Provide milestone gifts or bonus perks for long-term subscribers to encourage retention.

6. Reflection

- **Exclusive Rewards:** What rewards would attract and retain your audience as paying members?

- **Promotion Strategies:** How can you effectively promote membership tiers across your platforms?

7. Exercise

- **Design Membership Tiers:** Create three membership tiers with distinct benefits and pricing levels.

- **Develop a Marketing Plan:** Draft a strategy to promote these tiers, including visuals, testimonials, and limited-time offers to encourage sign-ups.

12.3 Turning Streams into Evergreen Content (Highlights and VODs)

Repurposing your live streams into evergreen content can create passive income opportunities while extending your reach. This section explores how to transform streams into lasting resources and revenue streams.

1. Repurpose Content for Multiple Platforms

Transforming streams into smaller, shareable formats helps maximize visibility and engagement across platforms.

- **Highlight Reels:** Edit short clips and post them as **YouTube Shorts**, **TikTok videos**, and **Instagram Reels** to attract new viewers.

- **Tutorials and Guides:** Extract educational segments and create standalone videos or blog posts to share insights and expertise.

- **Podcast Formats:** Convert Q&A streams or discussions into audio content using platforms like **Anchor** and **Spotify** for a broader audience.

- **Social Media Snippets:** Share impactful moments or quotes as teaser clips on **Twitter**, **Instagram Stories**, or **Facebook Reels** to generate interest.

2. Monetize Evergreen Content

Leveraging monetization tools allows you to generate passive income long after streams have aired.

- **YouTube Ads and Sponsorships:** Enable ad monetization and include sponsored mentions to boost earnings.

- **Affiliate Links in Descriptions:** Add referral links for equipment, software, or services mentioned in the content to earn commissions.

- **Bundle Highlights into Paid Courses:** Curate themed collections or tutorials and offer them as paid video series or premium downloads.

- **Membership-Exclusive Content:** Repurpose past streams into private playlists or archives for paying members.

3. Example

- **Tech Streamer's Video Course:** A tech streamer converted past tutorials into a 10-part video course and earned $8,500 in sales over six months.

- **Fitness Creator's Workout Library:** A fitness influencer compiled exercise routines into a premium membership library, generating recurring income.

- **Gaming Streamer's Highlight Reels:** A gamer edited gameplay highlights into YouTube Shorts, doubling subscribers and ad revenue in three months.

4. Tips

- **Optimize with SEO Tools:** Use tools like **TubeBuddy** and **VidIQ** to improve video titles, tags, and descriptions for better discoverability.

- **Create Thematic Playlists:** Organize related videos into playlists to keep viewers engaged and improve watch time.

- **Schedule Content Drops:** Release highlights and tutorials consistently to maintain audience interest.

- **Add Captions and Transcripts:** Improve accessibility and SEO by including captions and transcripts for repurposed content.

5. Reflection

- **Repurposing Opportunities:** How can you transform your past streams into evergreen content to expand reach and income?

- **Content Formats:** What new formats, such as podcasts or tutorials, could you explore to engage different audiences?

6. Exercise

- **Repurpose Content Ideas:** Select three past streams, outline repurposing ideas, and draft scripts for highlights or tutorials.

- **Test Monetization Strategies:** Create a monetization plan using affiliate links, ads, or premium bundles and track performance over 30 days.

12.4 Investing in Long-Term Partnerships and Brand Deals

Brand deals and sponsorships offer reliable income streams and growth opportunities when integrated effectively. This section explores strategies for identifying, securing, and scaling long-term partnerships with brands, supported by real-life examples from successful public figures.

1. Find and Secure Partnerships

Building partnerships with the right brands can create lasting collaborations and meaningful revenue streams.

- **Identify Relevant Brands:** Focus on companies that complement your content, such as tech tools, fashion brands, wellness products, or educational platforms.

- **Craft Professional Proposals:** Showcase audience demographics, engagement metrics, and case studies to demonstrate potential ROI.

- **Leverage Sponsorship Platforms:** Use tools like **Grapevine**, **Famebit**, **Upfluence**, and **Afluencer** to find partnership opportunities.

- **Network at Industry Events:** Attend expos, conventions, and webinars to connect with brands and decision-makers in your niche.

2. Structure Long-Term Deals

Clear agreements and performance tracking ensure lasting and scalable partnerships.

- **Define Deliverables:** Specify expectations such as product placements, sponsored video segments, or affiliate promotions.

- **Showcase Analytics Reports:** Provide brands with click-through rates, conversions, and impressions to highlight campaign performance.

- **Propose Multi-Phase Campaigns:** Offer scalable options like multi-month launches, seasonal promotions, or series-based sponsorships.

- **Incorporate Flexible Content Plans:** Adjust strategies based on performance, adding bonuses like Q&A sessions, giveaways, or exclusive reviews.

3. Example

- **David Dobrik's Automotive Partnership:** Popular YouTuber David Dobrik partnered with **SeatGeek**, integrating car giveaways into his content, which boosted engagement and built long-term brand trust.

- **Charli D'Amelio's Dunkin' Collaboration:** TikTok star Charli D'Amelio secured a partnership with **Dunkin'**, leading to the launch of her signature drink and increased brand visibility through viral campaigns.

- **MrBeast's Tech Sponsorships:** YouTube sensation MrBeast regularly partners with tech brands like **Honey** and **Shopify**, incorporating sponsorships naturally into challenge videos and giveaways, resulting in massive audience engagement.

4. Tips

- **Partner with Aligned Brands:** Focus on products and services that fit your audience's lifestyle or interests to build trust.

- **Use Performance Metrics:** Track engagement and conversion rates using tools like **Google Analytics** and **Social Blade** to provide sponsors with detailed reports.

- **Offer Scalable Packages:** Provide tiered sponsorship plans with multiple price points to accommodate different budgets.

- **Negotiate Extensions:** Propose long-term renewals based on successful results to create stability and growth.

5. Reflection

- **Audience Match:** What brands or products resonate most with your audience's interests?

- **Pitch Development:** How can you make your proposals stand out to potential sponsors?

6. Exercise

- **Brand Research Plan:** Identify five potential brands that match your niche and audience profile.

- **Create a Proposal Template:** Develop a sponsorship proposal with deliverables, analytics, and long-term growth opportunities.

12.5 Scaling Up with Teams, Editors, and Agencies

Hiring a team can help you grow faster by improving quality and freeing time to focus on creativity. This section explores strategies for building a support team and working with agencies to scale your streaming business effectively, using real-life public figure examples.

1. Build a Support Team for Growth

Outsourcing tasks allows you to focus on content creation while ensuring professional-quality production and engagement.

- **Editors and Designers:** Hire professionals to enhance video quality and branding. *Example: Jimmy Donaldson (MrBeast)* scaled his content by hiring editors and designers to produce engaging videos that attract millions of views.

- **Social Media Managers:** Delegate post-scheduling, replies, and campaigns. *Example: Chiara Ferragni* grew her fashion brand by relying on social media teams to manage Instagram and e-commerce strategies.

- **Community Moderators:** Employ moderators to manage chats and enforce rules. *Example: Tyler "Ninja" Blevins* uses moderators to maintain a positive chat environment during streams.

- **Virtual Assistants:** Handle emails, scheduling, and event planning. *Example: Marie Forleo* uses virtual assistants to streamline her coaching programs and online presence.

2. Work with Agencies for Professional Support

Agencies can manage marketing, sponsorships, and branding strategies to help scale faster.

- **Influencer Agencies:** Secure sponsorships and collaborations. *Example: Bretman Rock* leveraged influencer agencies to expand partnerships with beauty and lifestyle brands.

- **Marketing Consultants:** Optimize ads, SEO, and audience targeting. *Example: Graham Stephan* utilized marketing consultants to grow his personal finance YouTube channel and increase revenue streams.

- **Talent Management Firms:** Handle contracts and licensing deals. *Example: Lilly Singh* worked with talent managers to transition from YouTube success to hosting her own late-night talk show.

- **Production Agencies:** Access professional-level teams for visuals and branding. *Example: David Dobrik* collaborated with production teams to create cinematic-quality vlogs that attracted sponsorship deals.

3. Example

- **MrBeast's Scalable Production Team:** MrBeast hired editors, designers, and managers, enabling him to create high-quality content that has led to billions of views and major sponsorships.

- **Chiara Ferragni's Social Media Growth:** Chiara Ferragni scaled her fashion empire by employing marketing and design teams to manage branding and online campaigns.

- **Graham Stephan's Marketing Expansion:** Graham Stephan hired marketing consultants to optimize content and scale ad revenue, growing his finance-focused audience quickly.

4. Tips

- **Start Small and Scale Gradually:** Outsource specific tasks first, such as editing, before expanding your team.

- **Use Freelancer Platforms:** Find affordable experts on **Upwork, Fiverr,** and **PeoplePerHour** for short-term projects.

- **Track Performance Metrics:** Analyze growth and revenue improvements after hiring help.

- **Invest in Niche Skills:** Focus on experts in SEO, branding, and video transitions to improve quality.

5. Reflection

- **Task Delegation:** What tasks could you delegate to save time and improve quality?
- **Growth Plans:** How can you structure your team to support long-term scalability?

6. Exercise

- **Outsource Task List:** Make a list of tasks to outsource, such as editing and marketing.
- **Budget and Hiring Plan:** Create a budget and timeline for hiring freelancers or agencies to support growth.

Conclusion: Scaling Your Streaming Business for Growth

By leveraging advanced revenue strategies, streamers can build scalable and sustainable income streams. Whether offering courses, creating memberships, repurposing content, securing partnerships, or hiring a team, these techniques provide a roadmap for long-term success. Apply the tips, templates, and exercises in this chapter to turn your streaming career into a thriving business.

Chapter 12 Review: Advanced Revenue Streams

Chapter 12 explores advanced strategies for scaling your streaming business and creating long-term, sustainable revenue. The chapter covers offering online courses, creating paid memberships, repurposing content, securing brand deals, and scaling with teams and agencies to help you transform your streaming passion into a profitable business.

12.1 Offering Online Classes, Courses, and Consulting Services

- **Creating Online Courses** - Focus on topics your audience values and host courses on platforms like Teachable or Udemy. Structure the course with modules and engaging resources like worksheets and quizzes.

- **Providing Consulting Services** - Offer one-on-one coaching or group workshops on streaming setups, branding, or content growth strategies to generate income.

12.2 Creating Paid Membership Tiers and Special Content

- **Designing Membership Tiers** - Offer different levels of membership with exclusive perks such as private chats, bonus streams, and personalized shoutouts.

- **Platforms for Membership Programs** - Use platforms like Patreon, Ko-fi, or YouTube Memberships to manage subscriptions and offer rewards.

- **Promoting Membership Programs** - Highlight the benefits of membership during streams and offer limited-time bonuses to encourage sign-ups.

12.3 Turning Streams into Evergreen Content (Highlights and VODs)

- **Repurposing Content for Multiple Platforms** - Edit stream highlights for YouTube, TikTok, or Instagram, or turn Q&A sessions into podcasts.

- **Monetizing Evergreen Content** - Use ad revenue, affiliate links, and paid courses to generate passive income from repurposed content.

12.4 Investing in Long-Term Partnerships and Brand Deals

- **Finding and Securing Partnerships** - Partner with brands that align with your niche, and pitch proposals highlighting audience engagement and potential ROI.

- **Structuring Long-Term Deals** - Negotiate deliverables like product mentions and ad placements, and track performance to showcase ROI to brands.

12.5 Scaling Up with Teams, Editors, and Agencies

- **Building a Support Team** - Hire editors, social media managers, and community moderators to improve stream quality and free up time for creative work.

- **Working with Agencies** - Partner with influencer agencies or marketing consultants to secure sponsorships and optimize growth strategies.

Advanced revenue strategies enable streamers to diversify income streams and scale their businesses. By applying these techniques, streamers can create a profitable, sustainable career with long-term growth potential.

Chapter 13: Leveraging AI in Live Streaming

Artificial Intelligence (AI) is transforming the live streaming industry by enhancing content creation, improving audience engagement, and automating workflows. AI tools enable streamers to save time, optimize quality, and deliver highly personalized experiences. This chapter explores how AI can revolutionize your live streaming career and prepare you for an AI-powered future.

13.1 AI Tools for Automation, Editing, and Analytics

AI technology simplifies complex tasks, allowing streamers to focus more on creativity and engagement. This section explores how AI tools can streamline automation, improve editing workflows, and provide actionable insights.

1. Automate Repetitive Tasks

AI tools handle repetitive tasks, saving time and ensuring consistency.

- **Scheduling Tools:** Use platforms like **Streamlabs Chatbot** and **Zapier** to automate posting schedules, reminders, and announcements.

- **Moderation Bots:** AI-powered tools like **Nightbot** and **Moobot** filter spam, enforce chat rules, and manage interactions in real time.

- **Content Distribution:** Services like **Restream.io** allow multi-platform streaming without manual intervention, expanding audience reach.

2. Enhance Content with AI Editing Tools

AI editing tools simplify production workflows and elevate content quality.

- **Automated Video Editing:** Platforms like **Pictory AI** and **Descript** automate editing by cutting pauses, adding captions, and enhancing visuals.

- **Highlight Reels:** AI tools such as **Eklipse.gg** create highlight reels based on viewer reactions and key moments during streams.

- **Thumbnail and Graphic Design:** Design tools like **Canva** and **Fotor** use AI to create professional visuals quickly and efficiently.

3. Leverage Analytics and Insights

AI analytics tools provide actionable insights to optimize performance and audience engagement.

- **Audience Behavior Tracking:** Use **Google Analytics** and **Twitch Insights** to monitor trends, retention rates, and engagement spikes.

- **AI Sentiment Analysis:** Platforms like **StreamHatchet** evaluate viewer comments to gauge audience sentiment and preferences.

- **Keyword Optimization:** Tools such as **TubeBuddy** identify trending keywords to improve SEO for titles and descriptions.

4. Example

- **Gaming Streamer's AI Optimization:** A gaming streamer used **StreamElements'** AI-driven analytics to discover peak viewer times, boosting average viewership by 25% after adjusting their schedule.

- **Lifestyle Creator's Editing Efficiency:** A lifestyle influencer used **Descript** to edit long-form vlogs, reducing editing time by 50% and improving output consistency.

- **Tech Streamer's Keyword Optimization:** A tech-focused creator used **TubeBuddy** to optimize video descriptions, resulting in a 30% increase in search visibility.

5. Tips

- **Automate Early:** Implement AI tools for scheduling and moderation to free up time for creativity and interaction.

- **Focus on Trends:** Use AI analytics to track audience behavior and adjust content strategies based on data.

- **Test AI Tools Gradually:** Start with one AI platform to improve efficiency and scale up as needed.

- **Combine Tools for Impact:** Use multiple AI tools for editing, analytics, and automation to create a seamless workflow.

6. Reflection

- **Workflow Optimization:** What tasks in your streaming process could be automated to save time and improve efficiency?

- **Tool Evaluation:** Which AI tools can help you streamline editing, analytics, or audience engagement?

7. Exercise

- **Test AI Tools:** Experiment with one AI tool for analytics, editing, or scheduling.

- **Track Results:** Measure improvements in workflow efficiency, audience engagement, and content performance.

13.2 Customizing Viewer Experiences with AI Technology

AI allows streamers to deliver personalized and engaging experiences that make viewers feel valued. This section explores how AI tools can enhance viewer interactions, optimize streaming quality, and create immersive experiences.

1. Personalize Recommendations and Content

AI tools make it easy to deliver customized content that keeps viewers engaged.

- **AI Chatbots:** Platforms like **Botsify** and **Streamlabs Chatbot** answer FAQs, suggest personalized content, and guide viewers during streams.

- **Dynamic Content Feeds:** AI systems recommend clips, highlight reels, or upcoming streams based on viewer preferences and past behavior.

- **Interactive Overlays:** Tools like **Streamloots** and **StreamElements** enable customizable overlays for polls, mini-games, and viewer-driven actions to boost engagement.

2. Optimize Streaming Quality with AI

AI enhances video delivery to ensure a seamless viewing experience across devices.

- **AI-Optimized Video Delivery:** Platforms like **OBS Studio** and **XSplit** automatically adjust resolution and bitrate based on internet speed.

- **Multi-Device Compatibility:** AI ensures streams are optimized for desktops, mobile devices, and tablets without manual adjustments, providing consistent performance.

- **Real-Time Quality Adjustments:** Tools like **NVIDIA Broadcast** reduce background noise and improve audio clarity, maintaining professionalism.

3. Enhance Real-Time Interactions

AI-driven tools create immersive and interactive moments that increase viewer retention.

- **AI Voice Assistants:** Incorporate tools like **VoiceMod AI** to add sound effects, change voices, or create character-based personas during streams.

- **Augmented Reality (AR) Filters:** Platforms like **Snap Camera** and **Luppet** allow streamers to add interactive filters and animations to captivate audiences.

- **Audience Commands:** Use AI-enabled commands where viewers can trigger effects or animations using chat prompts.

4. Example

- **Art Streamer's Interactive Tutorials:** A creative streamer increased watch time by 30% by integrating AI-generated effects and viewer-controlled overlays into their art lessons.

- **Gaming Streamer's AR Filters:** A gamer used **Snap Camera** filters to create themed visual effects for holiday streams, leading to higher viewer participation.

- **Music Creator's AI Voice Effects:** A musician incorporated **VoiceMod AI** for interactive vocal effects during performances, attracting new subscribers.

5. Tips

- **Test AI Features Gradually:** Start with chatbots and overlays before expanding to AR filters or voice tools.

- **Focus on Engagement Tools:** Use AI features that promote audience participation, such as polls, reactions, and visual triggers.

- **Monitor Results Closely:** Track metrics like watch time, chat activity, and subscriber growth to measure impact.

- **Stay Current with Updates:** Explore new AI tools regularly to keep content fresh and innovative.

6. Reflection

- **Personalization Tools:** How can you customize viewer experiences to boost interaction and engagement?

- **Feature Testing:** What AI-powered features could make your streams more dynamic and memorable?

7. Exercise

- **Add AI Tools:** Integrate one AI-powered personalization feature, such as a chatbot, overlay, or AR filter.

- **Measure Impact:** Track its effect on viewer engagement, retention, and participation over the next three streams.

13.3 AI's Role in Moderation and Content Personalization

AI simplifies chat moderation and improves content relevance, creating safer and more enjoyable communities. This section explores how AI tools enhance moderation and deliver personalized content recommendations.

1. Use AI-Driven Moderation Tools

AI moderation tools help maintain a safe and welcoming environment for viewers.

- **Filtering Offensive Content:** Tools like **AutoMod** and **Streamlabs Chatbot** automatically detect and block inappropriate messages.

- **Sentiment Analysis:** AI platforms analyze chat tones to identify negative comments and prioritize them for moderator review.

- **Custom Commands and Responses:** Bots like **Nightbot** provide pre-set responses, rules, and warnings to streamline moderation.

- **Spam Prevention:** AI bots filter spam messages and links, ensuring clean and relevant conversations.

2. Personalize Content Recommendations

AI tools boost engagement by offering personalized suggestions and rewards.

- **AI-Powered Recommendations:** Platforms like **YouTube AI** and **Twitch Discoverability Tools** suggest streams and videos based on viewer preferences and behavior.

- **Custom Alerts and Rewards:** AI systems trigger personalized alerts for loyal viewers, such as badges, shoutouts, and exclusive rewards.

- **Dynamic Content Suggestions:** AI algorithms analyze viewing habits to suggest relevant playlists, highlight reels, or special events.
- **Audience Retention Strategies:** AI adjusts notifications and updates based on viewer activity to increase long-term engagement.

3. Example

- **Fitness Streamer's AutoMod Success:** A fitness streamer reduced inappropriate comments by 90% after integrating **Streamlabs Chatbot** and adjusting auto-moderation filters.
- **Gaming Creator's AI Recommendations:** A gamer saw a 25% boost in viewership after using **Twitch Discoverability Tools** to deliver personalized video suggestions.
- **Music Streamer's Loyalty Rewards:** A musician increased subscriptions by offering AI-triggered shoutouts and giveaways to loyal viewers during streams.

4. Tips

- **Balance AI and Human Oversight:** Use AI tools to automate tasks but keep human moderators for context-sensitive reviews.
- **Test and Refine Filters:** Adjust AI filters over time to prevent false flags or missed violations.
- **Engage Viewers with Rewards:** Set up AI-powered systems to celebrate milestones and incentivize participation.
- **Stay Updated on Features:** AI tools evolve quickly—keep testing new features to optimize performance.

5. Reflection

- **Moderation Needs:** What AI tools can you implement to improve audience safety and experience?
- **Personalization Opportunities:** How can AI recommendations and alerts enhance viewer engagement?

6. Exercise

- **Test AI Moderation Tools:** Integrate an AI moderation bot into your stream and refine its filters based on real-time performance.

- **Analyze Engagement Patterns:** Use AI analytics to track viewer behavior and optimize recommendations for better retention.

13.4 Ethical Considerations When Using AI

While AI offers incredible benefits, ethical concerns must be addressed to protect privacy, ensure fairness, and build trust. This section explores strategies for responsibly integrating AI tools into your streams.

1. Address Privacy Concerns

Transparency and consent are critical when using AI tools that collect and analyze data.

- **Data Transparency:** Inform viewers about data collection policies, especially when leveraging AI analytics or personalized recommendations.

- **Consent for AI Features:** Provide clear opt-ins for features like chat analysis, personalized suggestions, and data tracking.

- **Secure Data Storage:** Use platforms with encryption and privacy protection measures to safeguard sensitive information.

2. Ensure Algorithm Fairness and Inclusivity

AI algorithms should be monitored to prevent biases and promote fairness.

- **Avoid Discrimination:** Regularly evaluate AI performance to identify biases that might favor or disadvantage specific groups.

- **Test Algorithms Frequently:** Audit AI tools and retrain models to ensure fairness and inclusivity in content delivery.

- **Diverse Data Inputs:** Use broad data sets to train AI tools, minimizing the risk of systemic biases in recommendations.

3. Balance Automation with Authenticity

While AI improves efficiency, maintaining a human connection is essential for building trust.

- **Human Touch Matters:** Avoid over-reliance on AI by engaging in real-time, personal interactions with viewers.

- **Be Transparent About AI Usage:** Clearly explain how AI features enhance the viewing experience to foster trust.

- **Accountability for Errors:** Take responsibility for AI misjudgments and address viewer concerns promptly.

4. Example

- **Fitness Streamer's Privacy Policy Update:** A fitness influencer created a public transparency statement outlining data usage after implementing AI analytics, boosting audience trust.

- **Gaming Creator's Fairness Audit:** A gaming streamer tested AI recommendations and adjusted algorithms to avoid favoritism, improving viewer satisfaction.

- **Lifestyle Influencer's Human-AI Balance:** A lifestyle creator combined AI automation with live Q&A sessions to maintain authenticity and increase engagement.

5. Tips

- **Clarify AI Features:** Regularly communicate how AI tools are used in streams, including data collection and analysis methods.

- **Test for Biases:** Conduct audits to identify and address algorithmic biases early.

- **Emphasize Transparency:** Publish data privacy policies and provide opt-out options to respect viewer preferences.

- **Combine AI with Personalization:** Use AI for efficiency but maintain personal interactions to deepen viewer relationships.

6. Reflection

- **AI Transparency:** How can you clearly communicate AI usage and data practices to your audience?

- **Fairness Audits:** What steps can you take to test AI tools for biases and fairness?

7. Exercise

- **AI Tool Review:** Evaluate your AI tools for privacy, fairness, and inclusivity features.

- **Create Transparency Statements:** Draft a statement outlining how data is collected, stored, and used, and share it with your audience.

13.5 Preparing for an AI-Enhanced Streaming Future

AI technology is evolving rapidly, and adapting to its advancements ensures long-term growth and relevance. This section explores upcoming AI trends and essential skills to prepare for an AI-enhanced future.

1. Explore Future AI Trends

Understanding emerging trends helps streamers stay competitive and innovate their content.

- **AI-Driven Storytelling:** Platforms may use AI to script or generate stream narratives in real time, creating dynamic and engaging storylines.

- **Virtual Hosts and Avatars:** AI-generated avatars and virtual hosts can add diversity, interactivity, and flexibility to streaming setups.

- **Enhanced AI Analytics:** Real-time emotion tracking and predictive trends will shape personalized content strategies based on viewer behavior.

- **Voice and Language AI Tools:** Future advancements may include multilingual AI tools, enabling creators to reach global audiences seamlessly.

2. Develop Skills for AI Integration

Building AI proficiency ensures smooth adoption of new tools and features.

- **Learn AI Tools and Platforms:** Stay updated with tools like **OBS Studio, StreamElements, Canva AI**, and **Descript** to master editing, automation, and analytics.

- **Experiment with Emerging Features:** Test AI-driven overlays, filters, and effects to explore what resonates with your audience and keeps content fresh.

- **Expand Technical Knowledge:** Learn coding basics or AI tool customization to tailor features to your specific streaming needs.

- **Network and Collaborate:** Engage with AI developers and communities to gain early insights into cutting-edge innovations.

3. Example

- **Cooking Creator's Recipe Assistant:** A cooking influencer used AI-generated recipe suggestions and shopping lists to streamline content creation, leading to a 35% increase in engagement.

- **Travel Vlogger's Virtual Guide:** A travel vlogger incorporated AI-generated virtual tour guides in their videos, boosting viewer retention by 30% through interactive storytelling.

- **Fitness Trainer's AI Coaching Program:** A fitness creator launched AI-driven virtual coaching programs to personalize workout plans, doubling their subscriber count in six months.

4. Tips

- **Stay Informed About Trends:** Attend AI-focused webinars, workshops, and industry events to keep up with advancements.

- **Test Tools Gradually:** Incorporate AI features step-by-step to evaluate performance without overwhelming your workflow.

- **Collaborate with AI Experts:** Partner with AI developers to access early versions of tools and gain insights into future capabilities.

- **Track Performance Impact:** Use AI analytics to monitor viewer reactions and optimize content based on feedback.

5. Reflection

- **AI Adoption Plans:** How can you future-proof your streaming career by adopting AI innovations?

- **Skill Development:** What AI tools or skills could you learn to enhance your content and audience engagement?

6. Exercise

- **Create an AI Integration Plan:** Develop a 6-month strategy to test 2–3 new AI tools or features.

- **Track Results and Adjustments:** Evaluate tool performance and make adjustments to maximize their impact on your streaming goals.

Conclusion: Embracing AI for Sustainable Growth

AI is revolutionizing live streaming, enabling streamers to optimize content, automate workflows, and enhance viewer experiences. By integrating AI tools, maintaining ethical practices, and staying adaptable, you can future-proof your streaming career and continue growing in an evolving industry. Apply the strategies and exercises in this chapter to stay ahead of trends and embrace the future of AI-driven streaming.

Chapter 13 Review: Leveraging AI in Live Streaming

Chapter 13 explores the transformative potential of Artificial Intelligence (AI) in live streaming. It covers how AI tools can enhance content creation, audience engagement, and automation, ultimately helping streamers save time and optimize their workflows for a more personalized viewer experience.

13.1 AI Tools for Automation, Editing, and Analytics

- **Automating Repetitive Tasks** - Use AI-driven platforms like Streamlabs Chatbot and Zapier for scheduling, moderation, and content distribution across multiple platforms.

- **AI Editing and Content Enhancement** - Tools like Pictory AI and Eklipse.gg automate video editing, highlight reels, and thumbnail creation.

- **Advanced Analytics and Insights** - Platforms like Google Analytics and StreamHatchet provide data on audience behavior, engagement, and sentiment analysis to help optimize content.

13.2 Customizing Viewer Experiences with AI Technology

- **Personalized Recommendations and Content** - AI chatbots like Botsify suggest tailored content, while dynamic content feeds recommend clips and upcoming streams based on viewer preferences.

- **Adaptive Streaming Quality** - AI adjusts video resolution and bitrate based on the viewer's internet speed, ensuring optimal streaming across devices.

- **Enhancing Real-Time Interactions** - Use AI-powered voice assistants like VoiceMod AI and augmented reality filters from Snap Camera to create more immersive and interactive streams.

13.3 AI's Role in Moderation and Content Personalization

- **AI-Driven Moderation Tools** - Tools like AutoMod and Nightbot automatically filter offensive content and provide sentiment analysis to prioritize negative comments for review.

- **Personalized Content Recommendations** - AI systems, such as YouTube AI, suggest streams and videos based on past viewer behavior, enhancing content relevance.

13.4 Ethical Considerations When Using AI

- **Privacy Concerns** - Streamers must inform viewers about data collection practices and ensure consent for AI features like chat analysis and personalized recommendations.

- **Algorithm Bias and Fairness** - Monitor AI tools for biases and ensure they are regularly tested to maintain fairness and inclusivity.

- **Balancing Automation with Authenticity** - While AI offers automation, maintaining real-time personal interactions with viewers is key to preserving authenticity.

13.5 Preparing for an AI-Enhanced Streaming Future

- **Future AI Trends** - Upcoming AI developments include AI-driven storytelling, virtual hosts, and enhanced analytics for real-time emotion tracking.

- **Skills for AI Integration** - Streamers should stay informed by experimenting with new AI features and attending workshops to remain competitive.

AI technology is reshaping live streaming by automating workflows, optimizing content, and enhancing viewer interactions. By embracing these tools responsibly and staying adaptable, streamers can secure long-term growth and stay ahead of industry trends.

Chapter 14: Accessibility and Inclusivity in Streaming

Live streaming has the power to connect people from diverse backgrounds, but ensuring that content is accessible and inclusive requires careful planning. This chapter explores how to make streams welcoming for viewers of all abilities, languages, and cultural backgrounds. From adding subtitles to meeting legal compliance standards, this guide equips you with the tools to build an inclusive and engaging community.

14.1 Creating Accessible Streams with Subtitles and Audio Cues

Accessibility starts with removing barriers that might prevent people from engaging with your content. Subtitles and audio cues enhance accessibility for viewers with hearing or visual impairments. This section explores strategies to make streams inclusive and engaging for all audiences.

1. Provide Subtitles and Closed Captions

Captions make content accessible to viewers who are deaf or hard of hearing.

- **Auto-Generated Captions:** Use tools like **Twitch's Auto Captions**, **YouTube Live Captions**, and **Web Captioner** for live subtitles.

- **Manual Captions for Accuracy:** Edit and upload captions after streams for improved accuracy, especially for **VODs (Video on Demand)**.

- **Third-Party Software:** Tools like **Otter.ai** and **Rev.com** allow manual and AI-generated captions for better precision.

- **Language Options:** Add multilingual subtitles to reach a global audience and increase engagement.

2. Incorporate Audio Cues for Visual Elements

Audio descriptions assist visually impaired viewers by providing context for visual actions.

- **Verbal Descriptions:** Narrate visuals and actions happening on-screen to keep viewers informed.

- **Text-to-Speech Tools:** Integrate services like **Speechify** or **Voice Dream Reader** for auditory assistance and real-time text conversion.

- **Audible Alerts for Actions:** Include sound effects for notifications, polls, or chat interactions to enhance engagement.

3. Implement Best Practices for Accessibility

Optimizing streams for accessibility ensures inclusivity and professionalism.

- **Consistent Captions:** Provide captions for both live and recorded content to maintain accessibility at all times.

- **Readable Fonts and Colors:** Use high-contrast colors and legible fonts for captions and overlays to improve readability.

- **Volume Normalization:** Ensure clear audio and balanced sound levels to avoid overwhelming or inaudible content.

- **Testing Accessibility Features:** Regularly test captions and audio cues before streaming to identify errors and make adjustments.

4. Example

- **Gaming Streamer's Accessibility Upgrade:** A gaming streamer increased retention by 20% after adding live captions and integrating audio descriptions for non-visual elements, making streams more accessible to deaf and blind viewers.

- **Cooking Creator's Multilingual Captions:** A cooking influencer added captions in multiple languages, expanding their international audience and boosting engagement by 30%.

- **Fitness Instructor's Verbal Guidance:** A fitness streamer incorporated detailed verbal cues for exercises, ensuring visually impaired viewers could follow along effectively.

5. Tips

- **Test Features Before Streaming:** Verify caption accuracy and audio clarity to ensure accessibility tools function as intended.

- **Use High-Contrast Designs:** Opt for readable fonts and color schemes to enhance accessibility without straining the eyes.

- **Offer Language Options:** Expand your audience reach by including multilingual caption options.

- **Collect Feedback:** Ask viewers for feedback on accessibility features and make improvements based on their needs.

6. Reflection

- **Accessibility Features:** What features can you immediately implement to make your streams more inclusive?

- **Audience Needs:** How can you adapt captions and audio cues to better serve your audience?

7. Exercise

- **Enable Auto-Captions:** Test auto-captioning tools in your streaming software during a mock stream.

- **Add Audio Cues:** Incorporate verbal descriptions or sound alerts in your next stream and evaluate audience feedback.

14.2 Building a Welcoming and Inclusive Environment

Inclusivity goes beyond accessibility by creating a space where viewers feel respected, valued, and included. This section explores strategies for fostering inclusivity through language, events, and open conversations.

1. Promote Inclusive Language and Behavior

Creating an inclusive environment starts with intentional communication and behavior.

- **Use Gender-Neutral Terms:** Replace phrases like "guys" with "everyone" or "folks" to make all viewers feel welcome.

- **Acknowledge Diversity:** Celebrate different cultures, genders, and orientations through discussions, visuals, and chat themes.

- **Moderate Chat Effectively:** Establish clear guidelines to prevent hate speech, harassment, or discrimination, and use moderators to enforce them.

- **Highlight Pronouns:** Encourage viewers and moderators to share preferred pronouns to foster respect and understanding.

2. Host Inclusive Events and Themes

Incorporating diverse content themes builds community and encourages participation.

- **Cultural Celebrations:** Highlight international holidays, pride events, and heritage months with themed content.
- **Community Spotlights:** Feature diverse guests and collaborate with creators from underrepresented groups to amplify their voices.
- **Interactive Storytelling:** Use narratives and discussions that reflect different perspectives and life experiences to engage broader audiences.
- **Charity Events:** Organize fundraisers for causes that promote equality and inclusion, strengthening community bonds.

3. Encourage Open Conversations

Inviting feedback and fostering dialogue ensures ongoing improvement and inclusion.

- **Invite Feedback:** Ask viewers to share suggestions for improving inclusivity and regularly review input.
- **Recognize Contributions:** Highlight user-generated content, art, and shoutouts to make everyone feel valued and involved.
- **Create Safe Spaces:** Appoint moderators to handle inappropriate behavior quickly and support open conversations.
- **Interactive Q&A Sessions:** Host Q&As focused on diversity and inclusion topics to educate and inspire.

4. Example

- **Fitness Streamer's Cultural Challenges:** A fitness streamer boosted engagement by 30% after spotlighting diverse trainers and creating themed workout challenges celebrating different cultures.
- **Gaming Creator's Inclusive Panels:** A gamer collaborated with LGBTQ+ and minority creators in panel discussions, fostering conversations about representation and community growth.
- **Music Streamer's Multicultural Showcase:** A musician hosted performances celebrating global music traditions, attracting a wider and more diverse audience.

5. Tips

- **Post Community Rules:** Use pinned messages to display guidelines that promote inclusivity and respect.

- **Celebrate Diversity Regularly:** Plan events that highlight cultural moments and unique voices within your audience.

- **Engage Moderators:** Train moderators to enforce inclusivity standards and respond to issues quickly.

- **Amplify Voices:** Partner with creators from diverse backgrounds to showcase new perspectives.

6. Reflection

- **Inclusivity Planning:** What actions can you take to make your stream environment more inclusive?

- **Diverse Themes:** How can you incorporate events or collaborations that highlight underrepresented voices?

7. Exercise

- **Content Planning Ideas:** Develop three ideas for inclusive content themes or guest collaborations.

- **Implementation Schedule:** Plan a schedule to introduce these ideas and measure their impact.

14.3 Meeting Legal Compliance for Accessibility Standards

Legal standards ensure fair access to content and protect you from liability. Compliance demonstrates professionalism and care for your audience's needs. This section highlights key accessibility laws, implementation strategies, and legal protections for streamers.

1. Understand Key Accessibility Laws

Familiarity with accessibility laws helps you create inclusive content while avoiding legal risks.

- **Americans with Disabilities Act (ADA):** Requires digital platforms to accommodate people with disabilities by providing equal access.

- **Web Content Accessibility Guidelines (WCAG):** Sets global standards for captioning, screen reader compatibility, visual clarity, and alternative text.

- **Section 508 Compliance:** Ensures digital resources used by federal agencies are accessible to employees and the public.

- **Broadcast Accessibility Laws:** In some regions, live broadcasts may require closed captions and descriptive audio features to comply with local regulations.

2. Ensure Compliance with Accessibility Standards

Implementing compliance tools and strategies improves accessibility for all viewers.

- **Audit Your Stream Setup:** Use tools like **WAVE** and **Axe Accessibility Checker** to test compliance with WCAG standards.

- **Implement Captioning Features:** Provide auto-captions and manually edited captions for improved accuracy on both live and recorded content.

- **Optimize Layouts and Navigation:** Ensure layouts, buttons, and menus are keyboard- and voice-command-friendly.

- **Screen Reader Compatibility:** Verify that text elements and buttons are labeled for accessibility software.

- **Color Contrast Testing:** Use tools like **Contrast Checker** to confirm that text and visuals meet readability standards.

3. Protect Yourself with Legal Policies

Establishing clear policies safeguards your content and reinforces transparency.

- **Privacy Policies:** Clearly communicate how viewer data is collected, stored, and used, particularly with AI tools and analytics.

- **Terms of Service:** Include disclaimers about AI tools, third-party features, and accessibility tools used in streams.

- **Copyright and Fair Use Notices:** Clarify ownership of original and licensed content to avoid disputes.

- **User Agreements:** Require agreements for interactive features to ensure legal compliance.

4. Example

- **Gaming Creator's Accessibility Audit:** A gaming creator used **WAVE** to test and redesign overlays and captions, improving compliance and boosting viewer satisfaction.

- **Lifestyle Influencer's Caption Policy:** A lifestyle creator implemented multilingual captions and published a compliance statement, increasing international viewership by 20%.

- **Fitness Streamer's Legal Review:** A fitness instructor updated privacy policies and terms of service to cover AI features, ensuring transparency and avoiding legal issues.

5. Tips

- **Test Accessibility Regularly:** Use auditing tools frequently to identify and fix compliance gaps.

- **Update Features as Needed:** Keep captions, layouts, and AI tools aligned with evolving laws and technology.

- **Consult Accessibility Experts:** Work with legal and accessibility professionals to review and improve compliance efforts.

- **Publish Policies Publicly:** Make privacy policies and terms of service easily accessible to viewers.

6. Reflection

- **Accessibility Review:** Are your streams compliant with accessibility laws and best practices?

- **Improvement Areas:** What updates can you implement to ensure compliance and enhance viewer inclusivity?

7. Exercise

- **Accessibility Testing Tools:** Use a testing tool like **WAVE** or **Axe Accessibility Checker** to evaluate your stream setup.

- **Compliance Checklist:** Create a checklist for ongoing updates, including captions, privacy policies, and layout accessibility.

14.4 Catering to Non-English Audiences with Subtitles

Expanding to global audiences requires language support to make your content accessible worldwide. This section explores strategies for adding multilingual subtitles, localizing content, and promoting accessibility for international viewers.

1. Add Multilingual Subtitles

Subtitles help break language barriers and attract global viewers.

- **AI Translation Tools:** Use platforms like **Kapwing** and **Sonix AI** to auto-translate captions into multiple languages quickly.

- **Manual Translations:** Hire freelance translators on platforms like **Fiverr** or **Upwork** for higher accuracy and cultural relevance.

- **YouTube Auto-Translate:** Enable automatic subtitle translations to make VODs (Video on Demand) accessible to viewers worldwide.

- **Hybrid Approach:** Combine AI tools with manual editing to ensure both speed and accuracy.

2. Localize Content for Different Regions

Customizing content for cultural relevance improves engagement and relatability.

- **Adapt Language Tone:** Use culturally appropriate terms, humor, and expressions when addressing international audiences.

- **Highlight Global Themes:** Incorporate topics that resonate globally, such as international trends, holidays, and cultural celebrations.

- **Include Regional References:** Tailor visuals, stories, and examples to match regional preferences and traditions.

- **Multilingual Graphics and Text Overlays:** Ensure captions and on-screen text are localized for enhanced comprehension.

3. Promote Multilingual Support

Market your multilingual content to attract international audiences and build a global following.

- **Announce Features on Social Media:** Promote language options and subtitle features in posts, reels, and stories.

- **Create Playlists by Language:** Organize videos by language to make streams easier to find for non-English speakers.

- **Collaborate with International Influencers:** Partner with creators who speak different languages to expand reach.

- **Audience Polls:** Use surveys to determine which languages are most preferred by your viewers and prioritize translations accordingly.

4. Example

- **Travel Streamer's Multilingual Growth:** A travel streamer gained 15% more subscribers after adding Spanish and French subtitles to their VODs, attracting international viewers.

- **Cooking Creator's Language Expansion:** A cooking influencer offered subtitles in Italian and Portuguese, boosting recipe views by 25% in European markets.

- **Tech Reviewer's Global Impact:** A tech creator provided multilingual tutorials with Japanese and German translations, tripling their reach in international regions.

5. Tips

- **Test Subtitle Accuracy:** Review AI-generated translations for errors and make manual edits as needed.

- **Offer Popular Languages First:** Start with widely spoken languages like Spanish, French, and Mandarin before expanding further.

- **Highlight Language Options in Descriptions:** Clearly state available translations in titles and descriptions to attract international viewers.

- **Engage with Global Viewers:** Respond to comments in their preferred languages to build stronger connections.

6. Reflection

- **Language Expansion Plans:** Which languages could help you expand your audience reach?

- **Localization Improvements:** How can you make your content more relatable to international viewers?

7. Exercise

- **Translate Content:** Translate one video into another language using AI tools or manual services.

- **Promote Internationally:** Share the translated video on international forums and monitor audience engagement.

14.5 Tools to Boost Accessibility and Viewer Comfort

Several tools make it easier to implement accessibility features and enhance comfort for all viewers. This section highlights tools for captioning, audio, visual enhancements, and chat moderation to create a more inclusive streaming experience.

1. Captioning Tools

Captions improve accessibility for viewers with hearing impairments and expand audience reach.

- **Rev.com:** Provides professional transcription and captioning services for live and recorded content.

- **Web Captioner:** Offers free, real-time captions for live streams, ensuring immediate accessibility.

- **Otter.ai:** Generates automated captions and transcripts, ideal for post-stream edits and VODs.

2. Audio Accessibility Tools

Clear and high-quality audio ensures better engagement and accessibility.

- **Auphonic:** Enhances audio quality, reduces background noise, and balances sound levels for clarity.

- **Speechify:** Converts text into audio, offering support for visually impaired viewers through screen readers.

- **Krisp.ai:** Removes background noise during live streams and voice chats, improving clarity for listeners.

3. Visual and Chat Accessibility Tools

Visual enhancements and moderation tools create a user-friendly environment.

- **Streamlabs OBS Accessibility Extensions:** Improves visual clarity, supports screen readers, and adds customizable overlays.

- **Contrast Checker:** Tests color contrast to ensure visual elements meet accessibility standards.

- **Nightbot and AutoMod:** AI-powered moderation tools that filter offensive language and enforce community rules.

- **Colorblind-Friendly Tools:** Platforms like **Sim Daltonism** simulate colorblindness to help design inclusive visuals.

4. Example

- **Gaming Creator's Captioning Upgrade:** A gaming creator implemented **Rev.com** for captions, increasing engagement by 20% from hearing-impaired viewers.

- **Podcaster's Audio Enhancement:** A podcaster used **Auphonic** to improve audio quality, leading to clearer recordings and higher listener retention.

- **Fitness Streamer's Chat Moderation:** A fitness influencer added **Nightbot** to filter offensive comments, creating a safer and more positive community space.

5. Tips

- **Test Tools Before Streaming:** Verify compatibility and performance of accessibility tools to avoid disruptions.

- **Combine Tools for Maximum Impact:** Use a mix of captioning, audio, and visual aids for comprehensive accessibility.

- **Gather Feedback:** Ask viewers to share feedback about accessibility features and make improvements based on their needs.

- **Regular Updates:** Keep tools updated to maintain performance and ensure compliance with accessibility standards.

6. Reflection

- **Accessibility Tools:** What tools could immediately improve accessibility and viewer comfort in your streams?

- **Implementation Strategy:** How can you test and integrate new tools effectively?

7. Exercise

- **Test Accessibility Tools:** Use one accessibility tool, such as captions or noise reduction, in your next stream.

- **Measure Feedback:** Collect feedback from viewers and track engagement to evaluate the tool's impact.

Conclusion: Embracing Accessibility for Growth and Inclusion

Prioritizing accessibility and inclusivity enhances viewer satisfaction, builds stronger communities, and expands your reach. By implementing subtitles, ensuring legal compliance, catering to multilingual audiences, and leveraging accessibility tools, you can create a welcoming space for everyone. Apply the strategies in this chapter to make inclusivity a cornerstone of your streaming success.

Chapter 14 Review: Accessibility and Inclusivity in Streaming

Chapter 14 explores the importance of creating accessible and inclusive live streams that cater to a diverse audience. It covers strategies to make content welcoming for viewers of all abilities, languages, and cultural backgrounds, ensuring a more engaging and respectful community.

14.1 Creating Accessible Streams with Subtitles and Audio Cues

- **Subtitles and Closed Captions** - Use auto-generated captions (e.g., Twitch's Auto Captions, YouTube Live Captions) or edit manually for accuracy, especially for VODs.

- **Audio Cues for Visual Elements** - Incorporate verbal descriptions and text-to-speech tools to assist visually impaired viewers.

- **Best Practices for Implementation** - Ensure consistent captions and use high-contrast fonts and colors for readability.

14.2 Building a Welcoming and Inclusive Environment

- **Promoting Inclusive Language and Behavior** - Use gender-neutral language, acknowledge diversity, and establish chat moderation guidelines to prevent discrimination.

- **Hosting Inclusive Events and Themes** - Celebrate different cultures and collaborate with underrepresented creators to highlight diverse perspectives.

- **Encouraging Open Conversations** - Solicit feedback, recognize contributions, and create safe spaces through dedicated moderators.

14.3 Meeting Legal Compliance for Accessibility Standards

- **Key Accessibility Laws** - Understand compliance with the ADA, WCAG, and Section 508 to ensure your content is accessible.

- **Ensuring Compliance** - Audit your stream setup using tools like WAVE to test for accessibility standards and ensure all content includes captions.

- **Legal Protections** - Provide clear privacy policies and terms of service, particularly when using AI tools or third-party services.

14.4 Catering to Non-English Audiences with Subtitles

- **Adding Multilingual Subtitles** - Use AI tools like Kapwing and Sonix for automatic translation, or hire translators for greater accuracy.

- **Localizing Content for Different Regions** - Adapt language tone and content to be culturally relevant for international audiences.

- **Promoting Multilingual Support** - Announce multilingual features and organize content by language to attract global viewers.

14.5 Tools to Boost Accessibility and Viewer Comfort

- **Captioning Tools** - Use platforms like Rev.com for professional captions and Web Captioner for real-time captions during streams.

- **Audio Accessibility Tools** - Enhance audio quality with tools like Auphonic and Speechify for text-to-speech.

- **Visual and Chat Accessibility** - Use Streamlabs OBS accessibility extensions and moderation tools like Nightbot for better visual clarity and to filter offensive language.

Embracing accessibility and inclusivity in streaming creates a welcoming space that broadens your reach and fosters a more engaged community. By implementing these tools and strategies, you can ensure your streams are accessible to all viewers and build stronger, more diverse audiences.

Chapter 15: Staying Innovative and Adapting to Trends

The live streaming industry is constantly evolving, driven by technological advancements, changing algorithms, and shifting audience preferences. Streamers who embrace innovation and adapt quickly to trends can stay competitive, grow their reach, and maintain long-term success. This chapter explores how to leverage emerging technologies, track trends, and create flexible strategies to future-proof your career.

15.1 Exploring Emerging Technologies: VR, AR, and Interactive Tools

New technologies like Virtual Reality (VR), Augmented Reality (AR), and interactive tools are redefining live streaming by enhancing viewer engagement and offering immersive experiences. This section explores how to integrate these innovations into your streams.

1. Integrate Virtual Reality (VR)

VR creates fully immersive experiences that captivate tech-savvy audiences.

- **VR Streaming Platforms:** Use tools like **AltspaceVR** and **VRChat** to host virtual events, concerts, and meetups.

- **360-Degree Streaming:** Platforms like **YouTube VR** allow viewers to explore immersive 360-degree environments for dynamic storytelling.

- **VR Games and Tutorials:** Stream VR gameplay, walkthroughs, and training sessions to attract gaming and technology enthusiasts.

- **Virtual Tours:** Offer guided VR experiences for travel, art galleries, or real estate audiences to expand niche content.

2. Enhance Streams with Augmented Reality (AR)

AR overlays and filters add visual appeal and interactivity to streams.

- **AR Overlays:** Tools like **Snap Camera** add real-time effects, animations, and masks to personalize streams and engage viewers.

- **Interactive Filters and Tools:** Platforms like **Lightstream** enable dynamic AR effects and visuals that respond to viewer interactions.

- **Virtual Avatars:** AI-generated avatars from tools like **Luppet** create fun, character-based personas for interactive storytelling and gaming streams.

- **Product Demonstrations:** Use AR overlays to highlight product features during tutorials and reviews.

3. Engage Viewers with Interactive Tools

Interactive tools transform passive viewing into active participation.

- **Polls and Quizzes:** Platforms like **Streamlabs** allow viewers to vote, answer questions, and influence content decisions in real time.

- **Gamification Tools:** Add games like **Marbles on Stream** to encourage engagement and viewer interaction during broadcasts.

- **Live Donations and Reactions:** Tools like **Streamelements** enable live alerts for donations, comments, and reactions to boost excitement and community interaction.

- **Trivia Challenges:** Host trivia contests to keep audiences engaged while reinforcing themes in your content.

4. Example

- **Music Streamer's Virtual Concert:** A music streamer increased their audience by 35% by hosting a virtual concert with interactive AR effects and 360-degree video options.

- **Travel Vlogger's VR Tours:** A travel vlogger gained global traction by offering VR-based city tours and cultural explorations, attracting viewers from multiple countries.

- **Educational Creator's Interactive Tools:** An educator used polls and quizzes during science streams, improving viewer retention by 40%.

5. Tips

- **Test Emerging Tools Gradually:** Introduce VR and AR elements step-by-step to ensure smooth integration without overwhelming viewers.

- **Engage Early Adopters:** Market VR and AR features to tech-savvy audiences most likely to explore new technologies.

- **Optimize for Accessibility:** Ensure interactive tools and visual effects are compatible with accessibility features for inclusive engagement.

- **Track Engagement Metrics:** Measure viewer responses to new technologies and adjust content based on feedback.

6. Reflection

- **Technology Integration:** How can VR, AR, or interactive tools enhance your streams and attract a broader audience?

- **Content Ideas:** What themes or activities could leverage these technologies for maximum impact?

7. Exercise

- **Research New Technologies:** Explore one emerging technology, such as VR or AR, and analyze how it fits your niche.

- **Create a Technology Plan:** Develop a step-by-step plan to incorporate VR, AR, or interactive tools into your next live stream.

15.2 Keeping Up with Platform Updates and Algorithm Changes

Live streaming platforms frequently update algorithms, features, and monetization tools. Staying informed about these changes is essential for growth. This section highlights strategies for tracking updates, adapting to algorithm changes, and staying ahead of competitors.

1. Track Platform Updates

Keeping up with updates helps you leverage new features and tools effectively.

- **Follow Official Blogs and Forums:** Platforms like **Twitch Blog**, **YouTube Creators**, and **Facebook Newsroom** post regular updates about new features and policies.

- **Join Creator Communities:** Participate in forums like **Reddit Streaming Subreddits** or **Discord groups** to share insights and learn from others' experiences.

- **Use Analytics Tools:** Monitor changes in performance through **YouTube Studio** and **Twitch Dashboard** to quickly adapt to shifts in algorithms and viewer behavior.
- **Attend Webinars and Conferences:** Stay ahead by joining events like **VidCon** or **StreamFest** where updates and trends are discussed by industry experts.

2. Adapt to Algorithm Changes

Algorithms prioritize visibility based on optimization and engagement.

- **SEO Optimization:** Update titles, descriptions, and tags with trending keywords. Use tools like **TubeBuddy** and **VidIQ** for keyword research and tag suggestions.
- **Content Timing:** Schedule streams during peak engagement hours identified through analytics to maximize reach and visibility.
- **Focus on Engagement Metrics:** Boost likes, comments, and shares by encouraging participation with polls, questions, and giveaways.
- **Experiment with New Formats:** Test new features such as **YouTube Shorts**, **Twitch Clips**, and **Instagram Reels** to expand your reach.

3. Example

- **Gaming Streamer's Short-Form Success:** A gaming streamer boosted views by 20% by adopting **YouTube Shorts** immediately after its launch, repurposing clips from live streams into short, engaging highlights.
- **Lifestyle Influencer's Algorithm Adaptation:** A lifestyle creator used **Instagram Reels** to capitalize on algorithm preferences for video content, increasing follower engagement by 35%.
- **Tech Reviewer's Early Feature Adoption:** A tech creator leveraged **Twitch Predictions** to increase viewer participation, growing chat activity by 40%.

4. Tips

- **Test Features Early:** Experiment with new platform tools as soon as they're released to stay competitive.
- **Monitor Analytics Regularly:** Track performance metrics weekly to detect trends and adjust strategies quickly.

- **Engage with Platform Updates:** Provide feedback to platforms about features to stay involved and informed about upcoming releases.

- **Diversify Platforms:** Explore multiple platforms to reduce reliance on a single algorithm and expand audience reach.

5. Reflection

- **Update Strategies:** How do you stay updated on platform changes, and what tools can you add to track updates more effectively?

- **Adaptation Plans:** What adjustments can you make to align with recent algorithm updates and features?

6. Exercise

- **Subscribe to Updates:** Subscribe to at least three platform newsletters or communities to track news and trends.

- **Weekly Monitoring Checklist:** Create a checklist to review analytics, test features, and adapt strategies based on platform updates.

15.3 Combining Live and Pre-Recorded Content for Hybrid Models

Hybrid content models blend live and pre-recorded videos, offering flexibility and maximizing engagement. This section explores the benefits, ideas, and strategies for integrating hybrid content effectively.

1. Benefits of Hybrid Models

Hybrid models provide versatility and optimize content distribution.

- **Extended Reach:** Pre-recorded content attracts viewers outside live streaming hours, ensuring ongoing engagement.

- **Efficiency:** Streamers can create evergreen content, allowing live streams to focus on real-time interaction and audience engagement.

- **Content Recycling:** Repurpose highlights, tutorials, and Q&As into short videos, podcasts, or reels to maximize value.

- **Flexible Scheduling:** Pre-recorded content keeps channels active during breaks or travel periods without requiring live presence.

2. Ideas for Hybrid Content

Combining live and pre-recorded formats opens up creative possibilities for diverse audiences.

- **Live-to-Recorded Tutorials:** Stream live demonstrations, then edit and repurpose them into step-by-step guides for VODs or online courses.

- **Highlight Reels and Clips:** Use tools like **Eklipse.gg** and **Streamlabs Highlights** to extract and edit key moments for TikTok, Instagram, and YouTube Shorts.

- **Premieres and Watch Parties:** Schedule pre-recorded videos as "live premieres" to interact with viewers in real time through chat.

- **Countdowns and Trailers:** Create teasers for upcoming live events to build anticipation and increase attendance.

- **Product Demos and Reviews:** Combine live product launches with pre-recorded deep dives for detailed analysis.

3. Example

- **Tech Streamer's Growth Strategy:** A tech streamer grew their YouTube channel by 40% by combining live product reviews with pre-recorded tutorials optimized for SEO.

- **Fitness Influencer's Workout Series:** A fitness creator streamed live workout sessions and edited them into pre-recorded challenges, boosting subscriptions by 35%.

- **Cooking Creator's Recipe Tutorials:** A chef used hybrid content to share live cooking demos followed by edited recipe breakdowns, doubling views within three months.

4. Tips

- **Test Content Formats:** Use hybrid models to experiment with new ideas and formats without the pressure of live performance.

- **Repurpose High-Engagement Clips:** Analyze live streams for popular moments and turn them into short-form videos for social media.

- **Sync Themes Across Formats:** Maintain consistent branding by aligning live and pre-recorded themes for seamless viewer experiences.

- **Schedule Strategically:** Alternate between live and pre-recorded content to maintain consistency and avoid gaps in posting schedules.

5. Reflection

- **Content Balance:** What pre-recorded content can complement your live streams and extend audience engagement?

- **Optimization Strategy:** How can you repurpose live streams into evergreen content to maximize reach?

6. Exercise

- **Plan Hybrid Content Schedule:** Develop a one-month schedule combining live and pre-recorded videos.

- **Analyze Engagement Metrics:** Track performance across both formats to determine which strategies resonate most with your audience.

15.4 Trend Forecasting and Event Planning for Growth

Anticipating trends and planning events around them ensures relevance and keeps your audience engaged. This section highlights strategies for identifying trends and creating event plans to drive growth.

1. Track Trends for Content Inspiration

Staying ahead of trends helps streamers create timely, engaging content.

- **Monitor Social Media Trends:** Use tools like **Google Trends**, **TrendWatching**, and **BuzzSumo** to identify rising topics and viral hashtags.

- **Analyze Competitors:** Watch top creators in your niche to spot new formats, topics, and engagement strategies early.

- **Engage with Industry News:** Follow influencers, creators, and tech blogs for updates on technology, events, and streaming innovations.

- **Leverage Analytics Tools:** Use **Twitch Insights** and **YouTube Studio** to monitor trending content and audience preferences within your platform.

2. Develop Event Planning Strategies

Aligning events with trends creates excitement and draws in larger audiences.

- **Seasonal Themes:** Plan content around holidays, festivals, or trending challenges like #HalloweenStreams or #NewYearGoals.

- **Giveaways and Collaborations:** Organize giveaways tied to trends or partner with other streamers to host themed multi-streamer events.

- **Hashtag Campaigns:** Tie streams to trending hashtags and challenges for wider visibility across platforms.

- **Milestone Events:** Celebrate milestones like subscriber anniversaries, achievements, or product launches with themed content.

- **Countdown Streams:** Build anticipation with countdown events leading to major releases or announcements.

3. Example

- **Lifestyle Streamer's Holiday Growth:** A lifestyle streamer gained 50,000 views by participating in trending challenges and holiday-themed events promoted across TikTok and Instagram.

- **Fitness Influencer's Seasonal Challenge:** A fitness creator boosted memberships by 40% after launching a "30-Day Summer Challenge" aligned with health trends.

- **Tech Reviewer's Launch Event:** A tech streamer capitalized on a new product release by hosting a live review and Q&A session, increasing subscriber growth by 25%.

4. Tips

- **Act Quickly on Trends:** Incorporate trending topics promptly to maintain relevance while ensuring authenticity.

- **Promote Across Platforms:** Use social media, newsletters, and collaborations to maximize event exposure.

- **Engage Viewers in Planning:** Let your audience vote on themes, challenges, or prizes to increase interaction.

- **Track Event Performance:** Review analytics to measure success and refine future event strategies.

5. Reflection

- **Trend Integration:** What trends can you incorporate into your content to boost engagement?

- **Event Ideas:** How can you structure events to leverage seasonal themes or trending topics?

6. Exercise

- **Trend Tracking Plan:** Identify and monitor 3 emerging trends using tools like **Google Trends** and **BuzzSumo**.

- **Event Planning Brainstorm:** Develop event ideas related to each trend, including themes, formats, and promotional strategies.

15.5 Staying Flexible Amid Industry Changes

Adaptability is key to thriving in an industry that evolves rapidly. This section explores strategies to remain flexible, embrace change, and continue growing in a dynamic streaming environment.

1. Develop Strategies for Flexibility

Staying agile allows creators to adjust quickly to industry shifts and audience preferences.

- **Diversify Platforms:** Stream across multiple platforms like **Twitch**, **YouTube**, and **Facebook Live** to reduce dependence on any single source.

- **Experiment with Content Formats:** Test short-form videos, podcasts, Q&A sessions, and collaborations to explore new engagement methods.

- **Embrace Feedback:** Analyze viewer feedback and analytics to refine strategies and create content that resonates with your audience.

- **Pivot Quickly to Trends:** Stay open to incorporating emerging tools and formats, such as **TikTok Shorts** or **YouTube Clips**, to maintain relevance.

2. Invest in Lifelong Learning

Continuous learning helps creators stay ahead of industry developments and technological advancements.

- **Take Online Courses:** Learn new tools and techniques through platforms like **Skillshare, Coursera**, and **Udemy** to improve content creation and marketing.

- **Attend Webinars and Conferences:** Stay updated on trends and build connections by participating in events like **VidCon, StreamFest**, and niche-specific webinars.

- **Join Creator Communities:** Engage in **Discord groups** and **Reddit forums** for advice, support, and insight from fellow creators.

- **Follow Industry Leaders:** Track influencers and thought leaders for tips on adapting to new technologies and formats.

3. Example

- **Beauty Influencer's Algorithm Shift:** A beauty streamer adapted to algorithm changes on **Instagram Reels**, growing her follower count by 30% within 60 days.

- **Gaming Creator's Platform Expansion:** A gaming streamer expanded from **Twitch** to **YouTube Live** and **TikTok**, gaining 40% more engagement by reaching broader audiences.

- **Music Streamer's Content Experimentation:** A musician tested short-form covers on **YouTube Shorts**, leading to viral growth and doubling subscribers in three months.

4. Tips

- **Embrace Change as Opportunity:** Treat shifts in the industry as moments to innovate rather than setbacks.

- **Balance Testing and Stability:** Experiment with new formats while maintaining consistent core content to retain existing audiences.

- **Stay Informed and Proactive:** Monitor trends and industry updates to anticipate and prepare for changes.

- **Leverage Data:** Use analytics tools to track performance and adjust strategies based on data-driven insights.

5. Reflection

- **Adaptability Check:** What changes can you make today to improve flexibility and growth?

- **Learning Goals:** What new skills or tools can you learn to future-proof your streaming career?

6. Exercise

- **Create an Adaptability Plan:** Develop a 3-month plan with milestones for testing new content styles, tools, or platforms.

- **Track Progress:** Measure engagement and performance improvements as you experiment with new strategies.

Conclusion: Thriving in a Changing Streaming Landscape

Staying innovative and adaptable is critical for long-term success in live streaming. By embracing new technologies, keeping up with platform updates, blending live and pre-recorded content, forecasting trends, and maintaining flexibility, you can remain competitive and future-proof your career. Apply the tools and strategies in this chapter to lead the next wave of streaming innovation.

Chapter 15 Review: Staying Innovative and Adapting to Trends

Chapter 15 emphasizes the importance of staying ahead in the rapidly evolving live streaming industry. It covers emerging technologies, platform updates, hybrid content models, trend forecasting, and the flexibility needed to maintain long-term success.

15.1 Exploring Emerging Technologies: VR, AR, and Interactive Tools

- **Virtual Reality (VR) Integration** - Use VR platforms like AltspaceVR and 360-degree streaming on YouTube to offer immersive experiences.

- **Augmented Reality (AR) Enhancements** - Add AR overlays and interactive effects using tools like Snap Camera and Lightstream to engage viewers.

- **Interactive Tools for Engagement** - Platforms like Streamlabs allow for live polls, quizzes, and gamification to boost viewer participation.

15.2 Keeping Up with Platform Updates and Algorithm Changes

- **Tracking Platform Updates** - Stay informed by following official blogs, joining creator communities, and using analytics tools like YouTube Studio and Twitch Dashboard.

- **Adapting to Algorithm Changes** - Update SEO practices, optimize content timing, and focus on engagement metrics to boost visibility in platform algorithms.

15.3 Combining Live and Pre-Recorded Content for Hybrid Models

- **Benefits of Hybrid Models** - Hybrid content allows for greater reach, content recycling, and more efficient use of time.

- **Ideas for Hybrid Content** - Create live-to-recorded tutorials, highlight reels, and scheduled premieres to engage viewers in real-time and later.

15.4 Trend Forecasting and Event Planning for Growth

- **Tracking Trends** - Monitor tools like Google Trends and TrendWatching, and analyze competitors to spot rising topics early.

- **Event Planning Strategies** - Plan seasonal themes, giveaways, and collaborations, and use trending hashtags to amplify visibility and engagement.

15.5 Staying Flexible Amid Industry Changes

- **Strategies for Flexibility** - Diversify platforms, experiment with content formats, and embrace viewer feedback to remain adaptable.

- **Investing in Lifelong Learning** - Continuously learn new tools and techniques through online courses and webinars to stay competitive in the evolving landscape.

Adapting to trends and staying flexible is crucial to thriving in the streaming industry. By leveraging new technologies, staying updated on platform changes, and embracing emerging trends, streamers can remain innovative and future-proof their careers.

Chapter 16: Real-World Success Stories

Success in live streaming requires more than talent—it demands strategy, adaptability, and perseverance. In this chapter, we'll dive into real-world success stories, highlighting how top streamers overcame challenges, reinvented themselves, and scaled their brands into profitable ventures. These examples will help you gain insights, develop strategies, and apply proven methods to your own streaming journey.

16.1 Lessons from Top Twitch and YouTube Streamers

Top streamers didn't achieve success overnight—they built it step-by-step by identifying opportunities, adapting strategies, and prioritizing audience connections. This section explores lessons and tools from successful creators to inspire your growth.

1. Key Strategies from Successful Streamers

Successful streamers emphasize consistency, engagement, and diversification.

- **Consistency and Persistence**
    - **Ninja (Tyler Blevins):** Gained millions of followers by streaming daily, maintaining consistent themes, and interacting regularly with fans.
    - **Kai Cenat:** Dominated Twitch with high-energy content and consistency, becoming one of the platform's most-followed streamers.
    - **IShowSpeed (Speed):** Captivated younger audiences through humor, energy, and viral moments.
    - **Takeaway:** Stick to a regular schedule to build anticipation and trust.

- **Community Building and Interaction**
    - **Pokimane (Imane Anys):** Built loyalty through genuine interaction, humor, and transparent conversations about her journey.
    - **Ludwig Ahgren:** Grew a dedicated fan base by hosting events, challenges, and interactive Q&A sessions.

- o **Takeaway:** Engage viewers with polls, shoutouts, and personal stories to form deeper connections.

- **Diversification of Content**

  - o **Valkyrae (Rachell Hofstetter):** Expanded from gaming into lifestyle and vlogs, broadening her reach.

  - o **DrLupo (Benjamin Lupo):** Shifted focus to charity streams, raising millions and attracting new audiences.

  - o **Takeaway:** Introduce new formats like tutorials or behind-the-scenes footage to attract diverse audiences.

2. Growth Tools Used by Top Streamers

Top streamers leverage technology to optimize their streams and expand their reach.

- **Twitch Insights and Analytics:** Track growth patterns and engagement trends to refine strategies.

- **Streamlabs and OBS Studio:** Optimize production quality for professional-looking streams with overlays and alerts.

- **Social Media Integrations:** Use platforms like **Instagram**, **TikTok**, and **Twitter** to drive traffic to streams and expand audiences.

- **Editing Tools:** Utilize programs like **Premiere Pro** and **Canva** to create polished highlight reels and promotional material.

3. Example

- **Gaming Streamer's Expansion:** A rising gamer doubled subscribers by combining daily streams with edited highlight reels for YouTube.

- **Lifestyle Creator's Branding Growth:** A vlogger tripled engagement by adding personal vlogs and DIY tutorials alongside live streams.

- **Music Streamer's Viral Strategy:** A musician used TikTok trends to promote their streams, resulting in a 50% boost in live audience numbers.

4. Tips

- **Analyze Competitor Habits:** Study the branding, content types, and schedules of top streamers to refine your approach.

- **Balance Creativity and Consistency:** Experiment with new formats while sticking to a predictable schedule.

- **Use Analytics to Improve Performance:** Track metrics regularly and adjust based on viewer behavior and preferences.

- **Promote Across Platforms:** Build visibility by repurposing content for multiple platforms like **TikTok, Instagram**, and **YouTube Shorts**.

5. Reflection

- **Streamer Strategies:** What specific strategies can you borrow from your favorite streamer to improve your content?

- **Growth Tools:** How can you incorporate analytics or editing tools to boost quality and engagement?

6. Exercise

- **Analyze Top Streamers:** Select two successful streamers, analyze their top-performing videos, and identify at least three strategies to test in your own streams.

- **Content Planning:** Develop a 1-month schedule that integrates lessons learned from their approaches.

16.2 Creative Strategies That Transformed Channels

Streamers often stand out by creating unique, interactive, and innovative experiences that captivate audiences. This section explores bold experiments, gamification techniques, and strategies to make streams memorable.

1. Bold Content Experiments

Streamers who take risks and test creative formats often achieve viral success.

- **Ludwig Ahgren's Subathon:** Hosted a record-breaking, 31-day streaming marathon, engaging viewers with milestones, giveaways, and collaborations.

    - **Takeaway:** Plan special events that generate buzz and attract viral attention.

- **Mizkif's Interactive Polls:** Created live polls and audience-driven decisions, turning viewers into active participants.

- - **Takeaway:** Use chat polls and voting games to keep viewers invested in outcomes.
- **Amouranth's IRL Streams:** Combined lifestyle vlogging with live Q&A sessions, diversifying her audience base.
  - - **Takeaway:** Blend casual and structured content for variety and engagement.
- **DrLupo's Charity Streams:** Focused on charity fundraisers, raising millions and building goodwill with audiences.
  - - **Takeaway:** Organize meaningful events to create impact and long-term loyalty.

2. Gamification and Challenges

Adding interactive elements transforms passive viewers into active participants.

- **Viewer Challenges:** Introduce challenges like game mods, dares, or speedruns to create excitement and participation.
- **Giveaways and Trivia Contests:** Reward loyal viewers with prizes during trivia games or random draws.
- **Theme Nights and Role-Play Events:** Develop themed nights such as **Retro Gaming** or **Cosplay Contests** to attract niche audiences and spark creativity.
- **Community Goals and Unlockables:** Set donation or engagement milestones to unlock exclusive content or events.

3. Example

- **Fitness Streamer's Challenge Series:** A fitness creator launched a "30-Day Fitness Challenge" with prizes for participants, doubling their subscriber count.
- **Music Streamer's Song Requests:** A musician used viewer song requests as a form of gamification, increasing engagement by 45%.
- **Gaming Creator's Tournament Night:** A gamer hosted themed tournaments and prize giveaways, attracting competitive viewers and boosting subscriptions.

4. Tips

- **Experiment with Formats:** Test experimental formats like interactive games, role-play events, or challenge nights to keep streams dynamic.
- **Engage the Audience:** Create polls, Q&As, and interactive decisions to make viewers feel involved.
- **Celebrate Milestones:** Highlight achievements and recognize top contributors to maintain loyalty.
- **Promote Events in Advance:** Build excitement with countdowns and teasers across social platforms.

5. Reflection

- **Creative Planning:** What creative ideas can you incorporate to make your streams stand out and attract attention?
- **Engagement Strategies:** How can you make viewers feel more involved in your content?

6. Exercise

- **Plan a Themed Event:** Design a themed event, such as a challenge night or trivia contest, and outline tasks, rewards, and audience involvement strategies.
- **Review Audience Response:** Analyze feedback and performance metrics to refine future creative strategies.

16.3 Overcoming Failures and Reinventing Content

Every streamer faces setbacks, but the ability to adapt separates those who fail from those who thrive. This section explores strategies for learning from failures, rebranding, and reinventing content to sustain growth.

1. Learn from Failure

Failures can provide valuable insights that fuel growth and creativity.

- **Asmongold's Burnout and Reinvention:** Took breaks to overcome burnout and returned with commentary-based streams, leading to sustained growth.
  - o **Takeaway:** Pivot to new formats or focus areas when existing strategies stall.

- **Technical Failures Turned into Humor:** Many streamers use crashes or errors to create funny moments, making failures relatable and engaging.
    - **Takeaway:** Embrace authenticity, even during mishaps, to connect with viewers.
- **Tyler1's Comeback Story:** After being banned for toxicity, he reinvented his image, returned with reformed content, and built an even larger audience.
    - **Takeaway:** Address past mistakes transparently and focus on positive changes to rebuild trust.

2. Rebrand and Shift Content Strategies

Rebranding offers an opportunity to tap into new audiences and refresh stale content.

- **From Gaming to Education:** Creators shifted focus to tutorials and Q&A sessions, appealing to knowledge-seeking audiences.
- **Hybrid Models:** Incorporating pre-recorded content alongside live streams added variety and flexibility.
- **Cross-Platform Focus:** Some streamers diversified into podcasts, vlogging, or short-form videos to expand reach beyond live streaming.
- **Genre Shifts:** Streamers experimented with genres like IRL streams, fitness coaching, and reviews to find new niches.

3. Example

- **Music Streamer's Pivot to Tutorials:** A music streamer facing declining views transitioned to teaching instrument tutorials, boosting their subscriber count by 40% in six months.
- **Fitness Creator's Recovery Story:** A fitness influencer who experienced a content plateau shifted to motivational talks and mental health tips, revitalizing engagement.
- **Tech Streamer's Hybrid Model Success:** A tech creator mixed live product reviews with pre-recorded tutorials, improving content variety and sustaining growth.

4. Tips

- **Turn Setbacks into Lessons:** View obstacles as opportunities to pivot and reinvent your content strategy.

- **Test New Formats Gradually:** Experiment with new styles, themes, and platforms while retaining core elements that resonate with viewers.

- **Communicate Changes:** Keep your audience informed about transitions to maintain loyalty and curiosity.

- **Analyze Data:** Use analytics to assess performance and guide reinvention strategies.

5. Reflection

- **Challenge Analysis:** What challenges have you faced, and how could you reinvent your content to overcome them?

- **Adaptation Strategies:** What tools or approaches can you use to rebrand or pivot effectively?

6. Exercise

- **Identify Obstacles and Solutions:** List three obstacles you've experienced and outline potential solutions or content pivots.

- **Reinvention Plan:** Develop a 3-month strategy to test new formats or styles and track performance improvements.

16.4 Niche Market Successes and Underrated Tactics

Streamers often find untapped success by catering to niche audiences or exploring unconventional tactics. This section highlights how focusing on niche markets and using creative strategies can drive growth and build loyal communities.

1. Profiting from Niche Markets

Niche markets allow streamers to stand out by serving highly specific interests.

- **ASMR Streams (Gibi ASMR):** Focused entirely on relaxation and sensory triggers, tapping into an underserved market and attracting millions of followers.

- **Tabletop Gaming Channels:** Built communities around niche interests like **Dungeons & Dragons**, hosting campaigns, tutorials, and reviews for dedicated audiences.

- **Craft and DIY Streams:** Creators targeted hobbyists with art tutorials, sewing lessons, and cooking demonstrations, fostering engaged, creative communities.

- **Educational and Language Streams:** Streamers provided language-learning sessions or history lessons, appealing to knowledge-focused audiences.

2. Underrated Growth Techniques

Streamers can thrive by adopting overlooked strategies to enhance engagement and visibility.

- **Localized Streams:** Added multilingual subtitles and captions to attract international audiences, expanding their global reach.

- **Story-Driven Streams:** Developed episodic content with recurring themes, such as mystery games or role-playing series, to create binge-worthy experiences.

- **Early Adoption of Features:** Used platform beta features like **YouTube Shorts**, **Twitch Predictions**, and **TikTok LIVE** to capitalize on trends early and outpace competition.

- **Charity Streams and Community Events:** Organized fundraising events and collaborations to generate buzz and build goodwill.

- **Subscriber-Only Streams:** Rewarded loyal followers with exclusive content, building stronger relationships and increasing retention.

3. Example

- **ASMR Streamer's Relaxation Focus:** Gibi ASMR grew to millions of subscribers by tapping into the niche ASMR community and producing calming, immersive content.

- **Gaming Channel's Tabletop Success:** A D&D-focused creator gained a dedicated following by hosting live campaigns and tutorials, attracting role-playing enthusiasts.

- **Craft Streamer's DIY Series:** An artist built an audience by offering weekly craft tutorials, helping hobbyists learn new skills and complete projects.

4. Tips

- **Find Hidden Niches:** Research untapped markets aligned with your skills or passions and create tailored content.

- **Test Unconventional Strategies:** Experiment with story-driven episodes, multilingual captions, or interactive events to engage diverse audiences.

- **Leverage Early Tools:** Adopt new features and trends as they launch to stay ahead of competitors.

- **Monitor Niche Growth:** Use analytics to track niche trends and identify areas for further development.

5. Reflection

- **Niche Exploration:** What niche markets can you tap into, and how can you tailor your content to match their needs?

- **Content Planning:** How can you structure your streams to attract and retain niche audiences?

6. Exercise

- **Niche Market Research:** Research three niche communities and analyze their interests.

- **Stream Series Development:** Develop an idea for a stream series targeting one of these niches and outline episode topics to create engaging, specialized content.

16.5 Scaling Lessons from Influencers Turned Entrepreneurs

Scaling a streaming business requires leveraging influence to create multiple revenue streams and expand operations effectively. This section highlights strategies and examples of streamers who scaled their platforms into thriving businesses.

1. Business Models for Growth

Successful influencers expand revenue streams by diversifying their offerings.

- **Merchandise Stores:** Create branded apparel, mugs, and accessories using platforms like **Teespring** and **Printful** to monetize fandoms.

- **Subscription Services:** Offer exclusive content through platforms like **Patreon** and **Ko-fi**, providing paying subscribers with perks such as behind-the-scenes content, tutorials, and Q&A sessions.

- **Coaching and Courses:** Sell online courses about streaming setups, branding strategies, and content creation techniques to aspiring creators.

- **Affiliate Marketing and Sponsorships:** Partner with brands to promote products and earn commissions through affiliate links and partnerships.

- **Digital Products:** Sell e-books, templates, or toolkits tailored to niche audiences for passive income.

2. Building Teams for Growth

Streamers who scale successfully rely on teams to manage operations and maintain quality.

- **Editors and Designers:** Hire freelancers to create professional highlights, thumbnails, and branding materials.

- **Marketing Specialists:** Invest in ad campaigns and SEO strategies to expand reach and attract new audiences.

- **Community Managers:** Hire moderators to maintain chat engagement, enforce rules, and provide excellent audience interaction.

- **Virtual Assistants:** Delegate administrative tasks like scheduling, emails, and social media management to focus on creative growth.

3. Example

- **Ninja's Merch Empire:** Tyler Blevins (Ninja) expanded his brand by launching a merchandise line, boosting income beyond streaming revenue.

- **Valkyrae's Product Partnerships:** Valkyrae collaborated with major brands to promote products, turning her influence into profitable deals.

- **Ali Abdaal's Educational Courses:** Ali Abdaal, a productivity YouTuber, built a six-figure business by creating online courses and digital tools for creators.

4. Tips

- **Treat Your Channel Like a Business:** Track analytics, manage budgets, and reinvest profits into growth opportunities.

- **Focus on Branding:** Develop logos, taglines, and a professional image to stand out in competitive markets.

- **Automate Processes:** Use tools like **Streamlabs**, **Zapier**, and **Hootsuite** to streamline operations.

- **Expand Gradually:** Start with a few revenue streams and scale as you grow to avoid overextending resources.

5. Reflection

- **Scaling Strategies:** What steps can you take to scale your streaming business sustainably?

- **Team Development:** What roles could you delegate to improve efficiency and focus on content creation?

6. Exercise

- **Develop a 6-Month Scaling Plan:** Outline revenue goals, outsourcing tasks, and new monetization strategies.

- **Track Progress:** Evaluate milestones monthly and refine strategies based on performance data.

Conclusion: Building Success Through Lessons and Innovation

This chapter highlights the importance of persistence, creativity, adaptability, and scaling strategies in live streaming success. By studying top streamers, experimenting with content, learning from failures, and tapping into niche markets, you can turn your passion into a profitable business. Apply the tips and exercises outlined here to build and sustain long-term success.

Chapter 16 Review: Real-World Success Stories

Chapter 16 highlights how successful streamers built their brands, overcame challenges, and scaled their careers. Through real-world examples, the chapter provides valuable insights into strategies, creativity, and adaptability that aspiring streamers can apply to achieve long-term success.

16.1 Lessons from Top Streamers Across Platforms

- **Key Strategies from Successful Streamers** - Streamers like Ninja, Kai Cenat, IShowSpeed, and Valkyrae built thriving brands by maintaining consistency, engaging with audiences, and diversifying their content formats to reach wider audiences.

- **Growth Tools Used by Streamers** - Top creators leverage platforms like Twitch Insights, OBS Studio, and TikTok to optimize their performance, track metrics, and attract new viewers.

16.2 Creative Strategies That Transformed Channels

- **Bold Content Experiments** - Ludwig Ahgren's Subathon and Mizkif's interactive polls introduced unique formats like marathon streams and viewer-driven decisions to boost engagement.

- **Gamification and Challenges** - Streamers incorporated giveaways, themed events, and viewer challenges to create interactive and fun content that kept audiences engaged.

16.3 Overcoming Failures and Reinventing Content

- **Learning from Failure** - Streamers like Asmongold overcame setbacks by pivoting to commentary-based streams and maintaining authenticity, which reignited audience interest.

- **Rebranding and Content Shifts** - Many creators, including Amouranth, transitioned to lifestyle content, tutorials, and hybrid formats to expand their audiences and stay relevant.

16.4 Niche Market Successes and Underrated Tactics

- **Profiting from Niche Markets** - ASMR creators like Gibi ASMR and tabletop gamers built loyal communities by focusing on underserved audiences with specific interests.

- **Underrated Growth Techniques** - Streamers grew by adding multilingual content, developing story-driven series, and capitalizing early on new platform features like YouTube Shorts.

16.5 Scaling Lessons from Influencers Turned Entrepreneurs

- **Business Models for Growth** - Streamers expanded revenue through merchandise, online courses, and subscription-based memberships to build sustainable income streams.

- **Building Teams for Growth** - Influencers hired editors, marketers, and community managers to streamline operations and focus on creative content while outsourcing tasks.

By adopting these strategies and staying adaptable, streamers can build sustainable careers, turn challenges into opportunities, and scale their content into profitable businesses.

Chapter 17: Legal and Ethical Guidelines

Building a sustainable live streaming career requires more than technical expertise and creativity—it demands adherence to legal standards and ethical practices. This chapter covers critical areas like copyright laws, platform policies, sponsorship transparency, data security, and international compliance.

By mastering these topics, you can **protect your content, safeguard your reputation, and establish credibility** with audiences, platforms, and sponsors.

17.1 Copyright, Music Licensing, and Fair Use

Copyright laws protect intellectual property, and violations can lead to bans, fines, or lawsuits. Knowing how to use music, visuals, and media legally is essential for long-term success. This section covers the fundamentals of copyright, licensing options, and proactive protection strategies.

1. Understand Copyright and Its Impact

Streamers must respect copyright laws to avoid penalties and maintain professional credibility.

- **What Is Copyright?**
    - Copyright grants creators exclusive rights to their work (e.g., music, videos, images).

- **Why It Matters for Streamers:**
    - Unauthorized use can trigger **DMCA (Digital Millennium Copyright Act)** claims, resulting in takedowns, strikes, or account bans.

- **Common Violations:**
    - Playing copyrighted music in the background.
    - Displaying images or video clips without permission.
    - Using sound effects, logos, or designs owned by others without proper licensing.

2. Licensing and Legal Media Use

Using properly licensed or royalty-free media protects streamers from legal issues.

- **Royalty-Free Music Libraries:** Use platforms like **Epidemic Sound**, **Artlist**, or **StreamBeats** for DMCA-safe music.

- **Creative Commons Content:** Platforms like **Free Music Archive** and **Unsplash** provide free-to-use media with attribution.

- **Fair Use Considerations:** Transformative content, such as commentary, reviews, or parodies, may qualify as fair use, but this depends on legal interpretation and requires caution.

- **Public Domain Works:** Use materials that are free of copyright restrictions, such as classical music or archival images.

3. Proactive Copyright Protection

Taking proactive steps minimizes the risk of copyright strikes and legal disputes.

- **Mute Music on VODs:** Use tools like **Twitch's Audio Removal** to mute potentially copyrighted music automatically.

- **Keep Documentation:** Maintain records of purchased licenses, permissions, and agreements for proof of compliance.

- **Monitor Alerts:** Watch for **DMCA warnings** and address them promptly to prevent strikes or takedowns.

- **Use Custom Graphics and Sounds:** Design original overlays, logos, and effects to avoid relying on copyrighted materials.

4. Example

- **Gaming Streamer's Copyright Strategy:** A streamer switched to royalty-free background music from **StreamBeats**, avoiding DMCA strikes while maintaining production quality.

- **Music Creator's Licensing Success:** A musician secured licenses for cover performances through **Lickd** and **Songtradr**, ensuring legal uploads and monetization.

- **Educational Creator's Fair Use Case:** A teacher used short video clips under fair use to critique and explain content, carefully documenting references for legal compliance.

5. Tips

- **Audit Your Content:** Regularly review past broadcasts to identify and replace any unlicensed media.

- **Test Tools Before Streaming:** Verify that audio removal or copyright detection tools are functioning properly.

- **Consult Legal Resources:** Seek advice from copyright attorneys or trusted resources if unsure about usage rights.

- **Invest in Licenses Early:** Purchase commercial licenses for frequently used materials to future-proof content.

6. Reflection

- **Copyright Compliance:** Are there any copyrighted materials in your content? How can you legally replace or license them?

- **Content Planning:** What steps can you take to ensure your streams remain copyright-compliant moving forward?

7. Exercise

- **Content Audit:** Review your past broadcasts and replace copyrighted content with licensed or royalty-free media.

- **Licensing Plan:** Create a list of tools and resources for sourcing legal music, graphics, and videos to integrate into future streams.

17.2 Platform Policies: Avoiding Bans and Violations

Each streaming platform enforces rules to maintain community standards. Violations can result in suspensions or bans that may derail your growth. This section covers core rules, enforcement systems, and proactive strategies to avoid penalties.

1. Core Platform Rules to Follow

Understanding and adhering to platform guidelines ensures compliance and long-term success.

- **Content Guidelines:**
  - Avoid explicit content, harassment, or hate speech that violates platform policies.

- o Respect community standards, even during jokes or satire, to maintain professionalism.
- o Follow copyright laws when using music, images, or video clips.
- **Advertising Restrictions:**
  - o Ensure transparency in sponsored content and clearly label paid promotions.
  - o Follow ad placement rules and avoid misleading claims or deceptive practices.
- **Behavioral Expectations:**
  - o Maintain professionalism in chat interactions, gameplay, and collaborations.
  - o Avoid inflammatory language or inappropriate behavior that could trigger complaints.

2. Understand Enforcement Systems

Platforms monitor and enforce rules through strike systems and escalation processes.

- **Strike Systems:**
  - o **YouTube:** Three strikes within 90 days result in permanent bans.
  - o **Twitch:** Repeat offenses lead to indefinite suspensions or permanent bans.
  - o **Facebook Gaming:** Community standard violations result in temporary or permanent restrictions.
- **Appeals Process:**
  - o Most platforms allow appeals—document cases clearly and respond quickly to request reviews.
  - o Provide proof, including timestamps and context, when disputing strikes or violations.

3. Prevent Violations Before They Happen

Proactive measures reduce the risk of unintentional violations and protect your account.

- **Test Content Before Streaming:** Preview layouts, overlays, and audio for compliance with platform rules.

- **Automate Moderation:** Use tools like **Nightbot** and **Streamlabs Chatbot** to enforce rules in real time and filter inappropriate messages.

- **Backup Important Content:** Save all videos offline or to external storage to preserve proof in case of disputes or strikes.

- **Monitor Rule Changes:** Stay updated with platform newsletters, creator forums, and community guidelines to adapt to new policies.

4. Example

- **Gaming Streamer's Compliance Success:** A gamer avoided strikes by using **Streamlabs Chatbot** to filter chat and pre-check overlays for policy compliance.

- **Lifestyle Influencer's Appeal Win:** A vlogger successfully overturned a content strike by documenting permissions for music licensing and submitting proof during the appeals process.

- **Educational Creator's Proactive Moderation:** An educator used automated filters and human moderators to prevent policy violations in real-time chats.

5. Tips

- **Audit Content Regularly:** Review past streams and identify areas where rules might have been unintentionally violated.

- **Train Moderators:** Educate your team about platform rules and equip them to enforce standards effectively.

- **Track Policy Updates:** Use newsletters and forums to monitor rule changes and stay ahead of compliance requirements.

- **Test Content in Private Mode:** Run private test streams to verify compliance before going live.

6. Reflection

- **Policy Alignment:** Are your content and interactions aligned with platform policies and community standards?

- **Risk Assessment:** What areas in your streaming process might pose compliance risks, and how can you address them?

7. Exercise

- **Pre-Stream Compliance Checklist:** Review your platform's guidelines and create a checklist for pre-stream compliance checks.

- **Appeal Preparation Plan:** Outline a step-by-step plan to document content and handle violations in case appeals are necessary.

17.3 Transparency in Sponsorships and Paid Promotions

Transparency builds audience trust and keeps you compliant with legal standards when promoting products or services. This section explores sponsorship disclosure laws, ethical promotion practices, and tools for managing partnerships effectively.

1. Sponsorship Disclosure Laws

Streamers must follow disclosure laws to avoid fines and maintain audience trust.

- **FTC (Federal Trade Commission) Rules:**

    o Clearly label paid promotions with terms like **#ad** or **#sponsored** in titles, descriptions, and overlays.

    o Disclose partnerships verbally during streams and visually with pinned messages or on-screen notifications.

    o Avoid misleading claims and clearly separate advertisements from organic content.

- **Global Regulations:**

    o **EU's AVMSD (Audiovisual Media Services Directive):** Requires transparent advertising practices, including visible and verbal disclosures.

    o **UK ASA (Advertising Standards Authority):** Enforces strict rules about influencer promotions and sponsorship clarity.

2. Ethical Promotion Practices

Ethical partnerships create credibility and long-term audience loyalty.

- **Be Selective with Partnerships:** Only endorse products you've personally tested or genuinely believe in to maintain authenticity.

- **Balance Content with Ads:** Avoid overwhelming viewers with excessive promotions—integrate ads naturally within your content.

- **Use Contracts:** Formalize partnerships through contracts to define terms, expectations, and payment timelines clearly.

- **Highlight Sponsored Content:** Label sponsorships during sponsored giveaways, challenges, or unboxing videos to avoid confusion.

3. Tools for Managing Promotions

Streamers can simplify partnership tracking and compliance with the right tools.

- **Affiliate Platforms:** Use tools like **Amazon Associates**, **Impact**, and **Rakuten Marketing** to manage affiliate links and track earnings.

- **Sponsorship Dashboards:** Platforms like **StreamElements** and **HelloPartner** provide analytics on ad performance and payment tracking.

- **Brand Collab Managers:** Services like **Facebook Brand Collabs Manager** connect streamers with advertisers and streamline deals.

- **Content Labeling Tools:** Tools like **YouTube's Paid Promotion Tag** automatically label sponsored videos.

4. Example

- **Beauty Influencer's FTC Compliance:** A beauty creator labeled product reviews as #sponsored and included verbal disclosures, gaining trust while maintaining compliance.

- **Gaming Streamer's Affiliate Growth:** A gamer used Amazon Associates links in video descriptions and overlays, earning passive income while being transparent with viewers.

- **Tech Creator's Ethical Partnerships:** A tech reviewer only accepted partnerships with brands aligned with their niche, boosting credibility and revenue.

5. Tips

- **Prioritize Transparency:** Use clear labels and verbal disclosures to avoid legal risks and build audience trust.

- **Track Earnings and Performance:** Monitor affiliate and sponsorship data to evaluate profitability and refine strategies.

- **Test Product Relevance:** Only promote products that align with your brand and meet audience expectations.

- **Review Agreements Regularly:** Ensure contracts outline payment terms, deliverables, and compliance expectations.

6. Reflection

- **Promotion Practices:** Are your paid promotions labeled clearly and ethically aligned with your audience?

- **Compliance Checklist:** What steps can you take to strengthen transparency and manage partnerships effectively?

7. Exercise

- **Sponsorship Audit:** Review your sponsorships and add any missing disclosures to ensure compliance.

- **Promotion Plan:** Develop a strategy for integrating future promotions, including content labeling, product testing, and performance tracking.

17.4 Data Privacy and Security Practices

Handling sensitive viewer data requires strict privacy measures to avoid breaches and legal issues. This section explores strategies for protecting data, complying with privacy laws, and safeguarding content.

1. Protect Viewer Data

Streamers must prioritize security to build trust and protect sensitive information.

- **Secure Payment Systems:** Use trusted processors like **PayPal**, **Stripe**, or **Ko-fi** for donations and subscriptions to ensure safe transactions.

- **Enable 2FA (Two-Factor Authentication):** Add layers of security to streaming platforms, email accounts, and payment portals.

- **Limit Personal Sharing:** Avoid revealing private details such as addresses, phone numbers, or travel plans during live streams or chats.

- **Encrypt Sensitive Files:** Use encryption tools like **VeraCrypt** to protect stored data and backup files securely.

2. Comply with Privacy Laws

Streamers must adhere to data protection laws to avoid legal issues and build transparency.

- **GDPR (General Data Protection Regulation):** European law requiring consent for data collection and providing users access to their stored information.

- **CCPA (California Consumer Privacy Act):** U.S. regulation giving consumers control over how personal data is collected, stored, and shared.

- **COPPA (Children's Online Privacy Protection Act):** Requires parental consent for collecting personal data from users under 13.

- **Transparency Statements:** Post privacy disclaimers on websites and platforms outlining data collection practices and consent forms.

3. Safeguard Content and Transactions

Adopting protective measures reduces vulnerabilities and keeps your systems secure.

- **VPNs for Privacy:** Use services like **NordVPN** or **ExpressVPN** to encrypt internet connections and prevent data interception.

- **Password Managers:** Store and manage login credentials securely with tools like **LastPass, 1Password**, or **Bitwarden**.

- **Firewalls and Antivirus Programs:** Use trusted antivirus software and firewalls to block malware and phishing attacks.

- **Backup Systems:** Regularly back up content to cloud storage or external hard drives to safeguard against accidental loss or hacking.

4. Example

- **Gaming Streamer's Security Upgrade:** A gamer prevented hacking attempts by implementing **2FA** and using a **VPN**, improving privacy without interrupting streams.

- **Influencer's Privacy Policy Implementation:** A lifestyle creator updated privacy policies to comply with **GDPR**, reassuring viewers about data handling practices.

- **Business Streamer's Payment Security:** A coach switched to **Stripe** for secure payments, reducing fraud risks and boosting client confidence.

5. Tips

- **Review Privacy Tools Regularly:** Update passwords and software to stay ahead of security threats.

- **Simplify Compliance Processes:** Use templates for privacy statements and consent forms to save time.

- **Monitor Access Logs:** Track login attempts and unusual activity to detect potential breaches early.

- **Test Security Systems:** Perform periodic checks to ensure data encryption and firewalls are active.

6. Reflection

- **Security Checkup:** Is your data protection system strong enough to secure viewer and payment data?

- **Compliance Review:** Are your privacy policies aligned with global standards like GDPR and CCPA?

7. Exercise

- **Security Test:** Test your streaming setup's security features, including encryption, VPNs, and password managers.

- **Policy Updates:** Review and update your privacy policies to ensure compliance with current laws and regulations.

17.5 Staying Compliant with International Regulations

Streamers with global audiences must comply with international laws for content, advertising, and privacy. This section explores compliance standards, licensing practices, and secure payment processing for international markets.

1. Regional Compliance Standards

Understanding global regulations ensures lawful content distribution and audience protection.

- **Europe (GDPR):**

  o Prioritize consent for data collection, provide data access options, and offer deletion requests to comply with privacy laws.

- **Asia-Pacific Rules:**

  o Research country-specific regulations, such as content censorship, media licensing, and local advertising standards.

- **U.S. Regulations:**

  o Follow **FTC (Federal Trade Commission)** guidelines for advertising transparency and promotions.

  o Comply with **COPPA (Children's Online Privacy Protection Act)** when content targets children under 13.

- **Canada (CASL):**

  o Obtain consent for marketing emails and disclose sender details under anti-spam legislation.

2. Handle International Content Licensing

Licensing agreements should account for multiple regions to avoid copyright violations.

- **Music Rights Across Borders:** Ensure licenses cover usage in multiple countries through providers like **Artlist** and **Epidemic Sound**.

- **Video and Media Licensing:** Verify global distribution rights for clips, graphics, and templates before uploading content.

- **Multilingual Accessibility:** Offer captions and translations using tools like **Kapwing** and **Sonix AI** to increase accessibility and engagement.

- **Fair Use Standards:** Consult legal advisors to assess whether transformative content qualifies as fair use in different regions.

3. Payment Processing Across Borders

Secure and compliant payment systems simplify international transactions.

- **Global Payment Solutions:** Use services like **Wise, Payoneer**, and **Stripe** for multi-currency payments and tax reporting.

- **VAT Compliance:** Collect and remit value-added taxes (VAT) as required in regions like the EU.

- **Transaction Transparency:** Provide clear invoices and receipts for subscribers, sponsors, and clients.

4. Example

- **Gaming Streamer's Global Expansion:** A gamer expanded internationally by adding multilingual subtitles and switching to **Wise** for secure payments, increasing viewership by 20%.

- **Fitness Influencer's Licensing Success:** A fitness creator licensed royalty-free music globally to avoid takedowns, ensuring consistent monetization across platforms.

- **Educational Creator's Compliance Update:** An educator updated GDPR-compliant opt-ins and privacy policies to secure EU-based audiences and partnerships.

5. Tips

- **Hire Legal Advisors:** Work with professionals to ensure compliance in all target markets and avoid unexpected violations.

- **Regular Compliance Audits:** Review privacy policies, contracts, and licensing agreements quarterly to maintain accuracy.

- **Test Global Accessibility Tools:** Use multilingual captions, subtitles, and payment processors to simplify international scaling.

- **Stay Informed:** Monitor international law changes through industry blogs, newsletters, and legal forums.

6. Reflection

- **Global Compliance Review:** Are your content, licensing, and payment systems compliant worldwide?

- **Regional Strategy:** What markets could you expand into by updating legal frameworks and accessibility features?

7. Exercise

- **Market Research Task:** Research streaming laws in two target markets and identify compliance gaps.

- **Compliance Action Plan:** Update privacy policies, licensing terms, and payment settings to align with international regulations.

Conclusion: Protecting Your Career with Legal and Ethical Practices

Building a successful streaming career requires legal and ethical diligence. By following copyright rules, adhering to platform policies, ensuring transparency in sponsorships, protecting data privacy, and complying with international laws, you can **grow your audience confidently while avoiding legal risks**.

Apply the strategies, reflections, and exercises in this chapter to maintain professional integrity and secure long-term success.

Chapter 17 Review: Legal and Ethical Guidelines

Chapter 17 explores the importance of legal and ethical practices in building a successful live streaming career, covering key topics such as copyright, platform policies, transparency in sponsorships, data privacy, and international compliance.

17.1 Copyright, Music Licensing, and Fair Use

- **Understanding Copyright and Its Impact** - Copyright laws protect intellectual property, and violations can result in takedowns or legal consequences.

- **Licensing and Legal Media Use** - Use royalty-free music and Creative Commons content to avoid copyright violations and ensure compliance.

- **Proactive Copyright Protection** - Tools like Twitch's Audio Removal can help protect your content by muting copyrighted music in VODs and avoiding strikes.

17.2 Platform Policies: Avoiding Bans and Violations

- **Core Platform Rules to Follow** - Platforms enforce content guidelines to maintain community standards. Violations can lead to suspensions or bans.

- **Understanding Enforcement Systems** - Platforms use strike systems to penalize rule violations. It's important to understand the appeals process and follow platform rules to avoid penalties.

- **Preventing Violations Before They Happen** - Testing content for compliance and automating moderation with tools like Nightbot can help prevent violations during live streams.

17.3 Transparency in Sponsorships and Paid Promotions

- **Sponsorship Disclosure Laws** - The FTC requires paid promotions to be clearly disclosed with terms like #ad or #sponsored to maintain transparency with viewers.

- **Ethical Promotion Practices** - Only promote products you trust and balance content with ads to maintain authenticity and viewer trust.

- **Tools for Managing Promotions** - Use affiliate platforms and sponsorship dashboards to manage promotions, track performance, and ensure compliance with legal standards.

17.4 Data Privacy and Security Practices

- **Protecting Viewer Data** - Use secure payment processors and enable two-factor authentication to protect sensitive viewer and payment data.

- **Complying with Privacy Laws** - Adhere to privacy laws like GDPR and CCPA to protect viewer information and ensure compliance with data protection regulations.

- **Safeguarding Content and Transactions** - Use VPNs and password managers to protect personal and financial information during streaming and transactions.

17.5 Staying Compliant with International Regulations

- **Regional Compliance Standards** - Adhere to international laws like GDPR in Europe, and understand regional censorship and licensing requirements to stay compliant globally.

- **Handling International Content Licensing** - Ensure your content licenses cover multiple countries, and provide multilingual accessibility for global audiences.

- **Payment Processing Across Borders** - Use global payment solutions like Payoneer to securely process transactions and ensure compliance with cross-border payment regulations.

By mastering these legal and ethical practices, streamers can protect their content, reputation, and business, ensuring long-term success in the industry.

Conclusion

Congratulations on completing *HowExpert Guide to Live Streaming: The Ultimate Handbook for Building Your Live Streaming Channel, Growing Your Audience, and Monetizing Your Live Streams.* You've taken the first step toward building a successful streaming career by learning the tools, strategies, and insights to thrive in the competitive world of live content creation.

This guide has equipped you with everything you need to **launch, grow, and monetize your channel** while staying ahead of trends and maintaining legal and ethical standards. Now it's time to reflect, plan your next steps, and take action to turn your passion into a sustainable career.

I. Key Takeaways for Live Streaming Success

This guide has covered the essential pillars of live streaming, from laying the foundation to scaling and future-proofing your career. Here are the most important lessons to carry forward.

1. Start with Strong Foundations

Establishing a solid foundation sets you up for long-term success:

- **Choose the Right Platform:** Select platforms that align with your audience and niche for optimal growth and engagement.

- **Invest in Quality Equipment:** Optimize audio, video, and lighting to create professional-grade content.

- **Test and Troubleshoot:** Use reliable software, set up backups, and resolve technical issues efficiently to avoid disruptions.

2. Build Engaging Content That Connects

Creating compelling and consistent content fosters audience connection:

- **Plan Compelling Themes:** Develop challenges, events, and series that captivate viewers and keep them returning.

- **Maintain Consistency:** Follow a structured streaming schedule and create evergreen content to sustain long-term growth.

- **Boost Interaction:** Use polls, chatbots, and interactive games to foster engagement and build a strong community.

3. Grow Your Audience Strategically

Expanding your audience ensures visibility and long-term success:

- **Expand Visibility:** Leverage social media, collaborations, and giveaways to attract new viewers.

- **Optimize SEO:** Use keyword strategies and analytics tools to improve discoverability and reach targeted audiences.

- **Network and Partner:** Build relationships within the industry for cross-promotion, collaborations, and sustained growth.

4. Monetize and Scale Your Channel

Generating revenue and scaling operations turn your passion into a profitable business:

- **Diversify Revenue Streams:** Generate income through affiliate marketing, sponsorships, merchandise, and memberships.

- **Offer Premium Services:** Provide online courses, consulting, and exclusive content for advanced monetization.

- **Build a Team:** Hire editors, moderators, and marketing specialists to improve quality and efficiency.

5. Stay Innovative and Future-Ready

Remaining adaptable and innovative helps future-proof your career:

- **Embrace Emerging Technologies:** Use AI, VR, and AR to deliver unique, interactive experiences.

- **Adapt to Platform Changes:** Stay informed about updates, algorithms, and new features to remain competitive.

- **Analyze Data Trends:** Leverage analytics and forecasting tools to make informed decisions and refine strategies.

6. Protect Your Brand with Legal and Ethical Practices

Following legal and ethical standards builds trust and safeguards your career:

- **Follow Copyright and Licensing Rules:** Avoid violations by using royalty-free music and properly licensed content.

- **Be Transparent with Sponsorships:** Clearly label paid promotions to maintain credibility and compliance.

- **Ensure Data Privacy:** Prioritize security, privacy laws, and international regulations to protect your audience and business.

7. Tips

- **Consistency Drives Growth:** Develop a regular schedule to maintain audience trust and engagement.

- **Stay Adaptable:** Embrace changes in technology and trends to remain relevant and competitive.

- **Focus on Authenticity:** Connect with your audience through genuine interactions and content that reflects your values.

8. Reflection

- **Build a Solid Plan for Growth:** What foundational strategies will you implement to strengthen your content and platform presence?

- **Evaluate Future Goals:** How can you align your content and tools with long-term growth and monetization strategies?

9. Exercise

- **Develop a 30-Day Action Plan:** Write down three action steps you'll take in the next 30 days to implement the lessons you've learned.

- **Test and Analyze Results:** Experiment with interactive tools, themes, and collaborations, then evaluate metrics to identify what resonates most with your audience.

- **Focus on Expansion:** Outline strategies for building connections, improving production quality, and scaling revenue streams.

II. Staying Motivated and Adapting to Change

The world of live streaming is fast-paced, and success depends on your ability to stay motivated and adapt to change. Challenges like algorithm updates, technical failures, and slow growth are inevitable—but so is your ability to overcome them. This section focuses on strategies to maintain motivation, handle setbacks, and adapt to evolving trends.

1. Stay Inspired and Focused

Maintaining focus and enthusiasm ensures consistent growth and creativity:

- **Celebrate Small Wins:** Acknowledge milestones like subscriber growth, engagement boosts, or positive feedback to maintain morale.

- **Engage with Your Community:** Let your audience's support motivate you by celebrating their involvement, loyalty, and feedback.

- **Set Meaningful Goals:** Focus on impact—whether it's educating, entertaining, or building strong connections within your community.

- **Visualize Success:** Create vision boards or track progress to stay focused on long-term aspirations.

2. Handle Setbacks and Burnout

Setbacks are opportunities to learn and grow stronger:

- **Schedule Breaks and Rest Days:** Avoid burnout by planning downtime to recharge creativity and energy.

- **Experiment with Content Formats:** Refresh your approach with new ideas, themes, or collaborations to reignite passion.

- **Focus on Long-Term Impact:** Remind yourself of the bigger picture and the influence your content has on viewers.

- **Seek Support Networks:** Connect with other creators who can offer encouragement and advice during challenging periods.

3. Adapt to Change and Trends

Staying flexible and innovative ensures continued relevance and growth:

- **Monitor Industry Trends:** Stay ahead by following tech developments, platform updates, and audience preferences.

- **Test and Innovate:** Try out new formats, tools, and styles to keep content fresh, engaging, and competitive.

- **Learn Continuously:** Attend webinars, online courses, and workshops to gain new insights and skills.

- **Track Analytics:** Use data to identify patterns and opportunities for improvement, adapting content strategies as needed.

4. Example

- **Lifestyle Streamer's Adaptation:** A lifestyle creator overcame a slow growth phase by switching to TikTok highlights and short-form content, doubling their engagement in three months.

- **Gaming Influencer's Content Shift:** A gamer struggling with burnout shifted to tutorial-based streams, attracting new audiences and boosting subscriber counts.

- **Educational Creator's Innovation:** An educator introduced interactive quizzes and polls during streams, revitalizing viewer engagement and retention rates.

5. Tips

- **View Setbacks as Stepping Stones:** Use failures as learning experiences to refine strategies.

- **Refresh Your Approach Regularly:** Rotate themes, formats, and topics to prevent stagnation.

- **Stay Connected with Trends:** Follow influencers, industry updates, and creator forums to stay informed.

- **Track Emotional Health:** Monitor stress levels and address burnout before it impacts performance.

6. Reflection

- **Develop Motivation Strategies:** What strategies will you use to stay motivated during challenges?

- **Turn Obstacles into Growth Opportunities:** How can you turn obstacles into growth opportunities?

7. Exercise

- **Write a Motivational Journal:** Write a motivational journal entry about your goals for the next six months and the steps you'll take to reach them.

- **Plan Content Experiments:** Create a roadmap for experimenting with new content formats or tools to keep your streams engaging.

III. Next Steps for Growth and Career Expansion

Success in streaming doesn't end with launching your channel—it's an ongoing process of growth and expansion. This section outlines actionable strategies to level up your streaming career in the months and years to come.

1. Build a Scalable Business Model

Creating sustainable revenue streams and professional workflows allows you to scale effectively:

- **Diversify Revenue Streams:** Generate income through merchandise, courses, paid memberships, and consulting services.

- **Outsource Tasks:** Hire editors, graphic designers, and marketing specialists to free up time for content creation.

- **Partner with Brands and Sponsors:** Establish long-term partnerships to ensure reliable income opportunities and sponsorship deals.

- **Leverage Passive Income:** Develop pre-recorded tutorials, e-books, and templates to generate sales while focusing on live content.

2. Expand Your Audience Reach

Broadening your audience base ensures continued growth and visibility:

- **Repurpose Content:** Transform live streams into highlights, tutorials, and short-form clips for platforms like TikTok, Instagram Reels, and YouTube Shorts.

- **Explore Hybrid Models:** Combine live and pre-recorded videos to maximize flexibility and appeal to diverse audiences.

- **SEO and Paid Ads:** Use tools like TubeBuddy and Google Ads to optimize discoverability and run targeted ads.

- **Multilingual Subtitles:** Translate captions to attract global audiences and expand reach internationally.

3. Optimize for Retention and Engagement

Keeping viewers engaged ensures long-term loyalty and higher retention rates:

- **Create Recurring Events:** Plan weekly themes, contests, or challenges to keep audiences entertained and coming back.

- **Collect Viewer Feedback:** Use polls, surveys, and analytics tools to refine your content strategy.

- **Reward Loyalty:** Offer exclusive content, shoutouts, or giveaways for VIP subscribers to strengthen community bonds.

- **Personalize Engagement:** Use chatbots and interactive tools to provide customized viewer experiences.

4. Stay Professional and Protected

Professionalism and legal protection create a foundation for credibility and growth:

- **Review Platform Policies Regularly:** Stay updated with rules to avoid strikes, suspensions, or bans.

- **Update Privacy Practices:** Strengthen data protection measures as your audience expands.

- **Formalize Sponsorship Agreements:** Use contracts to clarify expectations, deliverables, and payment terms with partners.

- **Legal Compliance:** Ensure your content aligns with international regulations and copyright laws to avoid disputes.

5. Example

- **Fitness Influencer's Business Expansion:** A fitness creator scaled their business by launching branded workout gear, premium coaching programs, and an online course series.

- **Tech Streamer's Audience Growth:** A tech-focused streamer repurposed live Q&A sessions into tutorials and TikTok clips, gaining 50,000 new subscribers in three months.

- **Gaming Creator's Sponsorship Success:** A gaming streamer formalized sponsorship deals with multiple brands, turning part-time streaming into a full-time career.

6. Tips

- **Track Progress Regularly:** Use analytics tools to monitor growth, measure engagement, and assess ROI.

- **Set SMART Goals:** Focus on specific, measurable, achievable, relevant, and time-bound objectives.

- **Invest in Professional Development:** Take courses and attend industry events to sharpen skills and discover new strategies.

- **Plan Ahead:** Develop quarterly growth plans with deadlines and milestones to stay on track.

7. Reflection

- **Scaling Strategies for Growth:** What steps will you take to scale your streaming career in the next 6–12 months?

- **Professional Development Opportunities:** How can you leverage new skills and tools to accelerate growth?

8. Exercise

- **Growth Roadmap Development:** Create a detailed growth roadmap with specific goals, deadlines, and milestones.

- **Revenue Strategy Planning:** Outline monetization strategies for the next quarter, focusing on passive income streams and brand partnerships.

Final Thoughts: Your Journey Starts Now

Your journey as a live streamer is filled with opportunities to entertain, educate, and inspire audiences worldwide. With the tools, strategies, and insights from *HowExpert Guide to Live Streaming: The Ultimate Handbook for Building Your Live Streaming Channel, Growing Your Audience, and Monetizing Your Live Streams,* you're prepared to launch, grow, and scale your career confidently.

Key Principles for Success

- **Be Consistent:** Develop routines and schedules to keep your audience engaged and build trust over time.

- **Stay Creative:** Experiment with new content ideas, themes, and collaborations to remain fresh and relevant.

- **Focus on Value:** Prioritize audience needs by creating content that entertains, educates, or inspires.

- **Adapt and Evolve:** Embrace change, test new strategies, and remain flexible as trends and technologies shift.

- **Engage and Connect:** Build genuine relationships with your audience to foster loyalty and long-term support.

- **Invest in Growth:** Continuously upgrade your skills, tools, and knowledge to stay competitive and scalable.

The Future Is Yours

The future of streaming is limitless. With hard work, persistence, and creativity, you have the power to turn your passion into profit and leave a lasting impact in the streaming world.

Now it's time to take action—go live, grow your audience, and build your dream streaming career!

Appendices

The appendices offer valuable references, tools, and practical resources to help you implement the strategies outlined in *HowExpert Guide to Live Streaming: The Ultimate Handbook for Building Your Live Streaming Channel, Growing Your Audience, and Monetizing Your Live Streams.*

Appendix A: Glossary of Live Streaming Terms from A to Z

This glossary provides essential definitions and examples of **live streaming terminology** to help you navigate platforms, tools, and technologies with confidence.

A

- **Affiliate Program:** Monetization programs (e.g., Twitch Affiliate) that enable earnings through ads, subscriptions, and virtual tips.
- **Alerts:** On-screen notifications for follows, donations, and subscriptions to boost engagement.
- **Analytics:** Data tools that track audience behavior, retention, and growth metrics.
- **Aspect Ratio:** The proportional relationship between video width and height, commonly 16:9 for HD streaming.

B

- **Bandwidth:** The amount of data transferable over an internet connection, affecting streaming quality.
- **Bitrate:** The rate of data encoding, measured in kbps, impacting video clarity.
- **Bits:** Twitch's virtual tipping currency used to support streamers.
- **Broadcast Software:** Applications like OBS Studio and Streamlabs for managing streaming production.

C

- **Capture Card:** Hardware for recording external devices like gaming consoles. Examples: **Elgato HD60 S**.

- **Chat Bot:** Automated tools (e.g., **Nightbot**) that moderate chat, answer FAQs, and boost engagement.

- **Concurrent Viewers:** Number of viewers watching a stream at the same time.

- **Codec:** Software for compressing and decompressing video and audio data.

D

- **DMCA (Digital Millennium Copyright Act):** U.S. law protecting copyrighted content, often resulting in takedowns for violations.

- **Donation Alerts:** Notifications for monetary tips during streams.

- **Drop Frames:** Video frames lost due to slow internet speeds or hardware limitations, causing lag.

E

- **Emotes:** Custom emojis used in chat to express reactions and boost interaction.

- **Encoding:** Converting video and audio into digital formats for streaming.

- **Engagement Tools:** Polls, Q&A sessions, and giveaways to encourage viewer participation.

F

- **Fair Use:** Legal doctrine allowing limited use of copyrighted content for commentary, criticism, or education.

- **Follower Goal:** On-screen metrics to encourage audience growth.

- **FPS (Frames Per Second):** Video frame rate—higher FPS (e.g., 60fps) offers smoother visuals.

G

- **Green Screen:** Backdrop used for replacing or customizing backgrounds.

- **GPU (Graphics Processing Unit):** Handles visual rendering, essential for high-quality streaming.

H

- **Highlight Reels:** Edited clips showcasing key moments from live streams.

- **Hosting:** Broadcasting another creator's stream on your channel to share audiences.

I

- **IRL (In Real Life) Streams:** Non-gaming content focused on lifestyle, travel, or daily activities.

- **Ingest Server:** A server that processes live video before distributing it to viewers.

J

- **Jump Cuts:** Quick video edits used to skip unnecessary parts and maintain pacing in pre-recorded content or highlights.

K

- **Keyframe Interval:** Frequency of complete video frames sent during streaming. Optimizing intervals improves video quality.

- **Keywords:** SEO terms in titles and tags that improve content discoverability.

L

- **Latency:** The time delay between broadcasting and viewer reception. Lower latency improves real-time interaction.

- **Lurkers:** Viewers who watch streams without actively engaging in chat.

M

- **Monetization:** Earning revenue through ads, subscriptions, sponsorships, and merchandise.

- **Multistreaming:** Broadcasting to multiple platforms simultaneously for expanded reach.

- **Membership Tiers:** Paid levels offering exclusive perks and content.

N

- **Network Latency:** The delay caused by internet connectivity issues, impacting streaming performance.

- **Notifications:** Alerts sent to followers when a stream goes live to encourage attendance.

- **Niche Content:** Focused content targeting a specific audience interest, such as fitness, art, or gaming tutorials.

O

- **Overlay:** Custom graphics displayed on streams, including alerts and banners.

- **OBS (Open Broadcaster Software):** Free streaming software widely used for broadcasting and recording.

P

- **Partnership Program:** Advanced monetization levels providing higher revenue splits and premium tools.

- **Post-Stream Analytics:** Data showing retention rates, peak times, and engagement after broadcasts.

- **Podcast Streams:** Audio-focused live broadcasts featuring interviews or discussions.

Q

- **Quality Settings:** Viewer options for adjusting video resolution and bitrate to match internet speeds.

- **Queue System:** Features for organizing viewer requests or submissions during interactive streams.

- **Quick Actions:** Pre-configured shortcuts for managing overlays, transitions, or sound effects in real time.

R

- **Raid:** A Twitch feature that sends viewers to another streamer's channel to boost collaboration.

- **Resolution:** Video quality measured in pixels, such as 720p or 1080p.

S

- **Scenes:** Pre-designed layouts in streaming software used for intros, gameplay, and transitions.

- **Stream Key:** Unique codes connecting streaming software to platforms for broadcasting.

- **Sub Only Mode:** Chat setting limiting participation to subscribers.

T

- **Tags:** SEO keywords added to streams to boost visibility and relevance.
- **Thumbnail:** Preview image used in search results to attract viewers.
- **Transcoding:** Converting video formats to match devices or internet speeds.

U

- **UI (User Interface):** Design elements and layouts that improve usability in streaming software.
- **Upload Speed:** The rate at which data is sent from your device to the internet, critical for high-quality streaming.
- **Unlisted Streams:** Private streams only accessible via a direct link, often used for testing setups or exclusive events.

V

- **VOD (Video on Demand):** Archived streams saved for later viewing.
- **Viewer Retention:** A metric tracking how long viewers stay engaged during a stream.
- **Virtual Sets:** Digital effects or backgrounds added via green screens.

W

- **Webcam Capture:** Captures video from webcams for live streaming.
- **Widgets:** Tools like donation counters and timers displayed on-screen to engage viewers.

X

- **XML (Extensible Markup Language):** A data format used for configuring overlays and widgets in streaming setups.
- **XLR Microphones:** High-end microphones requiring audio interfaces for studio-quality sound.

Y

- **YouTube Studio:** YouTube's built-in analytics platform for tracking video performance and managing live streams.

- **Y-axis:** Vertical alignment often used in designing graphics or layouts for overlays.

Z

- **Zoom Features:** Tools for magnifying video or visuals during presentations, tutorials, or close-up demonstrations.

Conclusion: Mastering Streaming Terminology

This glossary is your **quick-reference guide** for building technical knowledge and confidence as a streamer. Keep it handy as you set up your tools, engage your audience, and experiment with new techniques.

Appendix B: Recommended Tools and Resources

This appendix provides a **comprehensive list of tools, software, and resources** to help you optimize your live streaming setup, enhance content quality, and streamline production workflows. Whether you're a beginner or a seasoned creator, these tools can elevate your streaming experience.

1. Streaming Software and Broadcasting Tools

A. OBS Studio (Open Broadcaster Software)

- **Description:** Free and open-source software for recording and broadcasting live streams.

- **Key Features:**
    - Customizable scenes and overlays.
    - Multiple input sources for video and audio.
    - Compatible with plugins for enhanced functionality.

- **Best For:** Beginners and advanced users looking for a versatile and free tool.

B. Streamlabs OBS

- **Description:** An upgraded version of OBS with built-in widgets and monetization features.

- **Key Features:**

- o Pre-designed themes and alerts.

- o Integrated donation tracking and chat management.

- o Cloud backup for settings and layouts.

- **Best For:** Streamers focused on audience engagement and monetization.

C. XSplit Broadcaster

- **Description:** Paid software with professional features for high-quality streaming.

- **Key Features:**

  - o Multistreaming support for multiple platforms.

  - o Advanced editing and scene transitions.

  - o Live annotations and drawing tools.

- **Best For:** Professional creators seeking premium features and customer support.

D. Restream.io

- **Description:** A cloud-based tool for broadcasting to multiple platforms simultaneously.

- **Key Features:**

  - o Stream to YouTube, Twitch, Facebook, and more at once.

  - o Built-in analytics and chat consolidation.

  - o Browser-based streaming with no downloads required.

- **Best For:** Multi-platform streamers focused on expanding audience reach.

2. Audio and Microphone Tools

A. Blue Yeti (USB Microphone)

- **Description:** A versatile USB microphone for high-quality sound.

- **Key Features:**

  - o Multiple polar patterns (cardioid, stereo, omnidirectional).

  - o Plug-and-play setup with volume and mute controls.

- **Best For:** Beginners and intermediate streamers needing professional audio.

B. Shure SM7B (XLR Microphone)

- **Description:** Studio-grade microphone requiring an audio interface.
- **Key Features:**
  - Dynamic cardioid pickup for noise isolation.
  - Smooth, flat frequency response for vocals.
- **Best For:** Advanced users creating professional audio setups.

C. Rode NT-USB Mini

- **Description:** Compact USB microphone designed for podcasting and streaming.
- **Key Features:**
  - Plug-and-play with no drivers required.
  - Built-in pop filter to reduce noise.
- **Best For:** Portable and budget-friendly audio solutions.

3. Video and Camera Equipment

A. Logitech C920 HD Pro Webcam

- **Description:** A widely recommended HD webcam for affordable, high-quality video.
- **Key Features:**
  - Full HD 1080p recording and streaming.
  - Autofocus and light correction.
- **Best For:** Beginners upgrading from built-in laptop cameras.

B. Sony Alpha a6400 (DSLR/Mirrorless Camera)

- **Description:** A compact and professional mirrorless camera for higher video quality.
- **Key Features:**
  - 4K video recording.

- o Interchangeable lenses for flexibility.
- **Best For:** Professional streamers aiming for cinema-quality video.

C. Elgato Cam Link 4K (Capture Card)

- **Description:** Connects DSLR cameras to computers for HD and 4K streaming.
- **Key Features:**
  - o Low-latency video capture.
  - o Supports DSLR, mirrorless, and action cameras.
- **Best For:** Creators upgrading to advanced video setups.

4. Lighting and Green Screens
A. Elgato Key Light

- **Description:** Adjustable LED panel light optimized for live streaming.
- **Key Features:**
  - o Wi-Fi-enabled brightness and temperature controls.
  - o Compact design for desktop setups.
- **Best For:** Consistent lighting without complicated setups.

B. Neewer Softbox Lighting Kit

- **Description:** Affordable lighting kit for professional illumination.
- **Key Features:**
  - o Soft, diffused lighting for reduced shadows.
  - o Adjustable stands for flexibility.
- **Best For:** Budget-friendly professional setups.

C. Green Screens (Elgato Green Screen)

- **Description:** Portable and collapsible backdrop for background replacement.
- **Key Features:**
  - o Wrinkle-free material for smooth chroma key effects.

o   Easy storage and setup.

- **Best For:** Streamers using custom digital backgrounds.

5. Engagement and Moderation Tools
A. StreamElements and Streamlabs Chatbot

- **Description:** Chat automation tools for interaction and moderation.

- **Key Features:**

    o   Auto-responders and commands for FAQs.

    o   Timed announcements and giveaways.

- **Best For:** Improving audience engagement and managing spam.

B. Nightbot

- **Description:** Free chatbot for managing chats and creating custom commands.

- **Key Features:**

    o   Spam filters and link blockers.

    o   Song requests and loyalty points for engagement.

- **Best For:** Basic moderation and community interaction.

C. Polling Tools (StreamPolls)

- **Description:** Tools to run live polls during streams.

- **Key Features:**

    o   Real-time voting for viewer engagement.

    o   Integration with Twitch and YouTube chats.

- **Best For:** Audience feedback and interaction.

6. Analytics and Growth Tools
A. TwitchTracker and SullyGnome

- **Description:** Analytics platforms for tracking Twitch performance.

- **Key Features:**

       o   Viewer metrics, follower growth, and chat activity reports.

- **Best For:** Tracking trends and optimizing strategies.

B. YouTube Studio and TubeBuddy

- **Description:** Growth tools for YouTube creators.
- **Key Features:**
  - o   SEO optimization and keyword suggestions.
  - o   Video analytics and performance tracking.
- **Best For:** Boosting discoverability and organic growth.

7. Monetization Platforms

A. Patreon

- **Description:** Subscription-based platform for recurring revenue.
- **Key Features:**
  - o   Paid memberships and exclusive content.
- **Best For:** Creating premium subscriber tiers.

B. Ko-fi and Buy Me a Coffee

- **Description:** Tip jar platforms for small donations.
- **Key Features:**
  - o   No mandatory fees and easy setup.
- **Best For:** Casual support and small-scale fundraising.

Conclusion: Tools for Success

The tools and resources in this appendix provide **everything you need to optimize your streaming setup, enhance engagement, and grow your audience.** Start with budget-friendly options and scale as your channel expands.

Appendix C: Top Platforms and Features Compared

This appendix provides a **detailed comparison** of the **top live streaming platforms**, covering their **features, monetization options, and ideal use cases** to help you make an informed decision about where to grow your channel.

1. Twitch – The Leader in Gaming and Interactive Streams

Overview:

Twitch, owned by Amazon, is the **largest platform for gaming streams**, **esports tournaments**, and **creative content** like art and music. It's built around **community engagement** and features robust monetization tools.

Key Features:

- **Affiliate and Partner Programs:** Monetize through ads, subscriptions, and Bits (virtual tipping).

- **Interactive Tools:** Emotes, badges, polls, and leaderboards enhance audience participation.

- **Extensions and Overlays:** Widgets like countdown timers and donation trackers.

- **Clips and Highlights:** Save and share top moments for ongoing promotion.

Monetization Options:

- **Subscriptions:** Paid tiers with exclusive perks.

- **Bits and Donations:** Direct financial support through tips.

- **Ad Revenue:** Ads shown during streams.

- **Affiliate Marketing and Sponsorships:** Partner with brands for sponsored content.

Best For:

- **Gamers, esports enthusiasts**, and creators looking for **interactive and niche communities**.

Challenges:

- **High Competition:** Standing out requires consistent effort and strategy.

- **Limited Discoverability:** Relies heavily on networking and algorithms.

2. YouTube Live – Versatility and SEO Optimization

Overview:

YouTube Live combines **live streaming** with **video-on-demand (VOD)** features, making it ideal for creators who want to build long-term visibility and evergreen content.

Key Features:

- **SEO-Driven Discoverability:** Videos rank on **YouTube and Google search engines** for organic growth.
- **Replay and Archive Features:** Streams are automatically saved for later viewing.
- **Integrated Ecosystem:** Combines live broadcasts with playlists and uploads.
- **Community Posts:** Allows creators to interact outside of live sessions.

Monetization Options:

- **Ads:** Display and pre-roll ads generate income.
- **Super Chats and Stickers:** Paid, highlighted messages during streams.
- **Memberships:** Paid subscription tiers for exclusive content.
- **Affiliate Marketing and Sponsorships:** Flexible revenue streams.

Best For:

- **Educators, businesses**, and **content creators** focused on **SEO and long-term growth.**

Challenges:

- **Algorithm Dependency:** Content success depends heavily on keyword optimization.
- **Less Interactive Features:** Compared to Twitch, tools for engagement are more limited.

3. Facebook Live – Community-Driven Content for Social Networks

Overview:

Facebook Live integrates with **existing social networks**, making it perfect for **businesses, influencers**, and **community engagement.**

Key Features:

- **Group and Page Integration:** Broadcast to groups or pages for targeted engagement.

- **Event Hosting Features:** Ideal for product launches and fundraisers.

- **Cross-Promotion Tools:** Share streams across groups and profiles.

- **Analytics Dashboard:** Provides insights into audience demographics and performance.

Monetization Options:

- **Stars:** Viewers send stars as virtual tips.

- **Fan Subscriptions:** Memberships with exclusive perks.

- **Ad Breaks and Sponsored Content:** Additional revenue opportunities.

Best For:

- **Businesses, influencers**, and **brands** focused on **community building** and **promotions.**

Challenges:

- **Algorithm Shifts:** Organic reach varies with platform updates.

- **Casual Content Preference:** Focuses on informal over polished broadcasts.

4. Kick – The Newcomer with High Revenue Splits

Overview:

Kick is a **newer streaming platform** gaining attention for **high revenue splits** and **fewer restrictions**, making it attractive to creators looking for **monetization flexibility** and **freedom of content.**

Key Features:

- **95% Revenue Split:** Creators keep 95% of subscription earnings, far higher than competitors.
- **Chat Features and Moderation Tools:** Interactive and flexible chat options.
- **Freedom of Content Rules:** Fewer content restrictions than other platforms.
- **Partnership Programs:** Early-stage partnerships for rising creators.

Monetization Options:

- **Subscriptions and Tips:** Higher payouts for memberships and tips.
- **Sponsorships and Partnerships:** Growing opportunities for brand deals.

Best For:

- **Gamers**, **free speech advocates**, and **niche content creators** who value **freedom and high payouts**.

Challenges:

- **Smaller Audience Base:** Still growing, so visibility may be lower than Twitch or YouTube.
- **Uncertain Future:** Being newer, long-term stability is yet to be proven.

5. TikTok Live – The Hub for Short-Form and Viral Content
Overview:
TikTok Live capitalizes on **short-form video trends** and appeals to **younger, mobile-first audiences** focused on **viral engagement.**

Key Features:

- **Virtual Gifts and Coins:** Viewers can send tips and virtual items during streams.
- **Filters and Effects:** Built-in tools for visual creativity.
- **Live Q&A and Polls:** Interactive features for viewer engagement.
- **Dual Streaming:** Collaborate with other creators to grow visibility.

Monetization Options:

- **Gifts and Diamonds:** Convert virtual gifts into income.

- **Brand Sponsorships:** Partnerships with businesses for promoted content.

Best For:

- **Younger audiences, influencers,** and **performers** creating **trendy, short-form content.**

Challenges:

- **Mobile-Only Format:** Limits creators who focus on desktop setups.
- **Short Content Focus:** Not ideal for long-form broadcasts.

6. LinkedIn Live – Professional Networking and Business Content

Overview:

LinkedIn Live caters to **businesses, professionals,** and **educators** focusing on **corporate branding, webinars,** and **networking.**

Key Features:

- **Professional Branding Tools:** Ideal for presentations and thought leadership.
- **Webinar Features:** Great for training sessions and Q&As.
- **Networking Focus:** Appeals to a business-minded audience.

Monetization Options:

- **Sponsorships and Paid Webinars:** Generate income through exclusive events.
- **Consulting Services:** Promote services for revenue growth.

Best For:

- **Corporate brands, consultants,** and **educators** targeting **professionals.**

Challenges:

- **Limited Casual Content Appeal:** Focuses more on formal content.
- **Niche Audience:** Smaller audience compared to platforms like Twitch.

Conclusion: Comparing Platforms for Your Goals

- **Twitch:** Best for **gaming and niche communities**.

- **YouTube Live:** Ideal for **education and SEO-based growth**.

- **Facebook Live:** Great for **community engagement** and **businesses**.

- **Kick:** Perfect for **high revenue payouts** and **freedom of content**.

- **TikTok Live:** Best for **trendy, short-form creators**.

- **LinkedIn Live:** Tailored for **business professionals and corporate events**.

Appendix D: Popular Streaming Events Worldwide

Live streaming events are a powerful way to **connect with audiences, showcase talent**, and **stay ahead of industry trends**. This appendix highlights **global events** that provide opportunities for networking, learning, and collaboration in the streaming world.

1. Gaming and Esports Events
A. The International (Dota 2 Championship)

- **Overview:** One of the largest esports tournaments in the world, hosted by Valve Corporation.

- **Key Highlights:**
  - Multi-million-dollar prize pools, attracting top gamers and massive audiences.
  - Live broadcasts and interactive streams with real-time analytics.
  - Special features like fantasy leagues and in-game viewing experiences.

- **Opportunities for Streamers:**
  - Co-stream matches and provide commentary.
  - Host watch parties to engage viewers and analyze gameplay strategies.

B. League of Legends World Championship

- **Overview:** Hosted by Riot Games, this is one of the most-watched esports events globally.
- **Key Highlights:**
  - High-quality production with in-game analysis and expert commentary.
  - Global reach with multilingual broadcasts.
- **Opportunities for Streamers:**
  - Cover the event with pre-game and post-game analysis.
  - Collaborate with other creators for predictions and giveaways.

C. Fortnite World Cup

- **Overview:** A global gaming competition by Epic Games with events for solos, duos, and squads.
- **Key Highlights:**
  - Massive audience engagement with interactive features like in-game drops.
  - Focus on casual and professional players alike.
- **Opportunities for Streamers:**
  - Stream reactions to matches and connect with Fortnite fans.
  - Organize parallel tournaments or themed gameplay streams.

D. EVO (Evolution Championship Series)

- **Overview:** The largest and longest-running **fighting game tournament** in the world.
- **Key Highlights:**
  - Showcases games like **Street Fighter**, **Tekken**, and **Super Smash Bros.**
  - Focuses on competitive skill and niche communities.
- **Opportunities for Streamers:**
  - Host commentary streams or post-match breakdowns.

- o Collaborate with fighting game enthusiasts to highlight key matchups.

2. Creative and IRL Streaming Events
A. TwitchCon

- **Overview:** Twitch's official convention celebrating creators and communities.
- **Key Highlights:**
  - o Panels, workshops, and networking opportunities.
  - o Livestreamed sessions for those unable to attend in person.
- **Opportunities for Streamers:**
  - o Showcase your content to attract followers and sponsors.
  - o Collaborate with creators and learn new strategies from panels.

B. VidCon

- **Overview:** A convention for online video creators and influencers, including streamers.
- **Key Highlights:**
  - o Focuses on creator education, branding, and marketing strategies.
  - o Networking with platform representatives and brands.
- **Opportunities for Streamers:**
  - o Connect with brands for sponsorships and collaborations.
  - o Broadcast live from the event to share insights with your audience.

C. DreamHack

- **Overview:** A combination of **gaming festival**, **esports tournament**, and **creative showcase**.
- **Key Highlights:**
  - o Includes gaming challenges, live music, and product demos.

- o 24-hour streaming stations for content creation.
- **Opportunities for Streamers:**
    - o Highlight behind-the-scenes moments and gameplay footage.
    - o Engage followers with live updates and challenges.

3. Tech and Industry Conferences
A. CES (Consumer Electronics Show)

- **Overview:** The largest tech trade show, showcasing innovations in streaming equipment and technology.
- **Key Highlights:**
    - o Cutting-edge advancements in cameras, microphones, and AI tools.
    - o Sessions focused on future trends in digital entertainment.
- **Opportunities for Streamers:**
    - o Stream product demonstrations and offer reviews.
    - o Cover keynotes on AI and virtual production tools.

B. NAB Show (National Association of Broadcasters)

- **Overview:** Focuses on **broadcasting and content creation technologies**.
- **Key Highlights:**
    - o Workshops and showcases for streaming setups and equipment.
    - o Interactive booths featuring the latest hardware and software.
- **Opportunities for Streamers:**
    - o Test and demo new tools for streaming setups.
    - o Share reviews and tutorials based on new tech discoveries.

C. PAX (Penny Arcade Expo)

- **Overview:** A gaming and technology expo with dedicated sections for indie developers and content creators.
- **Key Highlights:**

- o Game reveals and developer interviews.
- o Workshops and networking spaces for streamers.
- **Opportunities for Streamers:**
  - o Collaborate with indie developers for exclusive content.
  - o Stream gameplay demos and host post-event discussions.

4. Music and Entertainment Festivals
A. Coachella Live Stream

- **Overview:** One of the biggest music festivals, offering **live-streamed performances**.
- **Key Highlights:**
  - o Multichannel streaming of performances and interviews.
  - o VR and AR experiences for virtual attendees.
- **Opportunities for Streamers:**
  - o Host virtual watch parties or live-react to performances.
  - o Stream festival highlights and discussions on artists.

B. Tomorrowland Live

- **Overview:** A global electronic music festival streamed online for a massive audience.
- **Key Highlights:**
  - o High-definition visuals and interactive fan experiences.
  - o Global participation through VR and livestream broadcasts.
- **Opportunities for Streamers:**
  - o Provide commentary and fan reactions during live streams.
  - o Collaborate with DJs or creators in music-based niches.

5. Charity and Fundraising Events
A. Extra Life

- **Overview:** A **charity streaming marathon** that raises funds for children's hospitals.

- **Key Highlights:**
    - 24-hour streaming challenges to encourage donations.
    - Global participation from gaming and IRL creators.

- **Opportunities for Streamers:**
    - Host charity streams and engage viewers in donation drives.
    - Partner with other streamers to increase reach and impact.

B. Games Done Quick (GDQ)

- **Overview:** A speedrunning marathon for charity that draws huge audiences.

- **Key Highlights:**
    - Raises millions for charitable causes each year.
    - Features speedrunning challenges and fan engagement.

- **Opportunities for Streamers:**
    - Highlight favorite runs and analyze speedrunning strategies.
    - Organize charity streams aligned with GDQ themes.

Conclusion: Leveraging Events for Growth

Streaming events provide **valuable networking opportunities**, **inspiration**, and **collaborations** to expand your audience and content strategy.

Tips for Streamers:

1. **Plan Ahead:** Announce your participation in events to generate buzz.

2. **Engage Viewers in Real Time:** Use polls and giveaways during events to keep interactions high.

3. **Create Post-Event Content:** Upload highlights, reviews, and analysis to maintain momentum after the event ends.

By participating in these events—virtually or in person—you'll **enhance credibility**, **build connections**, and **boost visibility** in the streaming world. Let me know if you'd like more updates!

Appendix E: Interactive Reflection Questions and Checklists

This appendix provides **reflection questions** and **step-by-step checklists** to reinforce learning, assess progress, and create actionable goals for live streaming success. Use these exercises to evaluate your current setup, refine strategies, and prepare for future growth.

Section 1: Reflection Questions

1. Building Your Foundation

- What inspired you to start live streaming, and what are your primary goals?

- Who is your target audience, and what value will your content provide to them?

- How do you define success in live streaming—followers, income, engagement, or impact?

2. Choosing Platforms and Tools

- Which platform best aligns with your audience and content style (e.g., Twitch, YouTube, Kick, etc.)? Why?

- What features or monetization options influenced your platform choice?

- Are your streaming tools (software, cameras, microphones) optimized for quality and performance? What upgrades might improve your production value?

3. Content Creation and Engagement

- What niche or theme will set your content apart? Are there trends you can incorporate?

- How do you plan to engage your audience during streams—polls, games, Q&As?

- What steps have you taken to create a consistent content schedule? Are you staying organized with a calendar?

4. Growth and Monetization

- What social media strategies are you using to promote your streams? Are they effective?

- Have you established monetization strategies, such as affiliate programs, merchandise, or memberships? What areas could you expand?

- What analytics tools are you using to track performance? How often do you review data to refine strategies?

5. Future-Proofing and Innovation

- How do you plan to adapt to platform updates and new technologies like AI and VR?

- What steps have you taken to make your streams accessible and inclusive? Are there tools you could add?

- Are you setting long-term goals to scale your brand, such as offering courses or building partnerships?

Section 2: Checklists

Checklist 1: Streaming Equipment and Setup

☐ Camera or Webcam (HD or 4K)

☐ Microphone (USB or XLR)

☐ Lighting Setup (Ring light, softbox, LED panels)

☐ Green Screen for Virtual Backgrounds

☐ Capture Card for External Devices (e.g., Elgato)

☐ Reliable Streaming Software (OBS, Streamlabs, XSplit)

☐ Stable Internet Connection with Sufficient Upload Speed (at least 5 Mbps for HD)

☐ Backup Equipment (spare cables, batteries, or secondary cameras)

Checklist 2: Platform and Account Optimization

☐ Selected a Platform (Twitch, YouTube, Kick, Facebook, TikTok)

☐ Optimized Profiles (Banners, Profile Pictures, and Bios)

☐ Enabled Monetization Features (Ads, Subscriptions, Donations)

☐ Linked Social Media Accounts for Cross-Promotion

☐ Tested Platform Features (Overlays, Alerts, Polls)

Checklist 3: Content Planning and Scheduling

☐ Defined Content Niche and Theme

☐ Created a Weekly or Monthly Content Calendar

☐ Brainstormed Stream Ideas (Challenges, Events, Collabs)

☐ Prepared Scripts or Talking Points for Key Segments

☐ Tested Content Formats (Tutorials, Interviews, Panels)

Checklist 4: Audience Engagement and Moderation

☐ Enabled Chat Bots and Moderators for Interaction and Safety

☐ Prepared Interactive Tools (Polls, Giveaways, Challenges)

☐ Created Community Rules and Guidelines for Chats

☐ Added Visual Alerts for New Subscribers or Donations

☐ Designed Loyalty Rewards and Subscriber Badges

Checklist 5: Growth and Monetization

☐ Developed Social Media Marketing Plans for Promotion

☐ Collaborated with Other Creators for Shared Growth

☐ Set Up Merchandise Store or Digital Product Offerings

☐ Launched Exclusive Membership Tiers or Super Chats

☐ Reviewed Analytics to Optimize Strategies

Checklist 6: Backup and Emergency Plans

☐ Tested Backup Internet Connections or Hotspots

☐ Created Backup Streaming Devices (Laptops, Mobile Apps)

☐ Prepared Spare Equipment (Microphones, Cameras, Cables)

☐ Established Troubleshooting Steps for Audio/Video Errors

☐ Created Checklists for Technical Setup Before Streams

Checklist 7: Future-Proofing and Scalability

☐ Researched Emerging Trends (AI Tools, VR, AR Integration)

☐ Updated Accessibility Features (Subtitles, Audio Cues)

☐ Planned for Team Growth (Editors, Assistants, Agencies)

☐ Built Partnerships with Brands and Sponsors

☐ Expanded to Multiple Platforms Using Multistreaming Tools

Section 3: Action Planning Worksheet

Step 1: Define Your Goals

- Short-Term Goals (Next 30–60 days):
  Example: Grow follower count by 20% and improve video quality.

- Mid-Term Goals (3–6 months):
  Example: Launch a merchandise line and implement monetization strategies.

- Long-Term Goals (6–12 months):
  Example: Expand to multi-platform streaming and secure brand partnerships.

Step 2: Outline Key Actions

- What upgrades do you need for your setup?

- Which platforms will you prioritize?

- What steps will you take to improve audience engagement?

Step 3: Track and Measure Progress

- Use analytics tools to track performance.

- Adjust strategies based on engagement rates, donations, and retention.

- Schedule regular reviews of your progress every month.

Conclusion: Reflect, Plan, and Execute

Success in live streaming requires **ongoing reflection, planning, and execution.** Use this appendix to **evaluate your progress**, **set actionable goals**, and **fine-tune strategies** as you grow. Treat it as a **living document**—update it as you experiment with new tools, platforms, and approaches.

Appendix F: Frequently Asked Questions (FAQs)

Live streaming is an exciting and accessible way to share content, connect with audiences, and build a career. However, it also raises many questions, especially for new creators. This appendix answers **10 of the most frequently asked questions** about streaming, covering **setup, growth, monetization**, and **long-term success strategies.**

1. Getting Started with Live Streaming

Question 1: What is live streaming, and why is it so popular?

Answer:
Live streaming is the **real-time broadcasting** of video and audio over the internet, allowing direct interaction between creators and audiences. It's popular because it promotes **authentic engagement**, builds **communities**, and enables creators to **showcase talents** or **promote products** instantly.

Popular Uses:

- **Gaming Streams:** Tutorials, competitions, and gameplay walkthroughs.

- **Education and Training:** Webinars, coaching sessions, and how-to demonstrations.

- **Business Promotions:** Live Q&A sessions, product demos, and launches.

- **Entertainment and Lifestyle:** Music performances, travel vlogs, and cooking shows.

Question 2: What equipment do I need to start streaming?

Answer:
To get started, you'll need:

- **Camera:** Affordable options like **Logitech C920** or high-end options like **Sony Alpha a6400.**

- **Microphone:** Beginner-friendly **Blue Yeti** or professional **Shure SM7B** for premium sound.

- **Lighting:** Use **ring lights** or **LED panels** to improve visual clarity.

- **Streaming Software:** Tools like **OBS Studio**, **Streamlabs OBS**, or **XSplit** for overlays and transitions.

- **Internet Connection:** At least **5–10 Mbps upload speed** for HD quality.

Exercise: Test your gear with a **private stream** to identify and fix issues before going live.

2. Technical Setup and Optimization
Question 3: How can I prevent buffering and lag during streams?

Answer:

1. **Optimize Internet Connection:**

    o   Use a **wired Ethernet connection** instead of Wi-Fi.

    o   Ensure **upload speeds of 10+ Mbps** for 1080p streaming.

2. **Adjust Settings:**

    o   Lower the **bitrate** or **resolution** temporarily if lag occurs.

    o   Reduce frame rates for smoother performance.

3. **Close Unnecessary Programs:**

    o   Shut down background applications that drain resources.

Tip: Use **Twitch Inspector** or **Speedtest.net** to test connection stability before streaming.

Question 4: How can I test my stream setup before going live?

Answer:

- **OBS Studio Preview Mode:** Test overlays, audio, and transitions.

- **Private Streams:** Broadcast privately to test functionality and review playback.

- **Monitoring Tools:** Use **Streamlabs** and **Twitch Analytics** to track real-time performance.

Tip: Always test after **software updates** or adding new features to avoid unexpected issues.

3. Growing and Engaging Your Audience
Question 5: How can I attract more viewers to my live streams?

Answer:

- **Promote Your Streams:** Share highlights and announcements on **social media** platforms.

- **Collaborate with Streamers:** Co-stream or host guests to expand reach.
- **Optimize SEO:** Use **keywords**, **tags**, and **thumbnails** to boost visibility.
- **Host Contests:** Engage viewers with **giveaways**, **polls**, and challenges.

Tip: Develop a **content schedule** to keep viewers coming back regularly.

Question 6: How do I keep viewers engaged during long streams?

Answer:

- **Segment Your Content:** Rotate between activities, challenges, and Q&As to keep energy up.
- **Recognize Contributions:** Highlight **comments**, **donations**, and **milestones** during streams.
- **Interactive Tools:** Use polls and quizzes to involve viewers directly.

Tip: Plan themed content days (e.g., challenge days or giveaways) to maintain excitement.

4. Handling Challenges

Question 7: How do I handle trolls and negative comments?

Answer:

- **Set Rules:** Post chat guidelines and enforce them consistently.
- **Moderators and Bots:** Use tools like **Nightbot** or **Streamlabs Chatbot** to block offensive language automatically.
- **Stay Positive:** Redirect conversations to focus on **positive topics** and ignore intentional provocation.

Tip: Reward loyal viewers with **VIP badges** and shoutouts to encourage positivity.

Question 8: What if I face technical failures during a stream?

Answer:

- **Backup Equipment:** Have **spare microphones, cables, and internet connections** ready.

- **Troubleshooting Steps:**
  1. Restart software or devices.
  2. Reduce stream resolution or frame rate.
  3. Use **mobile streaming apps** as a temporary backup.

Tip: Create a **tech checklist** and rehearse emergency plans before streaming.

5. Monetization and Growth

Question 9: How can I make money as a live streamer?

Answer:

- **Subscriptions and Memberships:** Offer **exclusive perks** for paying subscribers.
- **Donations and Tips:** Use tools like **Ko-fi** or **Patreon** for support.
- **Sponsorships:** Partner with brands for product placements and ads.
- **Merchandise Sales:** Sell custom products through platforms like **Streamlabs Merch.**
- **Affiliate Marketing:** Promote products and earn commissions.

Exercise: Create a **monetization plan** outlining the top 2–3 strategies you want to start with.

Question 10: How can I use analytics to grow my channel?

Answer:

- **Track Viewership Trends:** Identify peak activity times and retention rates.
- **Engagement Insights:** Analyze likes, shares, and chat participation.
- **Content Testing:** Review performance data to see what works best.

Tools to Use:

- **Twitch Analytics Dashboard:** Tracks followers, chat activity, and tips.
- **YouTube Studio Analytics:** Monitors views, audience demographics, and watch times.

- **Streamlabs Reports:** Provides insights into revenue and viewer behavior.

Tip: Use data to refine **titles, formats**, and **content schedules** for higher engagement.

Conclusion: FAQs as Tools for Success

This FAQ section covers **10 of the most common questions** live streamers face, providing **practical strategies** and **tools for success.** From setting up equipment to scaling monetization, these answers are designed to help you navigate challenges and grow your career confidently.

Refer back to this section as you evolve, and keep experimenting with new ideas, tools, and features to stay ahead in the competitive world of live streaming!

About HowExpert

HowExpert publishes quick 'how to' guides on all topics from A to Z. Visit HowExpert.com to learn more.

About the Publisher

Byungjoon "BJ" Min (민병준) is an author, publisher, entrepreneur, and the founder of HowExpert. He started off as a once broke convenience store clerk to eventually becoming a fulltime internet marketer and finding his niche in publishing. He is the founder and publisher of HowExpert where the mission is to make a positive impact in the world for all topics from A to Z. Visit BJMin.com and HowExpert.com to learn more. John 14:6

Recommended Resources

- HowExpert.com – How To Guides on All Topics from A to Z.
- HowExpert.com/free – Free HowExpert Email Newsletter.
- HowExpert.com/books – HowExpert Books
- HowExpert.com/courses – HowExpert Courses
- HowExpert.com/clothing – HowExpert Clothing
- HowExpert.com/membership – HowExpert Membership Site
- HowExpert.com/affiliates – HowExpert Affiliate Program
- HowExpert.com/jobs – HowExpert Jobs
- HowExpert.com/writers – Write About Your #1 Passion/Knowledge/Expertise & Become a HowExpert Author.
- HowExpert.com/resources – Additional HowExpert Recommended Resources
- YouTube.com/HowExpert – Subscribe to HowExpert YouTube.
- Instagram.com/HowExpert – Follow HowExpert on Instagram.
- Facebook.com/HowExpert – Follow HowExpert on Facebook.
- TikTok.com/@HowExpert – Follow HowExpert on TikTok.

www.ingramcontent.com/pod-product-compliance
Lightning Source LLC
LaVergne TN
LVHW041208050326
832903LV00021B/533